MW00532270

ATHENIAN POLITICS
c. 800–500 BC

This book is designed to sharpen historical skills by a critical approach to the sources of information on ancient Athenian politics. It presents contemporary sources, later historical and biographical writings, archaeological evidence, inscriptions on stone, and papyri from Egypt. The reader has available in translation virtually all the documents on which scholars of this period base their conclusions.

The period covered embraces the reforms of Solon, the tyranny of Peisistratos and his sons, and the constitutional changes of Kleisthenes. When Athenian politics first become visible, the noble families are firmly in control. At the end of the period democracy is just beginning to emerge. Central to an understanding of the politics of the time are the conflict among aristocratic clans and the vertical ties between noble patrons and their supporters and dependants in the lower social strata. Paradoxically, democracy emerged from the actions of noble leaders who were certainly not of democratic disposition.

Professor Stanton, of the University of New England, challenges the ways in which professional scholars have viewed Athenian politics and presents us with a lucid and valuable new study, complete with explanatory notes, which will be most useful to students and teachers of ancient history, classical studies, and politics.

Professor Stanton is Associate Professor in the Department of Classics and Ancient History at the University of New England, Australia.

ATHENIAN POLITICS
c. 800–500 BC
A Sourcebook

G. R. Stanton

London and New York

First published 1990 by Routledge
11 New Fetter Lane, London EC4P 4EE

Simultaneously published in the USA and Canada
by Routledge
29 West 35th Street, New York, NY 10001

Reprinted 1991, 1994

© 1990 G. R. Stanton

Data converted by Columns of Reading
Set in 10/12pt Times
Printed in Great Britain by Clays Ltd, St Ives plc

All rights reserved. No part of this book may be reprinted or reproduced or utilized in any form or by any electronic, mechanical, or other means, now known or hereafter invented, including photocopying and recording, or in any information storage or retrieval system, without permission in writing from the publishers.

British Library Cataloguing in Publication Data
Stanton, G. R.
Athenian politics, c. 800–500 B.C.: a sourcebook.
1. Greece. Athens. Politics, ancient period
I. Title
320.9'38

Library of Congress Cataloging-in-Publication Data
Athenian politics, c. 800–500 B.C.: a sourcebook /
[edited by] G. R. Stanton.
p. cm.
Includes bibliographical references.
1. Athens (Greece) — Politics and government. 2. Athens (Greece) — Nobility — Political activity — History.
I. Stanton, G. R. (Greg R.), 1943–
DF277.A84 1990
938'.5 — dc20 89–71345

ISBN 0–415–04060–4 (hb)
ISBN 0–415–04061–2 (pb)

CONTENTS

PREFACE

'How do you know about events so long ago?' That question, whether articulated or implicit, repeatedly confronts people who teach or write about the ancient world. The question does not admit of a simple answer, because different types of evidence call for different techniques in handling them. This book presents evidence of very diverse kinds bearing on Athenian politics in the period down to (approximately) the Persian Wars. There is the poetry of an aristocrat highly involved in contemporary politics; Solon – for that is his name – reveals values of the times, but he does so within a poetic tradition. There are inscriptions carved on stone, often providing further clues by their finding places; but the inscriptions are frequently incomplete or damaged. There are coherent accounts written long after the events recorded; sometimes the sources are reliable or at least wear their prejudices openly, but sometimes they were written as long after the events recorded as our own time is from the Fourth Crusade. There are papyri found in the sands of Egypt, preserving accounts which have been repeatedly copied. And, of course, there is archaeological evidence, not only from Athens and the surrounding countryside but from sites scattered around the Mediterranean and Black Sea areas, that bears on political affairs in Athens; but one must keep in mind the limitations of archaeological evidence.

There have been various schools of thought about the nature of politics in Athens down to 500 BC. Some scholars have believed that economic interest groups developed during the last century of that period. Others have been prepared to believe the ancient assertion that parties conflicted with each other over the form of constitution Athens should have. The theme of this book, however, is that the politics of this early period in Athenian history are to be understood in terms of factions led by aristocrats. Each faction had vertical ties linking the noble family or families at its head with supporters (political 'friends', clients and dependants) in the lower strata of society. The interesting paradox, in this theme, is that democracy emerged from the actions of noble leaders who were certainly not of democratic disposition.

Many people and institutions have assisted me in writing this book. The University of New England has provided financial support and periods of study leave, and its successive professors of Classics, John Bishop and Trevor Bryce, have supported my applications for these resources. During repeated visits to Athens, the British School of Archaeology has done much more than provide accommodation and arrange permits for me to study inscriptions, sites and material in archaeological museums. The treasures of its library and the stimulating discussion and information provided by its fascinating range of students have been made readily available. A true home far from home. Across the garden the library of the American School of Classical Studies has often come to my rescue with desperately needed material. In Oxford the Ashmolean and the Bodleian libraries, in Cambridge the University and the Classical Faculty libraries, and in London the Institute of Classical Studies and the British libraries have opened their collections to me. For all these kindnesses I am grateful.

At an early stage Paul O'Keefe, Carole Tisdell and Dick Waring tried out some of my drafts on their classes and offered many suggestions about obscurities and ambiguities. David Lewis and Peter Rhodes generously annotated draft chapters and discussed many issues with me. Carole Tisdell returned to later drafts and devoted many hours to commenting on them. Brett Farrell checked references for me and identified many sentences which needed rewriting or correction. None of these friends is responsible for mistakes or infelicities that remain. I owe most of all to students of my department over the last twenty years who have listened to my views, raised difficult questions and shared their own thoughts with me.

GREG STANTON
The University of New England
Armidale, NSW, Australia
July 1989

ABBREVIATIONS

AC *L'Antiquité Classique*
AD *Arkhaiologikon Deltion*
Agora XV *The Athenian Agora*, vol. XV: *Inscriptions: The Athenian Councillors*, eds B. D. Meritt and J. S. Traill (Princeton 1974)
AJA *American Journal of Archaeology*
AJAH *American Journal of Ancient History*
AJP *American Journal of Philology*
AM *Mitteilungen des Deutschen Archäologischen Instituts* (Athenische Abteilung)
Anc. Soc. Inst. *Ancient Society and Institutions: Studies presented to Victor Ehrenberg on his 75th birthday* (Oxford 1966)
Andrewes, *Greek Tyrants* A. Andrewes, *The Greek Tyrants* (London 1956)
ANSMN *The American Numismatic Society Museum Notes*
AR *Archaeological Reports* (Supplement to *JHS*; cf. below)
ASNP[3] *Annali della Scuola Normale Superiore di Pisa*, serie III
Ath. Pol. *Athenaion Politeia* attributed to Aristotle
BCH *Bulletin de Correspondance Hellénique*
Bicknell, *Studies* P. J. Bicknell, *Studies in Athenian Politics and Genealogy* [Historia Einzelschriften, 19] (Wiesbaden 1972)
BICS *Bulletin of the Institute of Classical Studies* (University of London)
BSA *The Annual of the British School at Athens*
Burn, *Lyric Age* A. R. Burn, *The Lyric Age of Greece* (London 1960)
Burn, *Persia and the Greeks* A. R. Burn, *Persia and the Greeks:*

The Defence of the West, c.546–478 B.C. (London 1962)

C & M *Classica et Mediaevalia*

CAH^2 3 *The Cambridge Ancient History*, 2nd edn, vol. 3, eds J. Boardman and N. G. L. Hammond (Cambridge 1982–)

CAH^2 4 *The Cambridge Ancient History*, 2nd edn, vol. 4, eds J. Boardman, N. G. L. Hammond, D. M. Lewis and M. Ostwald (Cambridge 1988)

CEG P. A. Hansen (ed.), *Carmina epigraphica Graeca saeculorum viii–v a.Chr.n.* [Texte und Kommentare, 12] (Berlin 1983)

Chambers Aristoteles: ΑΘΗΝΑΙΩΝ ΠΟΛΙΤΕΙΑ, ed. M. H. Chambers (Leipzig 1986)

CJ *The Classical Journal*

CP *Classical Philology*

CQ *The Classical Quarterly*

CR *The Classical Review*

Davies, *APF* J. K. Davies, *Athenian Propertied Families 600–300 B.C.* (Oxford 1971)

Ehrenberg V. Ehrenberg, *From Solon to Socrates*, 2nd edn (London 1973)

FGrH F. Jacoby, *Die Fragmente der griechischen Historiker* (Berlin 1923–30; Leiden 1940–58) (*FGrH* 328 F 30, for example, refers to *Fragment* 30 of historian no. 328 [Philokhoros] in the collection.)

FHG C. and T. Müller, *Fragmenta historicorum Graecorum* (Paris 1841–70)

Fine, *Ancient Greeks* J. V. A. Fine, *The Ancient Greeks: A Critical History* (Cambridge, Mass. 1983)

Forrest W. G. Forrest, *The Emergence of Greek Democracy: The Character of Greek Politics, 800–400 B.C.* (London 1966)

French A. French, *The Growth of the Athenian Economy* (London 1964)

Friedländer and Hoffleit P. Friedländer and H. B. Hoffleit, *Epigrammata: Greek Inscriptions in Verse from the Beginnings to the Persian Wars* (Berkeley 1948)

G & R^2 *Greece and Rome*, 2nd series

Gentili and Prato *Poetarum elegiacorum testimonia et fragmenta*, eds B. Gentili and C. Prato (Leipzig 1979–85)

Gomme, *HCT* A. W. Gomme *et al.*, *A Historical Commentary on Thucydides* (Oxford 1945–81)

GRBS *Greek, Roman and Byzantine Studies*

Hammond² N. G. L. Hammond, *A History of Greece to 322 B.C.*, 2nd edn (Oxford 1967)

Hdt. Herodotos

Hignett C. Hignett, *A History of the Athenian Constitution to the End of the Fifth Century B.C.* (Oxford 1952)

How and Wells W. W. How and J. Wells, *A Commentary on Herodotus* (Oxford 1912)

HSCP *Harvard Studies in Classical Philology*

IG I³ *Inscriptiones Graecae*, vol. I, 3rd edn, ed. D. M. Lewis (Berlin 1981–)

IG II² *Inscriptiones Graecae*, vol. II, editio minor, ed. J. Kirchner (Berlin 1913–40)

Jeffery L.H. Jeffery, *Archaic Greece: The City-States c. 700-500 B.C.* (London 1976)

JHS *The Journal of Hellenic Studies*

JÖAI *Jahreshefte des Österreichischen Archäologischen Institutes in Wien*

LCM *Liverpool Classical Monthly*

Macan R.W. Macan, Commentary on Herodotos Books 4–6 (London 1895)

Meiggs and Lewis R. Meiggs and D. M. Lewis, *A Selection of Greek Historical Inscriptions to the End of the Fifth Century B.C.* (Oxford 1969)

Moore J.M. Moore, *Aristotle and Xenophon on Democracy and Oligarchy* (London 1975)

MSS Manuscripts (of an ancient author's work)

*OCD*² *The Oxford Classical Dictionary*, 2nd edn (Oxford 1970)

PACA *The Proceedings of the African Classical Associations*

Piccirilli Plutarco, *La vita di Solone*, eds. M. Manfredini [text and translation] and L. Piccirilli [introduction and commentary] (Verona 1977)

PP *La Parola del Passato*

QUCC *Quaderni Urbinati di Cultura Classica*

RA *Revue Archéologique*

Raubitschek, *DAA* A. E. Raubitschek, *Dedications from the Athenian Akropolis: A Catalogue of the Inscriptions of the Sixth and Fifth Centuries B.C.* (Cambridge, Mass. 1949)

RE Pauly-Wissowa-Kroll, *Real-Encyclopädie der classischen Altertumswissenschaft*

RFIC *Rivista di filologia e di istruzione classica*

RhM *Rheinisches Museum für Philologie*

Rhodes P.J. Rhodes, *A Commentary on the Aristotelian* Athenaion Politeia (Oxford 1981)

Rosén Herodoti Historiae, ed. H. B. Rosén (Leipzig 1987–)

Sandys[2] J. E. Sandys, *Aristotle's Constitution of Athens*, 2nd edn (London 1912)

Sayce A. H. Sayce, Commentary on Herodotos Books 1–3 (London 1883)

SBAW *Sitzungsberichte der Bayerischen Akademie der Wissenschaften zu München* (Philos.-Hist. Klasse)

Sealey B. R. I. Sealey, *A History of the Greek City States ca.700–338 B.C.* (Berkeley 1976)

SHAW *Sitzungsberichte der Heidelberger Akademie der Wissenschaften* (Philos.-Hist. Klasse)

Stein H. Stein, Commentary on Herodotos, 4th and 5th edn (Berlin 1881–3)

Talanta *Τάλαντα: Proceedings of the Dutch Archaeological and Historical Society*

TAPA *Transactions and Proceedings of the American Philological Association*

Thomsen R. Thomsen, *The Origin of Ostracism: A Synthesis* [Humanitas, 4] (Copenhagen 1972)

Traill, *Demos and Trittys* J. S. Traill, *Demos and Trittys: Epigraphical and Topographical Studies in the Organization of Attica* (Toronto 1986)

Traill, *Political Organization* J. S. Traill, *The Political Organization of Attica: A Study of the Demes, Trittyes, and Phylai, and their Representation in the Athenian Council* [Hesperia Supplements, 14] (Princeton 1975)

Vanderpool E. Vanderpool, 'Ostracism at Athens', in *Lectures in Memory of Louise Taft Semple: Second Series* (Cincinnati 1973) 215–70

von Fritz and Kapp K. von Fritz and E. Kapp, *Aristotle's Constitution of Athens and Related Texts* (New York 1950)

Wade-Gery, *Essays* H. T. Wade-Gery, *Essays in Greek History* (Oxford 1958)

West *Iambi et elegi Graeci ante Alexandrum cantati* 2, ed. M. L. West (Oxford 1972)

ZPE *Zeitschrift für Papyrologie und Epigraphik*

NOTE ON TRANSLITERATION

In order to bring the reader closer to Greek names and terms as they were seen by the Athenians, and to avoid such mispronunciations as 'ch' (as in 'church') for Greek χ, a fairly strict transliteration is used in this book. Thus I use Attike, Hipparkhos, Kleisthenes and Peisistratos, whereas one will find Latinised and semi-Latinised forms (Attica, Hipparchus, Cleisthenes, Pisistratus or Peisistratus) in many modern books and articles. However, complete consistency is virtually impossible and I adopt the familiar spelling for some names, such as Plato and Thucydides.

INTRODUCTION

The Bronze Age civilisations of Crete and Mycenae ended with the destruction of the palaces about 1200 BC. Literacy disappeared from the Greek world until the eighth century. Even then, the great epic poems which reached substantially their final form in that century – the *Iliad* and the *Odyssey* – ostensibly refer to the Bronze Age period. So they repeatedly leave the reader wondering just how much of the social and political life reflected in the epics belongs in the era of their monumental composition. The didactic poetry of Hesiod does refer to the agricultural and religious assumptions of the eighth century, and something is revealed by the lyric poets of the seventh century about life in that period. But we know nothing from contemporary sources about the political structure of their world, apart from references to 'kings' and 'tyrants'.

Then in the sixth century BC there emerges a politician who indicates his values and who writes, after the event, about what he was trying to achieve. This is Solon of Athens, and we have this striking effusion of political information because he was a poet as well as a politician. We do not possess the full corpus of his poetry – indeed we have fragments rather than complete poems. Nevertheless, we can discern his concern for his reputation and for his political actions to be favourably remembered (posthumous glory was greatly valued in Greek as well as Roman society). The fragments throw direct light on the economic and political problems which he tried to solve and on the constitutional changes which he made. But for a more complete picture we rely heavily on sources written much later, on an historical account comprising the first part of a document known as the *Athenaion Politeia* ('Constitution of the Athenians'), written in the fourth century BC, and even on Plutarch, who depended particularly on sources written in the fourth and third centuries (though he had, of course, more of Solon's poetry than we have), but who was writing his biographies at the very end of the first or early in the second century of our era.

It will be clear from these comments on Solon that this book concentrates on an important issue for historians: how we know about what happened in the distant past. The historian of ancient Greece is frequently forced to assess the evidence of sources written many centuries after the events he or she is studying. Hence I do not hesitate to include most of the ancient accounts of a significant event (such as the attempted tyranny of Kylon), so that skills in detecting bias, in interpreting, evaluating and marshalling evidence, and in constructing a case, are sharpened. Of course, assessment of the sources is a dynamic process: as we determine our view of what happened and why, our opinion of the worth of a particular source will be changing.

Moreover, we are not restricted to written sources. Archaeological evidence bearing, for example, on the success of Solon's economic changes or on the public building programme undertaken by the tyrants in Athens is of great value. But the limitations of archaeological evidence for political history must also be kept in mind. To take an example from the Bronze Age period in Greece: we can talk so readily as I did above about the destruction of the 'palaces' of Crete[1] not because the dominance of one immensely complex building at Knossos tells us that the system of government was monarchical, but because an archaic form of the later Greek word for 'king' occurs on tablets which were accidentally baked (and thus preserved) in the conflagration which destroyed that building. It is true that, fifty years before those tablets engraved with Linear B script were deciphered, Sir Arthur Evans designated one room at Knossos, which contains a large stone chair and benches on either side of it, the 'Throne Room'. But this was (and remains) a sheer guess. We do not know whether the benches were occupied by a council of advisers or a college of priests or someone else. (To put the limitations of purely archaeological evidence starkly, dare I suggest the parents of pre-school children? After all, there is an excellent stone-lined hole for a pre-school sandpit – called a 'lustral basin' by Evans – adjacent to this room. Just as the Victorian gentleman thought first of a bath fit for Ariadne or an ornamental fish tank, a parent of the late twentieth century might think of other amenities.)[2] There are no purely archaeological indications – nor could there be – that a king sat on the 'throne'. Similarly, in a later period, there are limitations on the use of archaeological evidence. The remains of houses and cemeteries, though indicating habitation in the fifth or fourth rather than the sixth century, may point to a population centre which formed the basis of one of Kleisthenes's electorates. But identification of the electorate depends on other evidence, of a written kind (see Chapter V, pp. 163–5).

One of these forms of written evidence – bearing not only on the constitutional changes by Kleisthenes, but on many other aspects of Athenian politics – is commonly found in archaeological field surveys and excavations. This is the inscription, usually engraved on a thin stone slab which was set upright in the ground (like modern tombstones). The study of such inscriptions, known as epigraphy, illuminates many facets of politics in our period. One, for example, reveals collaboration with the tyrants by an Athenian family which managed to convey the impression in our earliest literary source, Herodotos, that it had been the strongest opponent of the tyrants (see Chapter IV, pp. 111–12 and Chapter VI, pp. 202–4). The body of evidence is constantly growing through the discovery of inscriptions by archaeologists and their interpretation by epigraphers. Another form of written evidence is found in the sands of Egypt. The invaluable papyrus document on the constitution of Athens, the *Athenaion Politeia*, was found in an ancient rubbish heap or tomb in Egypt and was first published less than 100 years ago.[3] The recent edition by M. H. Chambers and the observations and judgments of papyrologists reported in P. J. Rhodes's commentary on the document show that progress is still being made. But other, far more flimsy, scraps of papyrus preserve ancient views on the politics of archaic Athens (see document [**4**] and note 4 on document [**29**]).

Along with the emphasis on the way in which conclusions are reached about the distant past in Greece there coexists in this book a view about the nature of Athenian politics in the period to 500 BC. Some have thought that politics in archaic Athens are to be explained in terms of conflict between different economic interest groups. Others, including some ancient commentators, have suggested that the basic struggle was over different forms of constitution (oligarchic, democratic, middle-of-the-road). I believe that conflict between aristocratic clans[4] is the key to an understanding of politics in this period. In this conflict vertical ties between aristocratic patrons and their supporters in the lower classes are seen as crucial. The model which seems most useful was suggested by W. G. Forrest[5]: a set of pyramids; at the head of each stands an aristocratic clan (or possibly a coalition of clans), linked with their political 'friends' in the next social class and then on through the remaining classes, with the numbers of clients growing more numerous as one descends. In the normal game of archaic politics the poorest inhabitants (citizens from the time of Solon) are distributed among bodies of clients led by aristocratic families. Danger for the system arises if one particular family disrupts the 'pyramids' and wins over the retainers of other families.

Of course, out of this period in Athens' history democracy emerged. The paradox is that the steps which led to democracy, only realised in its fully fledged form in the fifth century BC, were all taken by aristocratic leaders in the preceding period. Solon betrays in his poetry a strongly aristocratic bias. He claims that he gave to the common people such status 'as is sufficient' for them and did not 'offer them too much' (document [**24**]). He tried to avoid the collapse of aristocratic government which would be involved in the sweeping away of lower-class supporters by another Kylon, someone who attempted to become tyrant. But in seeking to protect aristocratic control he gave some privileges to the lower classes, which can be seen (and were seen in antiquity) as a step on the road to democracy. Again, Peisistratos was not a democrat; he wanted a tyranny – with himself as tyrant. Yet the effect of the long period of tyranny by himself and his sons was to suppress the position of other aristocratic clans. And, at the end of our period, Kleisthenes did not win the common people to his faction because he believed in democracy. They had previously been spurned by his own family as well as by others. It was only when he was losing in the game of aristocratic politics resumed after the overthrow of the tyrants that he embraced them as political allies. He convinced them to support a revision of the constitution which was intended, I believe, to give special advantages to his own family. But the thorough redistribution of citizens for electoral purposes served not just to handicap rival families and promote the cause of Kleisthenes's family, the Alkmeonidai. It also strengthened the hand of the common people, who used their power to act against their former patrons. Even the Alkmeonidai and their connections found themselves victims of ostracism in the 480s BC. The aristocrats who unintentionally promoted the development of Athenian democracy are central to this book. But my intention is to provide in it a fairly complete presentation of sources, and sufficient explanation of them, for readers to evaluate the prominence given to the role of aristocratic factions in Athenian politics down to 500 BC.

Notes

1 G. Cadogan, who has published a book entitled *Palaces of Minoan Crete* (London 1976), momentarily questions the terminology in *The End of the Early Bronze Age in the Aegean* [Cincinnati Classical Studies, n.s. 6] (Leiden 1986) 169–70.

2 Evans's considered view appeared in *The Palace of Minos at Knossos* 4 (London 1935) 904–7, 915 with supplementary plate LXIII. For his earlier views and his work on the 'Throne Room' see A. J. Evans, *BSA* 6 (1899–1900) 3–70 at 35–42; P. M. Warren, *The Aegean Civilizations* (Oxford 1975) 21, 85; A. Brown, *Arthur Evans and the Palace of Minos* (Oxford 1983) 37–52.

3 By F. G. Kenyon of the British Museum, on 30 January 1891. E. A. T. W. Budge, who bought the papyrus for the Museum in Port Said on 8 April 1889, claimed that it was found near Malawi (*By Nile and Tigris: A Narrative of Journeys in Egypt and Mesopotamia on behalf of the British Museum* [London 1920] 2.136–7, 147–50), but other evidence points to the vicinity of Asyut (see A. H. Sayce, *Reminiscences* [London 1923] 332–4 and E. G. Turner, *Greek Papyri: an Introduction*² [Oxford 1980] 22, 184 n. 12).

4 For an introduction to the power, tenacity and adaptability of hereditary ruling groups, from a long chronological perspective based on Western Europe in medieval and modern times, see J. K. Powis, *Aristocracy* (Oxford 1984). The best book on Greek aristocracy is M. T. W. Arnheim, *Aristocracy in Greek Society* (London 1977); see especially chapter 2. Unfortunately, the only book devoted specifically to the Athenian aristocracy, P. MacKendrick, *The Athenian Aristocracy, 399 to 31 B.C.* [Martin Classical Lectures, 23] (Cambridge, Mass. 1969) has other limitations apart from the restricted period it covers. MacKendrick provides a parade of individual *gennetai* (members of clans) from a later period, but he does not discern clans acting as groups. There is some odd use of evidence; for example, he mentions the honouring of *prutaneis* as if it were a new diversion in the period 294–263 BC (p. 38), although he is aware (p. 25) of earlier lists such as [**86**]. He identifies many people as *gennetai* on flimsy evidence; indeed, some identifications are contradicted elsewhere in the book (cf. pp. 3 and 8 with 10–11, 13 with 30).

5 Forrest 48–9.

I

ATTIKE BEFORE SOLON

The transference of power from the kings to the aristocracy

When the political structure of Athens and the territory controlled by the city (called *Attike ge*, the land of the Athenians, or 'Attike' for short) first becomes visible in any detail, aristocratic families are in control. But originally there must have been kings in Attike, for the term for 'king', *basileus*, was retained as the name of one of the chief offices (or 'arkhonships'). The arkhon known as Basileus was responsible in classical Athens for some of the most sacred rituals of the state, such as the union of his wife with the god Dionysos mentioned in passage [**1**]. The Athenians of later times had traditions about their kings (as illustrated in passages [**3**] and [**4**]), but it is extremely difficult to extract from these traditions anything which can seriously be held to be historical. At some time before 700 BC the noble families succeeded in wresting control from a royal family. The outline of how this happened has to be deduced largely from two passages ([**1**] and [**2**] below) in the *Athenaion Politeia*, the 'Constitution of the Athenians' attributed (wrongly, in my view) to Aristotle. Unfortunately, the beginning of this work is itself lost.

1 Athenaion Politeia *3*

3 The ancient constitution, before Drakon's time,[1] was organised along the following lines. Offices were filled according to qualifications of noble birth[2] and wealth. At first offices were held for life, but later for a period of ten years.[3] (2) The most important and earliest of the offices were those of Basileus, Polemarkhos and Arkhon. Of these the earliest was the office of Basileus (for it stems from ancestral antiquity) and the second to be established was that of Polemarkhos, because of the inadequacy of some of the Basileis in matters of war. For this reason Ion was sent for in a threatening crisis. (3) The last office to be established was that of Arkhon.[4] Most authorities place its establishment in the time of Medon; but some date it to the time of Akastos, citing as evidence the fact that the nine arkhons now swear that they will carry out their oaths 'as in the time of Akastos',[5] suggesting that it was in his time that the descendants of Kodros withdrew from the kingship in return for the privileges granted to the Arkhon.[6] Whichever way it was, it would make little difference to the date.[7] But that the office of Arkhon was the last to be established is shown by the fact that the Arkhon does not control any of the ancient functions, as the Basileus and Polemarkhos do, but only the ones added later. So it is only of recent times that the Arkhonship has become important, having been augmented by the added functions. (4) Many years later, when the offices had already become annual appointments, the Thesmothetai[8] were appointed for the task of recording statutes and preserving them for judgment between litigants. So their office, alone of those discussed, was never of more than one year's duration.

(5) Chronologically, then, this is the order of precedence of these offices, relative to one another. The nine arkhons did not all occupy the same building. The Basileus had what is now called the Boukoleion, near the Prytaneion (and there is proof: for even now the union and marriage of the Basileus's wife to the god Dionysos takes place there).[9] The Arkhon occupied the Prytaneion, and the Polemarkhos the Epilykeion (which was formerly called the Polemarkheion, but after Epilykos rebuilt and refurbished it during his term as Polemarkhos, it was called the Epilykeion). The Thesmothetai occupied the Thesmotheteion, where the whole nine came together in the time of Solon.[10] The arkhons' authority was sufficient to make final decisions in lawsuits and not merely, as now, to conduct preliminary investigations. Such, then, was the character of the offices. (6) The Council of the Areopagos had the constitutional position of watching over the laws,[11] but it administered the largest and most important part of the state's affairs, even summarily inflicting personal punishment and fines on all offenders. This was natural since the arkhons were elected on qualifications of noble birth and wealth, while the Areopagos consisted of men who had served in that capacity.[12] For this reason membership of the

Areopagos is the only office which has remained to the present day a life appointment.[13]

Notes

1 That is, before the late seventh century BC. The words 'the one before Drakon's time' were probably inserted in the text when the 'Drakonian constitution' was inserted in chapter 4 [**15**]; see note 1 on that passage.

2 This may well have been an unspoken qualification for centuries before the idea that office should be restricted to nobles was challenged. The term for the prominent families that emerged as leaders from the dark age following the fall of the Mycenaean kingdoms and were regarded as a nobility of birth in the seventh and sixth centuries was Eupatridai ('people born of noble fathers'); cf. Rhodes 75–6.

3 The idea (expressed in 'at first offices were held for life') that the nobles forced the kings to stand down only to allow them or fellow nobles to retain the substance of monarchical powers as arkhons for life is improbable. It is better to presume that the arkhonship was of limited tenure from the beginning. We can place no faith in the surviving lists of kings (including the legendary Ion, mentioned below), arkhons for life and ten-year arkhons. All that is certain is that an aristocratic regime, with three chief offices, followed on a monarchy.

4 It seems clear that the official called 'king' (Basileus) retained only the religious power of the king, while the latter's administrative power was transferred to the Arkhon and his military power to the Polemarkhos.

If one of the officials who took over the powers of the kings was called Basileus, it seems that the term had no derogatory connotations (unlike the Roman term for 'king', *rex*) and thus that the transition from monarchy to aristocracy was relatively peaceful (cf. Hignett 46). Basileis is the plural form of Basileus.

The office of Polemarkhos ('military leader') is here stated to have been introduced after that of Basileus, but it should also be regarded, on linguistic grounds, as having been introduced after the office of Arkhon. One hardly needs to refer to the 'military leader' unless the term 'leader' (*arkhon*) is already in use. The term *arkhon* ('leader, ruler, regent') was used for the Arkhon but also for 'the nine arkhons' as a group (Basileus, Polemarkhos, Arkhon and the six Thesmothetai), as in the second sentence of *Athenaion Politeia* 3.3. Indeed the word translated 'offices' (*arkhai*) in *Athenaion Politeia* 3.1–2 could equally well be translated 'arkhonships'. To avoid confusion modern scholars sometimes refer to the Arkhon as the eponymous arkhon (i.e. the arkhon after whom the year was named; cf. the use of the arkhon's name as a date in, for example, *Athenaion Politeia* 14.1 [**55**] and 22.2 [**90**]).

5 This is surely the intended sense, although the reading of the papyrus at 'as' is uncertain (I prefer Kenyon's [ὥ]σπ̣ερ̣ to Oppermann's ἦ ‹μὴν› τά for the meaning; but, according to J. D. Thomas [Rhodes 100] and M. H. Chambers [Teubner text], neither word really suits the traces on the papyrus) and it is not easy to find parallels for the meaning 'carry out their oaths'. The oath of the arkhons is mentioned also in *Athenaion Politeia* 7.1 [**42**] and 55.5.

6 The text of the papyrus at this point has been challenged and its meaning

disputed. The word translated 'kingship' is *basileia*.

7 A justifiable conclusion, since in the traditional king lists (for which see Kastor of Rhodes, *FGrH* 250 F 4), Akastos was the son of Medon.

8 The six junior arkhons who bring the total to nine. The task here assigned to them cannot be correct if the laws were not written down before Drakon's time (see pp. 26–33), so it is probably a guess based on the presumed etymology ('lawgivers') of the term for their office.

9 This ritual wedding took place on the evening of the central day of the festival called Anthesteria; for a description see H. W. Parke, *Festivals of the Athenians* (London 1977) 112–13 or E. Simon, *Festivals of Attica: An Archaeological Commentary* (Madison, Wisc. 1983) 96–7.

10 For bibliography and brief discussion of the location of the buildings mentioned in this section, see Rhodes 103–4, 105–6.

11 Rhodes (107, 316–17) has suggested that the Council of the Areopagos was given a title such as 'guardian of the laws' from a very early period (no later than the codification by Drakon) and that it used the vagueness of the title to assume and exercise more powers than it formally possessed. But it was natural for a Council composed of nobles, some of whom had been members for several decades, to exert pressure on the noble cadets who were not yet members of the Council and who were currently holding office as arkhon.

12 For the procedure whereby arkhons passed into the Areopagos at the end of their year of office, see D. M. MacDowell, *Athenian Homicide Law in the Age of the Orators* (Manchester 1963) 40–1.

13 The author wrote the *Athenaion Politeia* about 330 BC. He makes clear in this section the predominance of the Areopagos in the aristocratic state.

2 Athenaion Politeia *41.2*[1]

(2) In number, this was the eleventh of the changes.[2] For the first alteration of the original situation took place when Ion and those with him came as settlers.[3] Then for the first time the Athenians were divided into four tribes, and they instituted tribe-kings.[4] The second alteration, which had some semblance of a constitution, and the first after this, was the one made in the time of Theseus, which deviated slightly from a monarchical constitution. After this was the alteration in the time of Drakon, in which they first wrote down the laws.[5] The third alteration was that in the time of Solon, after civil conflict; from it arose the beginning of democracy.[6] The fourth alteration was the tyranny in the time of Peisistratos. The fifth was that of Kleisthenes after the overthrow of the tyrants and was more democratic[7] than that of Solon. The sixth was that after the Persian Wars, when the Council of the Areopagos was in charge . . . .

Notes

1 Only about half of this long section (41.2) is given here. Because the early part of the *Athenaion Politeia* is lost, we have to rely on the author's summary of the changes in the constitution, and on the epitome of Herakleides (see [**3**]), to deduce what was said in the lost beginning of the work. Here we learn that the Athenians were originally divided into four tribes, each with a leader called *phulobasileus* (see also *Athenaion Politeia* 8.3 [**42**]), and that there was a transition from monarchy to aristocracy, beginning (it is said) with the mythical king Theseus.

2 In the constitution. The eleventh change was the restoration of democracy in Athens in 403 BC, after the removal of 'the Thirty' installed by Sparta following her victory over Athens in the Peloponnesian War. In our author's view, stated explicitly later in the chapter, the constitution set up after the return of the democrats lasted to his own day (c. 330 BC).

3 Ion was, according to legend, the son of king Xouthos of the Peloponnese and Kreousa, the daughter of Erekhtheus, king of Athens. He led the Athenians to victory over a coalition of Eleusis (in the western part of Attike) and the Thracians under Eumolpos. See Thucydides 2.15.1 [**5**] and note 3.

4 The term *phulobasileis* (translated 'tribe-kings') must refer to nobles who were leaders of the four tribes (note 1 above).

5 This sentence, oddly attributing the writing down of the laws to the Athenians rather than to Drakon, was probably inserted when the 'Drakonian constitution' was inserted in chapter 4 [**15**]. The words 'and the first after this', which make the previous sentence rather clumsy, were possibly added at the same time to mask the fact that Drakon's change breaks the numbered sequence of alterations. The interpolator sought to give the impression that the numbered sequence of changes began with Theseus, not Ion.

6 The comments here and (below) on Kleisthenes about the growth of democracy have an Aristotelian flavour, but do not support the close parallel with biological growth seen by J. Day and M. H. Chambers, *Aristotle's History of Athenian Democracy* [University of California Publications in History, 73] (Berkeley 1962), especially viii–ix, 38–50. They support the belief that this work was written in the Aristotelian school, not that Aristotle personally wrote it.

7 Although *metastasis*, 'alteration', is to be understood with 'second', 'third', 'fourth', 'fifth', 'sixth', etc., a word such as 'constitution' seems to have been in the author's mind when he wrote 'was more democratic'; cf. *Athenaion Politeia* 22.1 [**90**].

3 *Anonymous, excerpt from Herakleides Lembos,* On Constitutions[1]

Constitution of the Athenians

1 The Athenians had a monarchy in the beginning. When Ion settled with them, they were then called Ionians for the first time. Pandion, who was king after Erekhtheus, divided the rule among his sons, who were in continual conflict. Theseus made a proclamation and reconciled them on terms of equal and similar shares . . . .[2] From the time of the sons of Kodros kings were no longer appointed because they seemed to be effeminate and had become inadequate.[3]

Notes

1 Herakleides Lembos lived in Alexandria in the second century BC. His epitome *On Constitutions* was later excerpted by an unknown author. When the *Athenaion Politeia* was discovered in 1889, it confirmed that Herakleides's work comprised an epitome (relating to forty-four constitutions) derived directly from some 158 *Constitutions* written in the school of Aristotle. Either Herakleides or his excerptor made a poor job of his work. The end product provides less and less detail as it proceeds; it has political figures blatantly out of order; and it frequently fails to indicate the antecedents of words such as 'who' or 'they'.

This excerpt indicates some of the topics covered in the lost beginning of the *Athenaion Politeia*. The author of that work evidently agreed with other sources that the Athenians lived under a monarchy until the sons of Kodros.

2 The rest of Theseus's story is summarised.

3 The final epithet 'inadequate' probably refers to matters of war; cf. *Athenaion Politeia* 3.2 [**1**].

4 *Herakleides Lembos,* Epitome *of Hermippos,* On Lawgivers

Book 2

Kekrops, the earthborn man of [double form], is said to have been the first to give the [Ath]eni[a]ns [law]s, when he w[a]s ki[n]g, and of his [law]s the . . . [are] highly esteemed. But according to [Phi]lokhoros the . . . .[1]

Note

1 This is a papyrus fragment of the second century AD (the square brackets are intended to indicate letters which have been restored) which was used to reinforce a papyrus roll which has part of Plato's *Politikos* written on it. This patch preserves the end of Book 1 and the beginning of Book 2 of an epitome made by Herakleides Lembos (second century BC) of a treatise *On Lawgivers* by Hermippos (third/second century BC). Another patch gives the title of the work that was copied on the original papyrus: 'Ep[i]tome by [Her]akleides son of [S]arapion of the works of Hermippos *On Lawgivers*, *On the S[ev]en Sages* and *On [P]ythagoras*.' The fragments of this papyrus were first published by B. P. Grenfell and A. S. Hunt in volume 11 of *The Oxyrhynchus Papyri* (London 1915); it is referred to as *POxy* 1367. A commentary is provided there and by I. Gallo in volume 1 of *Frammenti biografici da papiri* [Testi e commenti, 1] (Rome 1975) 13–55.

The fragment indicates the kind of tradition current in the third and second centuries BC about the first king of Athens. Kekrops is described like other primeval men as 'earthborn'. The description of Kekrops as 'of double form' is variously explained as his being part man and part serpent, or as being male in the upper part of his body and female in the lower part, or as being of double citizenship (Egyptian and Greek). On this see Diodoros of Sicily 1.28.7 and A. Burton, *Diodorus Siculus, Book I: A Commentary* [Études préliminaires aux religions orientales dans l'empire romain, 29] (Leiden 1972) 122–3. Note also that Hermippos quoted conflicting opinions of the local historians of Attike. Unfortunately the patch is broken just as Philokhoros's opinion is about to be given. We know from the eighth-century monk Georgios Synkellos that Philokhoros explained the epithet 'of double form' as a reference to the extraordinary size of Kekrops's body (*FGrH* 328 F 93).

The unification of Attike

An important process in Athenian politics after 800 BC was the unification of the town of Athens and the large territory (about 2,650 square kilometres) of Attike. (I use the strictly transliterated form 'Attike' – see the introduction on p. 6 – although 'Attika' and 'Attica' have been widely accepted in modern discussions.) The vast majority of the people continued to live in scattered villages from which they went out to farm the surrounding land. But they were now a part of a political unit which controlled a large territory by Greek standards – rivalled, in fact, only by the territory (Lakonia) controlled by Sparta.

Later Athenians attributed this unification to a king, Theseus (passages [**5**]–[**7**]). But it seems likely that, even if such a large area had been united under the Mycenaean kings, a further *sunoikismos* was necessary after 800 BC, that is, long after the traditional dates (thirteenth century) for Theseus's reign in the king lists. It is, moreover, likely that the process of unification was piecemeal (as suggested in the notes on passage [**5**]), and that villages in the west and the far north-east were incorporated in the Athenian *polis* at a later stage.

5 *Thucydides 2.14.1–2.15.2, 2.16.1*[1]

14 The Athenians were convinced by what they heard[2] and brought in from the country their wives and children and all their household possessions; they even tore the timber off their houses. Their sheep and cattle they transported across to Euboia and the adjacent islands. (2) The move was a painful experience for them since most of them had always been accustomed to living in the country.

15 This had been characteristic of the Athenians from very early times more than of the other Greeks. From the time of

Kekrops and the first kings down to the time of Theseus the pattern of settlement in Attike was always in separate communities with their own town halls and officials. Unless there was some threat they did not meet to confer with the king, but they each conducted their own affairs and made their own decisions. On occasion some of them even fought with the king, as the people of Eleusis under Eumolpos did with Erekhtheus.[3] (2) But when Theseus became king he used his power as well as his intelligence to reorganise the country. One of his main changes was to abolish the councils and governments of the various communities and unite all the inhabitants in the present city,[4] setting up a single council and town hall. They all continued to live on their own lands, but he compelled them to have this one city, which became great when they were all registered as Athenian citizens. This city Theseus bequeathed to his descendants and from his day to this the Athenians hold a national festival in honour of the goddess Athene called the Sunoikia.[5] . . . *16* So for a long time the Athenians had lived in independent communities throughout Attike[6] and even after their unification the common experience from the time of the ancient inhabitants right down to the present war was to be born and live in the country. It was not easy to move with all their households, especially since they had just restored their properties after the Persian Wars.

Notes

1 The important information (for us) in this passage is provided in passing by Thucydides, who is intent on expounding his point that the Athenians found it difficult in 431 BC to uproot themselves from the districts where their families had lived for generations and become squatters in the town. The author of the *Athenaion Politeia* (to judge from the excerpt from Herakleides's epitome [**6**]) probably described the unification of Attike in its own right, but the early part of that work is lost.

2 At the beginning of the Peloponnesian War (431 BC), when the Spartans and their allies were about to invade Attike, Perikles son of Xanthippos, one of the ten generals of Athens, advised the Athenians to bring their property into the city and prepare for defensive action. He suggested that encouragement could be derived from the financial reserves, income and armed forces of Athens. This passage gives the response of the citizens.

3 Thucydides makes it clear that Attike was settled in separate communities in early times. Only when there was general alarm would the inhabitants come together and confer with the king who had general suzerainty over the whole of Attike. As evidence of the independence of the local communities Thucydides cites the war between the legendary king Erekhtheus and the Eleusinians, who lived west of Athens beyond the Aigaleos range but still within what was later

known as Attike (*Attike [ge]*, the land of the Athenians), under the leadership of Eumolpos.

4 This passage illustrates the reason why many scholars use the unwieldy term 'city-state' for *polis*. *Polis* is the word which I have translated by 'community' in 2.15.1–2 and then by 'city' here and in the next sentence. Thucydides calls the early communities of Attike *poleis* (the plural of *polis*) because they were politically independent. Then he uses *polis* for the city of Athens in his time, which was a political unit comprising both the town and the villages of Attike.

5 The name of the festival and the verb which Thucydides uses for Theseus's act of unification (*sunoikizein* in 2.15.2 and 2.16.1) suggest that it was a process of *sunoikismos*, 'living together'. But Thucydides emphasises in this passage that most of the people of Attike continued to live in the country. The unification was purely political and did not involve a transplant of population. For the festival, see note 4 on [**7**].

6 Although some scholars (e.g. R. A. Padgug, *GRBS* 13 [1972] 135–50) have vigorously defended the view that Attike was unified once for all in the Mycenaean period, many others have doubted the attribution of the unification to the legendary figure of Theseus, a king before the Trojan war. Hignett (pp. 36–7), for example, argues that there was disunion after the Mycenaean period and that the basic unification of Attike for the classical period took place in the eighth century. A. M. Snodgrass, *Archaeology and the Rise of the Greek State* (Cambridge 1977) 14–21 argues that Attike was so drastically depopulated in the centuries before 800 BC that any act of unification over such a large area (about 2,650 square kilometres) in the Bronze Age would need to be implemented afresh; and that it is only in the eighth century that pottery from outlying areas becomes indistinguishable in style and quality from that of the town. Even if one accepts a basic unification then, it is likely that Eleusis in the west and probably the area around Marathon in the north-east were incorporated in the Athenian *polis* at a later date. The Homeric hymn to Demeter suggests that Eleusis was still independent (cf. the references to the *polis* of Eleusis in verse 318 and to the *demos* of Eleusis in verse 490, and the complete lack of reference to Athens in the hymn) when it was composed in the seventh century (for a discussion of the date of composition see N. J. Richardson, *The Homeric Hymn to Demeter* [Oxford 1974] 5–11). The incorporation of Eleusis in the Athenian state may even belong to the sixth century. In Herodotos's story of the meeting between Solon of Athens and Kroisos of Lydia (1.29–1.34), a meeting which many consider legendary, Solon tells Kroisos about a certain Tellos the Athenian who brought help to his fellow-citizens 'when there was a battle between the Athenians and their neighbours at Eleusis' (1.30.5). It is not clear whether the battle was against the Megarians (but fought at the border town of Eleusis) or against the people of Eleusis. If the latter, then the passage suggests that Eleusis was not part of the Athenian *polis* in the time of Solon's contemporary Tellos – that is, at the beginning of the sixth century. J. McK. Camp II, *Hesperia* 48 (1979) 397–411, especially 404–5, argues that the backwardness of the political development of Athens (as seen, for example, in her lateness in colonisation and tyranny) may have been caused by a drought – and the epidemic which he postulates accompanied it – which is suggested by the closure of many wells in the Agora

in the second half of the eighth century BC. (For a summary of his theory see *The Athenian Agora: Excavations in the Heart of Classical Athens* [London 1986] 33–4.) Snodgrass, in R. Hägg (ed.), *The Greek Renaissance of the Eighth Century B.C.: Tradition and Innovation* [Skrifter Utgivna av Svenska Institutet i Athen, 4° 30] (Stockholm 1983) 167–71, especially 169–71, questions the existence of such a drought on the grounds that the Agora may not be representative and that a much higher proportion of young children should appear in the known burials of the period. Camp does, however, have a point in asking why the number of graves discovered in Attike from the period 700–650 BC is only a quarter or a fifth of those for the preceding half-century (ibid. 211). This phenomenon could be explained by the slowness of recovery after a disaster which greatly reduced the population.

6 *Anonymous, Excerpt from Herakleides Lembos,* On Constitutions

1 . . . Pandion, who was king after Erekhtheus, divided the rule among his sons, who were in continual strife. Theseus made a proclamation and reconciled them on terms of equal and similar shares.[1]

Note

1 For the context of this excerpt from the 'Constitution of the Athenians', see [3] above. According to the text, it was specifically the sons of Pandion who persisted in conflict and were reconciled by Theseus. But the lost beginning of the *Athenaion Politeia* probably indicated that Theseus reconciled the Athenians as a whole. This is suggested not only by the account of Thucydides (whom the author of the *Athenaion Politeia* was capable of using) but more especially by Plutarch (see [7]), who probably based his account on the same kind of local history of Attike as was used extensively for the *Athenaion Politeia*.

7 *Plutarch,* Theseus *24.1–2, 24.3–4*

24 After the death of Aigeus Theseus conceived a marvellous, large-scale project. He united the inhabitants of Attike in a single town[1] and made them one people belonging to one city. Hitherto they had been scattered and difficult to summon for the common interest of all and there were occasions when they had quarrelled and fought with one another. (2) So he went round and tried to persuade them village by village and clan by clan. . . .[2] (3) He abolished, then, the separate town halls, councils and governments in the various communities and established one common town hall and council for all where the town is now situated. He called the city Athens and established a common festival called the Panathenaia.[3] (4) He also celebrated on the sixteenth of Hekatombaion the Metoikia, which is still celebrated today.[4] Then he laid down the royal power, as he had undertaken,[5] and began to arrange the constitution with the sanction of the gods.

Notes

1 *Astu*, referring to the town which has grown into the modern city of Athens. In general Plutarch's account of the unification follows that of Thucydides closely. But Plutarch is surely mistaken in thinking that Theseus compelled everyone to move to the town. The political nature of the unification is correctly presented in the following clause: the inhabitants of Attike became one *demos*, a single citizen body meeting in a single assembly, and were members of one *polis*, a single self-governing community (although they continued to live in their villages; cf. Thucydides 2.15.1 [**5**]).

2 This sentence shows the nature of the opposition to unification: regional interests and the interests of nobles. The conflict among groups of landed aristocrats (their power having a largely regional basis; cf. *Athenaion Politeia* 13.5 [**52**]) existed both before and after Solon's reforms and it provides support for Hignett's contention (p. 123) that there was no effective unification of Attike until the tyranny of Peisistratos.

3 The greatest state festival, at which 'all' the Athenians honoured the city's patron goddess Athene. The evidence on the Panathenaia is collected and discussed by J. A. Davison, *JHS* 78 (1958) 23–42 and 82 (1962) 141–2 (= *From Archilochus to Pindar: Papers on Greek Literature of the Archaic Period* [London 1968] 28–69). Note in particular his demonstration that there was another tradition which attributed the Panathenaic festival to Erikhthonios, a son of the god Hephaistos. These stories of a foundation by a son of Hephaistos and a re-foundation or reorganisation by Theseus 'must have been addressed to an audience which had reason to believe that the Panathenaic festival in some form had existed since time immemorial' (*JHS* 78 [1958] 25 [= *From Archilochus to Pindar* 32]).

4 'Metoikia' refers to the change of residence which Plutarch thinks was involved in the unification. The festival is presumably the same as the Sunoikia mentioned by Thucydides and, if so, Plutarch's account provides its date of celebration (accepted, for example, by J. D. Mikalson, *The Sacred and Civil Calendar of the Athenian Year* [Princeton 1975] 29–30).

5 In the omitted portion of 24.2 Plutarch says that Theseus persuaded some of the powerful to his project by offering them a constitution without a king, and democracy. The idea that Theseus abolished the monarchy and established *demokratia* (24.2, 25.2) arose in the fifth century BC (it is present, for example, in Euripides, *Suppliant Women* 399–408). The author of the *Athenaion Politeia* (41.2 [**2**]) in the fourth century does not go so far.

Kylon's unsuccessful attempt to establish a tyranny and its aftermath

During the seventh century BC there was a wave of Greek aristocrats setting themselves up as tyrants in their respective cities. Many ambitious nobles saw what their counterparts in other cities had done and seized power in their own city. Sometimes they formed an alliance with an already established tyrant. Kylon of Athens married the daughter of Theagenes, the tyrant of neighbouring Megara. He relied on his fame as a victor at the Olympic Games and sought support from others in Attike. He seized the Athenian Akropolis during the Olympic festival (perhaps mistaking advice from the oracle at Delphi), but in this case the other noble families were able to muster their retainers and eventually overcome the attempted tyranny. The Kylonians were not able to detach the lower-class supporters from their aristocratic patrons.

The sources differ over several details; hence the incident provides a challenging exercise in source interpretation. But the incident also reveals something of the structure of politics at Athens in the late seventh century.

8 *Herodotos 5.70.2–5.72.1*

(2) First Kleomenes sent a messenger to Athens and tried to expel Kleisthenes and many other Athenians with him, describing them as 'accursed'. The messenger and proclamation were sent on the instruction of Isagoras, for the Alkmeonidai and the members of their faction were accused of the bloodshed which led to the label 'accursed', whereas he himself and his supporters had no connection with it.[1]

71 This is the reason why some Athenians were called 'accursed'. There was an Athenian named Kylon who had won a victory at Olympia.[2] He aimed at a tyranny, won over a faction of his contemporaries and attempted to seize the Akropolis. Unable to hold it, he sat as a suppliant in front of the statue of Athene. (2) The chiefs of the Naukraroi, who were at that time in charge of Athens,[3] made them leave[4] on the understanding that they were liable to any penalty but death. When they were murdered the Alkmeonidai were blamed.[5] These events took place before the time of Peisistratos.[6]

72 When Kleomenes sent instructions and tried to expel Kleisthenes and the 'accursed', Kleisthenes himself left the country secretly. But Kleomenes nevertheless arrived in Athens with a small force and drove out as 'accursed' 700 Athenian families[7] which were suggested to him by Isagoras.

Notes

1 Kleisthenes the Alkmeonid and Isagoras were leaders of two rival factions in Athens after the overthrow of the tyrants (511/10 BC). Kleisthenes, who was losing the struggle, formed an alliance with the common people and thus carried his proposals and overcame his opponents. Isagoras's response was to summon Kleomenes, a Spartan king. This is the context in which the story of Kylon is introduced (for the full story see Chapter V, pp. 138–45). Macan (on Herodotos 5.71.1) points out that none of our sources tells the story from Kylon's point of view. Herodotos and Thucydides tell the story in order to explain the term 'accursed', as applied to the Alkmeonidai; the *Athenaion Politeia* was presumably interested in its relevance to constitutional history; while Plutarch introduces the story because he thought that Solon was involved in the trial of the Alkmeonidai and the purification of the city. M. Lang, *CP* 62 (1967) 243–9 argues that Herodotos's version includes practically all that was known of the conspiracy and its aftermath in his time, and that the additional material in Thucydides and the later sources are accretions to the facts. But her attempt to demythologise the accounts starts with the assumption that Herodotos did not abbreviate his knowledge of the affair, except in the details of Kylon's status and of the help from Megara. Such an assumption seems inadmissible for an account which is explicitly a digression.

2 Herodotos does not bring out the significance of this Olympic victory. Thucydides (1.126.5, below [**9**]) shows that it led Kylon to attack during the Olympic festival.

3 Thucydides (1.126.8, 11 [**9**]) says that the nine arkhons were the officials involved in the negotiations and explains, in view of their unimportance in his time, that 'at that time the nine arkhons conducted most of the public business'. Since he indicates that the people came in from all districts of Attike, tribal officials may also have been involved. But the Naukraroi, though tribal officials, had *financial* duties (see *Athenaion Politeia* 8.3 [**42**], 21.5 [**84**]) and it is difficult to see how they came to be involved. B. Jordan, *California Studies in Classical Antiquity* 3 (1970) 173–4 suggests that they were treasurers responsible for revenues stored on the Akropolis and also for the statue of Athene. If so, how were they able to offer the conspirators immunity from capital punishment? Their interest in the statue would be obvious, but their power to keep their guarantee of immunity would not be. There is a further difficulty in Herodotos's statement that the Naukraroi were at that time in charge of Athens. Jordan (ibid. 153–75) solves this problem by adopting the reading of one manuscript ἐνέμοντο τότε instead of the generally accepted ἔνεμον τότε ('who were at that time in charge') and translating 'who at that time collected the revenues from Athens'. I prefer the reading of most manuscripts because Thucydides must have read ἔνεμον τότε (to which his τότε . . . ἔπρασσον ['at that time conducted'] corresponds). For bibliography on the Kylonian conspiracy and the evidence on Naukraroi and the usage of the verb νέμεσθαι see Jordan's article. Recently T. J. Figueira has linked Herodotos's reference to the 'chiefs (*prutaneis*) of the Naukraroi' with the ostrakon cast

against Xanthippos which is translated in Chapter V, p. 183 [**94** (iii)]. He argues that the executive of the Council known as *prutaneis* (see *IG* II^2 1750 [**86**] with notes) did not exist when the ostrakon vote was cast, so that it alludes to the *prutaneis* of the Naukraroi, allegedly still existing in the 480s (*Historia* 35 [1986] 257–79). However, if trierarchs had replaced the Naukraroi by the time of the Persian Wars (see *Chiron* 14 [1984] 14), the action of Xanthippos which so offended one voter probably had nothing to do with the duties of Naukraroi, whose office was by then obsolete. Moreover, the ostrakon makes no mention of Naukraroi, only of *prutaneis*. It is better to consider this word on the ostrakon as a general reference to political leaders in Xanthippos's time. Thucydides's statement that the nine arkhons were responsible seems more reliable than Herodotos's reference to an obscure office.

S. D. Lambert, *Historia* 35 (1986) 105–12 suggests that the word for 'at that time' has a much more specific reference: the arkhons were away at the festival (whether the Olympic festival or the Diasia; cf. Thucydides 1.126.5–6 [**9**]), the chiefs of the Naukraroi were responsible for the initial response to the crisis at Athens, and the arkhons took over later in what was a long siege (Thucydides 1.126.8 [**9**]). But this involves rejecting the main clause of the sentence ('made these men leave on the understanding that they were liable to any penalty but death'), which clearly makes the chiefs of the Naukraroi responsible for the final negotiations with the Kylonians.

4 The verb ἀνίστημι, used here and in Thuc. 1.126.11, means 'make to stand up, raise up' and is used in a technical sense of making suppliants rise from their suppliant posture and leave the sanctuary.

5 To make clear why the Alkmeonidai, the family from which Kleisthenes was descended, was blamed, Herodotos needs to mention, as Plutarch (*Solon* 12.1–2 [**11**]) does, that an Alkmeonid named Megakles was arkhon (probably eponymous arkhon) at the time of Kylon's attempted *coup*. When we turn from the exigencies of Herodotos's story to what actually happened, we might well conclude that responsibility for the murder of the Kylonians rested with all nine arkhons, as Thucydides implies (see note 3 above and note 10 on [**9**]). But when the Alkmeonidai were put on trial a generation or more after the attempted *coup* (see note 3 on [**10**]), the fact that Megakles had been arkhon at the time was used against the family. The Alkmeonidai continued to be thought responsible, as the context for Thucydides's story [**9**] shows. Thucydides himself, however, takes a line more favourable to the Alkmeonidai by making the nine arkhons and not just Megakles (even if he was eponymous arkhon) responsible for the conduct of the siege (1.126.8 [**9**]). Herodotos gives a pro-Alkmeonid version by omitting all mention of an Alkmeonid arkhon and perhaps also by implying that it was not the arkhons but other officials who were responsible for the massacre. (For a different view see H.-F. Bornitz, *Herodot-Studien* [Berlin 1968] 53–4, 57, 139, 163 and R. Develin, in J. W. Eadie and J. Ober (eds), *The Craft of the Ancient Historian: Essays in Honor of Chester G. Starr* [Lanham, Maryland 1985] 125–39 at 129–30.) While the Alkmeonidai may well have been the victims of propaganda spread by their opponents, they nevertheless had people in the fifth century (as the accounts of Herodotos and Thucydides reveal) propagating a version of the attempted *coup* of Kylon which was more in their interests.

6 This is a vague date. Kylon's Olympic victory is dated to 640 BC and his attempt at establishing a tyranny is generally put in one of the Olympic years 632, 628 or 624 on the assumption that he was probably a young man when he competed at Olympia (in one of the sprints: Pausanias 1.28.1), but should not have been too old for his faction of contemporaries to be past the age to make an assault on the Akropolis.

7 Although this refers to households or extended families, not clans, the number seems too high both for expulsion by 'a small force' and for effective opposition to be mounted by the remaining Athenians against Kleomenes and Isagoras (Herodotos 5.72.2 [**80**]).

9 *Thucydides 1.126.1–1.127.1*

126 In the meantime[1] Sparta sent embassies to Athens with various charges, so that she might have as strong a reason as possible for making war, if Athens paid no attention. (2) The first embassy she sent ordered the Athenians to drive out the curse of the goddess.[2] The story of the curse was as follows.

(3) There was in ancient times an Athenian named Kylon who had won a victory at Olympia. He came from a noble family and was influential. He had married the daughter of a Megarian named Theagenes, who was tyrant of Megara at that time.[3] (4) When Kylon consulted the god at Delphi he was told that he should seize the Akropolis in Athens at the greatest festival of Zeus. (5) He received a force from Theagenes and persuaded his friends to support him,[4] and when the Olympic Games came on in the Peloponnese he seized the Akropolis with a view to establishing a tyranny;[5] for he thought that the Olympic Games was the greatest festival of Zeus and was somewhat appropriate for himself, an Olympic victor. (6) Whether the greatest festival was meant to be in Attike or somewhere else he did not even consider and the oracle did not make clear. (The Athenians have a festival, the Diasia, which is called the greatest festival of Zeus the Gracious; it is held outside the city and at it the whole people assemble and sacrifice not ordinary victims but local offerings.)[6] He felt that his interpretation was correct and he made his attempt. (7) But when the Athenians realised this they all came in from the countryside[7] and joined in besieging them on all sides. (8) After some time most of the Athenians grew tired of the siege and went away, entrusting the blockade to the nine arkhons, who were given full authority to settle the whole matter in whatever way they decided was best. At that time the nine

arkhons conducted most of the public business.[8]

(9) Those besieged with Kylon were in a bad state because of the lack of food and water. (10) Kylon and his brother escaped, but the rest, because they were distressed and some of them were dying of hunger, sat down as suppliants at the altar on the Akropolis. (11) When those Athenians who were entrusted with the blockade saw them dying in the sanctuary, they made them leave on the understanding that they would not harm them in any way. But after leading them out they murdered them. Some of those killed had taken refuge, as they passed, at the altars of the dread goddesses.[9] For this reason the murderers and the family descended from them[10] were called 'accursed and committers of sacrilege against the goddess'. (12) So the Athenians drove out these 'accursed' men. But later Kleomenes the Spartan with a faction of Athenians drove out the living members of the family and dug up and cast out the bones of the dead.[11] However, they returned later and their family still lives in Athens.

127 It was this curse that the Spartans ordered to be driven out. The main reason they put forward was to take vengeance for the gods, but they knew that Perikles son of Xanthippos was connected with the curse on his mother's side and they thought that if he were expelled it would be easier for them to gain concessions from the Athenians.

Notes

1 Thucydides refers to the period between the decision of the Peloponnesian League in August 432 BC to go to war with Athens and the open outbreak of war with the invasion of Attike in the following May. This period, he says (1.125.2), was taken up with preparations for war by the various members of the League.

2 The singular presumably refers to Athene, whose altar ('statue' in Herodotos 5.71.1) is probably meant in 1.126.10 below.

3 The potential tyrant, Kylon, formed a marriage alliance with the tyrant of Megara, who subsequently provided troops for Kylon (1.126.5).

4 Kylon's upper-class supporters (*philoi*) in Thucydides's account are equivalent to his faction (*hetaireia*) of contemporaries in Herodotos's account. For Herodotos's use of *hetaireia* see note 6 on Herodotos 5.66.2 [**80**].

5 This is one of two minor discrepancies between Herodotos (who says that Kylon tried to seize the Akropolis but was unable to hold it) and Thucydides. The other minor discrepancy concerns the negotiations. Herodotos says that Kylon himself became a suppliant and that the faction agreed to stand trial. Thucydides (1.126.10–11) says that Kylon and his brother escaped, but that his supporters negotiated an amnesty. The scholia on Aristophanes, (b) and (c) [**12**], also have Kylon escape, but an historian of uncertain date, Aristodemos

(*FGrH* 104 [Anhang] F 2), who confuses Megakles (see note 5 on Herodotos 5.71.2 [**8**]) with the more famous Perikles, says that Kylon was killed on his way down from the Akropolis. There is no conclusive argument for preferring Thucydides to Herodotos on these two points, but the more detailed account provided by Thucydides suggests that it may be wiser to think that Kylon did succeed in seizing the Akropolis but that during the subsequent siege he and his brother escaped, leaving their faction to negotiate an amnesty.

6 This translates the text of the manuscripts for the last clause. For arguments against the widely accepted emendations and for a discussion of the Diasia see M. H. Jameson, *BCH* 89 (1965) 165–72.

7 This clause seems to mean that the great majority of the citizens still lived in farming communities at the time of Kylon's attempt, and came in prepared for a siege lasting several days, rather than that the city dwellers were the only ones concerned and they were out working on the land during the day.

8 This is the most significant difference with the account of Herodotos who says that 'the chiefs of the Naukraroi, who were at that time in charge of Athens' were the officials involved in the siege negotiations. Thucydides appears to be deliberately contradicting Herodotos and his version is to be preferred; see note 3 on Herodotos 5.71.2 [**8**] above.

9 A reference to the avenging deities called Erinues. The supporters of Kylon had apparently reached the Areopagos, just north-west of the Akropolis, before being attacked.

10 Thucydides does not name the Alkmeonidai because he assumes that his readers will identify 'the family' with the Alkmeonidai when he says (1.127.1) that Perikles was connected with the curse on his mother's side. On the basis of what Thucydides has told us, one would have expected that all nine arkhons (who must have belonged to several families) were equally guilty. His narrative needs an explanation such as that provided by *Athenaion Politeia* 13.2 [**52**] for the period after Solon, that the arkhon (that is, the eponymous arkhon) had the greatest power. Plutarch (*Solon* 12.1 [**11**]) highlights the role of one arkhon, Megakles the Alkmeonid.

11 The first expulsion of the Alkmeonidai can be dated from *Athenaion Politeia* 1 [**10**] and Plutarch, *Solon* 12.3-4 [**11**] to the period shortly before Solon's reforms. The Alkmeonidai returned by about 590 BC, if Alkmeon, son of the Megakles involved in the Kylon affair, commanded the Athenian forces in the First Sacred War (Plutarch, *Solon* 11.2 [**103**] with note 4). The second expulsion mentioned by Thucydides occurred in 508/7 BC (cf. Herodotos 5.70.2 [**8**]).

10 Athenaion Politeia *1*

1 . . . [The Alkmeonidai were tried by a jury chosen][1] on qualifications of noble birth[2] who took oath over the sacrifices, with Myron [acting as prosecutor]. When the curse was pronounced, the bodies of the offenders themselves were cast out of their graves,[3] while their family was exiled for ever. On these terms Epimenides of Krete performed a ceremonial purification of the city.[4]

Notes

1 The words in square brackets are supplied. The beginning of the *Athenaion Politeia* is lost. The portion preserved on papyrus begins in mid-sentence and towards the end of a chapter which presumably dealt with Kylon's attempt to establish a tyranny and the action of other nobles, under the leadership of Megakles the Alkmeonid, in murdering Kylon's supporters. This is deduced from the summary of the work, made by Herakleides Lembos in the second century BC, which reads: 'Those who joined Kylon in his attempt at establishing a tyranny fled to the altar of the goddess and were killed by Megakles and his followers. Those responsible for the murder were banished as accursed.' (*On Constitutions* 2). From Plutarch, *Solon* 12.4 [**11**] we learn that Myron was the accuser of the Alkmeonidai. If the beginning of the *Athenaion Politeia* is thus correctly reconstructed, it reveals that its author was influenced by the propaganda of generations of factional opponents of the Alkmeonidai more than by the pro-Alkmeonid accounts of Herodotos and Thucydides. .

2 Naturally only nobles were acceptable jurors for the trial of nobles such as the Alkmeonidai.

3 This action against dead members of the family is mentioned also by Plutarch (*Solon* 12.4; Thucydides 1.126.12 [**9**] connects it with the second expulsion of the 'accursed' in 508/7 BC). It shows that the trial of the Alkmeonidai took place at least a generation after the massacre of the Kylonians. The delay may have been because the Alkmeonidai were sufficiently powerful at the time of Kylon's attempt to have had Megakles elected eponymous arkhon and to escape immediate conviction. Alternatively, all nine arkhons were held responsible and too many families were implicated for an immediate trial to be held. Whatever the explanation for the delay, shortly before the reforms of Solon a coalition of families used the sacrilege charge to remove the Alkmeonidai from Attike for ever (they hoped). This is of importance for an understanding of the reforms of Solon; the expulsion of the Alkmeonidai is an example of the kind of clan conflict which led to Solon's extraordinary appointment.

4 Plutarch, *Solon* 12.8-9 [**11**] dates this purification by Epimenides to the time of Solon. See note 6 on that passage.

11 *Plutarch,* Solon *12.1–4, 12.7–9 (abridged)*

12 The Kylonian curse had been troubling the city for a long time. It stemmed from the occasion on which those who had sworn to support Kylon and who were sitting as suppliants of the goddess[1] were persuaded by Megakles the arkhon to come down and stand trial. They attached a woollen thread to the goddess's statue and held on to it, but when they had descended as far as the shrine of the dread goddesses the thread broke of its own accord. Megakles and his fellow arkhons rushed to seize them on the pretext that the goddess rejected their appeal. Those outside sacred precincts were stoned to death, while those who took refuge at the altars were slaughtered there. The only men spared were those who appealed to the arkhons' wives. (2) For this deed they were hated and called 'accursed'. The surviving supporters of Kylon regained their strength and were continually in conflict with the descendants of Megakles. (3) At this particular time the conflict had reached an extreme peak and the common people were divided between the two factions.[2] With his reputation already high Solon[3] intervened along with the most prominent Athenian citizens and by entreaty and argument he persuaded those called 'accursed' to submit to trial and be judged by a jury of 300 men chosen on qualifications of noble birth.[4] (4) Myron of Phlya acted as prosecutor and the men were convicted. The living members of the family were exiled and the corpses of the dead were dug up and cast outside the borders of the country . . . .[5]

(7) So they summoned from Krete Epimenides of Phaistos . . . . (8) When he came he formed a friendship with Solon, assisting him greatly in the preparation of his legislation and in paving the way for its acceptance. . . .[6] (9) His greatest contribution was to sanctify and consecrate the city by various propitiatory and purificatory offerings and by religious foundations and thus to make it observant of justice and more inclined to harmony.

Notes

1 Athene.

2 Note the political vocabulary here. There was continual *stasis* between the Kylonian faction and the Alkmeonidai and the *stasis* reached a high peak with the division of the *demos* into supporters of one side or the other.

3 There is a tendency in the tradition represented by Plutarch's *Solon* to associate Solon with more events than is plausible. If Solon persuaded the Alkmeonidai to submit to trial, he or they underestimated the strength of the coalition of clans opposing them. Among other things, the coalition presumably had the support of Delphi for the sacrilege charge, for Delphi had encouraged Kylon earlier against the powerful Alkmeonidai (cf. W. G. Forrest, *BCH* 80 [1956] 39–42). In any case it is significant that Plutarch, like the author of the *Athenaion Politeia*, conceives of the trial of the Alkmeonidai as belonging to the period shortly before Solon's reforms. Indeed, if Solon's reputation was already high, as Plutarch indicates, he may already have held the arkhonship. This would strengthen the case (see note 3 on [**18**] and note 5 on [**29**]) for

placing Solon's reforms some time after his arkhonship.

4 This and the following sentence enable us to reconstruct the fragmentary opening sentence of *Athenaion Politeia* 1. The *Athenaion Politeia* and Plutarch appear to be following the same tradition on the punishment of the Alkmeonidai (living and dead) and on the employment of Epimenides. Probably both accounts are based on an *Atthis*, a local history of Attike.

5 Plutarch goes on to speak of further troubles (the loss of Nisaia and Salamis to Megara) and the view of seers that the city needed purification from curses and pollution.

6 Apparently this is a political friendship, for Epimenides used his prestige to disseminate Solonian propaganda. Diogenes Laertios (1.110) dates the purification by Epimenides to the 46th Olympiad (596–593 BC) and, like Plutarch, assumes that Epimenides gave advice to Solon (1.112–13).

12 *Scholia*[1] *on Aristophanes,* Hippeis *445*

(a) 'from the committers of sacrilege': Those involved in the Kylonian curse, which seems to have been an act of impiety against Athene, inasmuch as those who were blockaded with Kylon on the Akropolis came down for trial in the Areopagos, after fastening a chain of suppliants' branches to the statue of Athene. But when it collapsed, the Athenians hit them with stones. Aristophanes says 'committers of sacrilege' instead of 'accursed'.[2]

(b) 'committers of sacrilege': Those who wronged Athene. For Kylon, an Athenian, having married a Megarian wife, the daughter of Theagenes, and wanting to become tyrant, received an oracle to attack the city at the great festival of Zeus. He made his attack during the Olympic Games, thinking that this was the great festival, and received the added support of a force from Theagenes, not realising that the Diasia was the great festival. He attacked the Akropolis, began to plunder it and was caught. He was taken prisoner while looting the sanctuary of Athene. Kylon himself escaped, but they killed the rest. Some, indeed, they murdered after dragging them away from the altars where they were suppliants. So they used to call those who wronged the suppliants 'committers of sacrilege'. They were expelled from the city because they had transgressed the ancient laws in killing the suppliants.[3]

(c) Kylon seized the Akropolis with a view to gaining a tyranny. He was taken prisoner in the act of looting the sanctuary of Athene, and was blockaded by the Athenians. He himself found an opportunity to escape, but his supporters fled to the altars of the gods.[4] These men[5] dragged them away and murdered them; for this reason they were called 'committers of sacrilege'.

Notes

1 Scholia are explanatory comments, generally written in the margins of manuscripts, by ancient scholars and teachers. (For a photograph of scholia written in all four margins of the first page of another play by Aristophanes, see K. J. Dover, *Aristophanic Comedy* [London 1972] plate 3 [facing p. 7].) The three explanations offered here reveal a fair degree of overlap, especially between (b) and (c), which use as a heading the same quotation from verse 445 of the play. Aristophanes's character (representing the fifth-century politician Kleon) says threateningly: 'From the committers of sacrilege against the goddess I say that you are descended.'

2 Thucydides (1.126.11 [**9**]) uses both 'accursed' and the word being explained here, which I have translated 'committers of sacrilege'.

3 Both attempting to set up a tyranny and violating the sanctuary sought by suppliants were serious offences. Comment (b) follows Thucydides's account fairly closely, echoing phraseology such as 'received a force from Theagenes' and having Kylon himself escape. But the scholiast embellishes the version of our other sources by having Kylon loot the treasures kept in the sanctuary of Athene. The added detail helps to excuse the Alkmeonidai (who, incidentally, are not mentioned in any of these three comments).

4 The scholiast runs together the altar of Athene (Thucydides 1.126.10 [**9**]; cf. Plutarch, *Solon* 12.1 [**11**] with note 1) and the altars of the dread goddesses (1.126.11).

5 This should refer, in the context, to 'the Athenians', but it may originally have referred specifically to the Alkmeonidai (and their associates).

The codification of laws by Drakon

At some time late in the seventh century (the traditional date is 621/0 BC) laws were enacted or written down by a certain Drakon. They almost certainly did not amount to a constitution, and so passage [**15**] is highly suspect, probably a forgery. Specific information is virtually restricted to a law on homicide, which was republished with the retention of anachronistic clauses some 200 years later (passage [**13**]). The provisions of this law seem designed to eliminate a vicious circle of feuding and murder by aristocratic clans. If we look at the law in the light of the Kylonian affair (pp. 17–26 above), it seems that one clan in particular, the Alkmeonidai, stood to gain protection from vengeance attacks following their leadership in the slaughter of the Kylonians.

13 *Meiggs and Lewis no. 86* = IG *I^3 104 (409/8* BC)[1]

Diogn[e]tos of the deme Phrearrhioi was secreta[ry]
Diokles was arkhon[2]

It was resolved by the Council and the Assembly, Aka[m]antis held the p[r]ytany,[3] [D]io[g]netos was secretary, Euthydikos [w]as chairman, ..e...anes moved the motion. [L]et the recorders of the laws pub[l]ish on a marble block th[e] law of Drakon concerning homi[ci]de, after receiving it from the B[a]s[i]le[us,[4] wi]t[h the he]lp of [the secr]etary of the Council and le[t them] pl[a]c[e it in fr]on[t] of the Stoa of the Basileus.[5] The *poletai* [are to] let the [cont]ract [in accordance with the l]aw; the Hellenotamiai are to make the pa[y]m[e]n[t].[6]

First Axon.[7]

Even if [someone k]i[lls someone] without [pr]emedita[ti]on, [he is to be] ex[iled].[8] The Basileis are to [pr]onounce responsib[le] for the homici[de] either . . . (seventeen letters illegible) . . . or the one who [in]stigated it. The Ephetai are to reach [a v]er[di]ct.[9] [Pardon is to be granted, if] there is a [fathe]r or brothe[r] or sons, by al[l], or else the one who op[poses it is to prevail. In the] absence of these relatives, [pardon is] to be granted by relatives as distant as cou[sin's] son and [cousin, if all] agree to it; the one who op[pos]es it [is to p]rev[ail. But if not even one of these is alive,] and he [ki]lled unintention[ally,] and the [F]i[fty-One, the Ephetai,] determine that he killed [unintention]ally, le[t] me[mbers of the ph]r[atry, ten in number,] admit him, [if they agree to it. Let] the Fif[ty-]One [select these men on qualifications of] nob[le bi]rth. [And let those] who ki[l]le[d pr]evi[o]usly [be covered by] th[is statute.] . . .[10]

Notes

1 A revised text of this inscription was provided for Meiggs and Lewis by R. S. Stroud, who subsequently published a full discussion of the inscription and Drakon's work as lawgiver in *Drakon's Law on Homicide* [University of California Publications: Classical Studies, 3] (Berkeley 1968). Traces of fifty-eight lines are preserved before the inscription breaks off, but only the first twenty lines are translated here. Words and letters in square brackets represent restorations not visible on the stone.

2 Since we know that Diokles was arkhon in 409/8 BC the heading of the whole inscription provides a firm date for the republication of Drakon's law on homicide. In 411/10 there was an oligarchic revolution in Athens which set up

a Council of Four Hundred as the government. After its overthrow the newly restored democracy began to revise and republish the laws of Athens. This inscription is one of the results of that republication.

3 This clause indicates that Akamantis was the tribe providing the executive of the Council when the decree was passed, but we do not know when the prytany of Akamantis fell in 409/8 BC.

4 This sentence strongly suggests that Drakon's law on homicide was to be republished without alteration. The Basileus (that one of the nine arkhons called 'king'; cf. *Athenaion Politeia* 3.2–3 [**1**]) probably had the original *axones* (wooden tablets) of Drakon in his archives; see note 2 on *Athenaion Politeia* 7.1 [**42**].

5 The law was to be publicly exhibited in the Agora, the administrative and commercial centre of Athens, in front of the portico named after the office of Basileus. The portico was found in the north-west corner (see note 2 on [**42**]) of the Agora in 1970: T. L. Shear Jr, *Hesperia* 40 (1971) 243–60 with plates 45–50 and 44 (1975) 365–70 with plate 82; H. A. Thompson and R. E. Wycherley, *The Athenian Agora* 14 (Princeton 1972) 83–90; H. A. Thompson, *The Athenian Agora: A Guide to the Excavation and Museum*, 3rd edn (Athens 1976) 82–7. The stone was discovered in 1843 at the site of the modern cathedral of Athens, about 700m away, and is now in the National Epigraphical Museum.

6 The decree passed in 409/8 BC finished with financial arrangements for the republication of Drakon's law on homicide. The *poletai* ('sellers') are to let the contract for the purchase of the marble block, the inscribing of the law and the erection of the block in the place designated. The Hellenotamiai ('treasurers of the Greeks') are to make the payments for these services.

7 When the law of Drakon was republished in 409/8 BC the engraver took over this heading from his source. Lines 11–55 of the present inscription represent the content of the first *axon*, or wooden tablet, containing Drakon's law. Stroud convincingly shows by means of careful measurements that there was a heading in line 56 and he restores with reasonable certainty '[Sec]ond [*axon*]' (op. cit. 16–18). Since the law on homicide was copied from at least two *axones*, it is unlikely that only part of the homicide law was republished in 409/8 BC. Some, however, take the opening word καί in line 11 as a connective ('and') and conclude that part of the homicide law (presumably that dealing with intentional homicide) was not republished for some reason. But this view conflicts with the decision to publish 'the law of Drakon concerning homicide' and one would in any case expect a connective 'and' to be deleted along with a preceding clause if that existed. That καί means 'even' was defended by Stroud (op. cit. 34–40). It is interesting to note that the law began with unintentional homicide and moved on to intentional homicide in that part of the inscription which has been lost. This seems to follow from the headings and from the evidence that death was a penalty for intentional homicide in the late fifth and fourth centuries. But M. Gagarin, *Drakon and Early Athenian Homicide Law* [Yale Classical Monographs, 3] (New Haven 1981), suggests that intentional homicide was dealt with only by implication in Drakon's code (he stresses 'Even if' in line 11) and that the procedures and penalties for intentional homicide were the same as for

unintentional homicide. This would require that the Athenians later increased the penalty for intentional homicide. Moreover, as pointed out in note 8, Drakon's law seems intent on distinguishing (and protecting the life of) the person who commits involuntary homicide.

8 The opening provision of Drakon's law on homicide emphasises that even where there was no premeditation the penalty for homicide is exile (the restoration of exile as the penalty is supported by Demosthenes 23.52, 72 and other passages). This penalty hardly fits the tradition that Drakon's law code prescribed death as the penalty for most offences (Plutarch, *Solon* 17.2 [**16**]). Indeed, the burden of the law on homicide as preserved in this inscription is protection of the person who commits involuntary homicide. (For the view that 'unpremeditated' homicide is restricted to what we would call accidental homicide, and did not cover an act intended to harm but which resulted in death, see W. T. Loomis, *JHS* 92 [1972] 86–95.) By making the basic penalty exile Drakon reduced the likelihood of a succession of killings and consequent feuds between noble clans.

9 The decision as to guilt rests with fifty-one Ephetai (identity uncertain, but jurors in the homicide courts). In the preceding sentence Basileis (plural) could refer either to the Basileus ('king') arkhons over the years or the Basileus arkhon and the tribal heads (*phulobasileis*; see note 4 on [**2**]). Their task, apparently, is to pronounce the sentence and to name the person responsible for the death.

10 Lines 13–20 appear to provide for the pardon of the involuntary homicide on the unanimous wish of the closest relatives of the victim available, or for re-admission to Attike on the recommendation of the Ephetai and the phratry (apparently everyone belonged to a 'brotherhood' before Kleisthenes; see the introduction to Chapter VI, p. 191 and note 4 on [**96**]) if no relative as close as cousin's son was still alive. About half of each line is illegible, but lines 13–14 and 16–20 can be restored from the law quoted in Pseudo-Demosthenes 43.57. Lines 26–9 (not translated here) are very fragmentary but appear to be identical with the law cited in Demosthenes 23.37, which provides for the punishment of anyone who kills the homicide while he is in exile. This provision also constituted a safeguard against the vicious circle of noble feuds.

* * *

Does the inscription preserve Drakon's law on homicide from the seventh century? The case against the authenticity of the law rests on the assumptions that a law recorded on wooden tablets would not have survived for 200 years and that revisions must have been made in the homicide law by the Athenians over that period. Against these assumptions of historical probability it can be shown that the similar wooden tablets of Solon survived much longer than 200 years (E. Ruschenbusch, *Σόλωνος νόμοι: Die Fragmente des solonischen Gesetzeswerkes mit einer Text- und Überlieferungsgeschichte* [Historia Einzelschriften, 9] [Wiesbaden 1966] 23–52 and note 1 on Plutarch, *Solon* 1.1 [**31**]). It can also be shown that Drakon's law on homicide was not revised or incorporated into a new code at the time of Solon's reforms (*Athenaion Politeia* 7.1 [**42**]; Plutarch, *Solon* 17.1 [**16**]; R. S. Stroud, op. cit. 32–4). The religious nature of the law on homicide and the attitude to it of the orators suggest that it was considered inviolable. Certainly the recorders of the law in 409/8 BC preserved several items in the law which were obsolete in the late fifth century: the selection of representatives on the basis of aristocratic birth (line 19), a clause making the provisions for pardon retroactive (lines 19–20) – relevant only for a generation or so after the legal innovation of pardon – and a reference to frontier markets (lines 27–8). For an extended argument that the present inscription preserves a faithful copy of Drakon's law on homicide see R. S. Stroud, op. cit. 60–4.

Finally, we might consider the effect of Drakon's law on homicide on the feuding which followed the unsuccessful attempt of Kylon to become tyrant in Athens (pp. 17–26 above). The Alkmeonidai stood to gain more than the supporters of Kylon from the codification of this law on homicide. This law offered the Alkmeonidai protection against vendettas; they would not be as vulnerable to vengeance attacks by noble families which had lost men when Megakles the Alkmeonid led the massacre of the Kylonians. Now public authorities rather than the family of the deceased would administer an institutionalised mechanism for dealing with both involuntary and intentional homicide. Compare R. S. Stroud, op. cit. 72–4.

14 *Aristotle,* Politics *1274b 15–19*

(15) Laws of Drakon are extant, but he legislated within an already existing constitution. No peculiarity in the laws is worthy of mention except their severity, which results from the heavy penalties prescribed. Pittakos also was the creator of laws but not of a constitution.[1]

Note

1 Aristotle is listing characteristics of sundry lawgivers. The definite statement here (first and third sentences) that Drakon did not enact a constitution should oblige us to approach the following document with extreme caution.

15 Athenaion Politeia *4*[1]

4 The above is an outline of the earliest constitution. Not long after these events, in the arkhonship of Aristaikhmos,[2] Drakon enacted his statutes. His organisation had the following characteristics. (2) The franchise was given to all those who could provide themselves with military equipment. These citizens elected the nine arkhons and the treasurers from the owners of unencumbered property worth not less than 10 minas; they elected the other, less important officials from those who could provide themselves with military equipment and the Strategoi and Hipparkhoi from those who declared their unencumbered property to be worth not less than 100 minas and who had legitimate sons, born in wedlock, over 10 years of age. These officials were required to exact security from retiring *prutaneis*, Strategoi and Hipparkhoi until their audit, taking four sureties of the same property qualification as the Strategoi and Hipparkhoi.[3] (3) There was to be a Council of Four Hundred and One, chosen by lot from those who possessed the franchise. Men over 30 years of age were to be eligible for this and the other offices governed by lot; no one was to hold the same office twice until everyone else had had a turn; after this the lot was to be cast over again. There were fines for any member of the Council who failed to attend a meeting of the Council or of the Assembly – 3 drakhmas for a Pentakosiomedimnos, 2 for a Hippeus and 1 for a Zeugites.[4] (4) The Council of the Areopagos was guardian of the laws and watched over the officials to see that they governed in accordance with the laws. Anyone who felt himself wronged could lay a complaint before the Council of the Areopagos, declaring what law had been broken by the injustice he claimed to have suffered. (5) As stated above,[5] the security for loans was the debtor's person and the land was in the hands of a few.

Notes

1 This chapter is almost certainly a later forgery and the statements made in it should be used with great caution. There is no mention anywhere else of the Council of Four Hundred and One or of many other provisions in this constitution, although some are so remarkable that they should have attracted much comment from later writers. The qualifications in terms of money (4.2) are clearly anachronistic; even Solon used a division in terms of landed wealth (*Athenaion Politeia* 7.3–4 [**42**]). Higher qualifications are demanded for generals and cavalry commanders than for arkhons and treasurers, contrary to all expectations for Drakon's era. The classes used by Solon are introduced without warning in 4.3 after being ignored in 4.2. The fact that the description of the constitution begins with imperfect indicatives ('elected', 'were required'), changes to the accusative-and-infinitive construction ('there was to be a Council', etc.) and finally reverts to imperfect indicatives ('the Council of the Areopagos was guardian', etc.) suggests that 'the man responsible for the insertion made a half-hearted job of recasting the "constitution" in narrative

form' (Rhodes p. 112). Some, however, have attempted a defence of this constitution. R. Develin, *Athenaeum* 62 (1984) 295–307, for example, while dissatisfied with earlier attempts (such as that of K. von Fritz, *CP* 49 [1954] 73–93 = *Schriften zur griechischen und römischen Verfassungsgeschichte und Verfassungstheorie* [Berlin 1976] 71–98) to defend chapter 4 as part of the *Athenaion Politeia*, argues that the reference to Drakon in 41.2 [**2**], which many have thought an adjustment coinciding with the interpolation of chapter 4, refers not to the arrangements detailed in chapter 4 but to the publication of laws (which Develin believes was treated in the lost beginning of the work). However, he rightly accepts (p. 296) the text which reads 'His [not 'this'; i.e. an explicit reference to Drakon] organisation had the following characteristics.' So what follows, which are clearly constitutional arrangements, *are* linked to Drakon. Overall, the arguments of the sceptics concerning chapter 4 are convincing: see, for example, J. W. Headlam, *CR* 5 (1891) 166–8; Sandys[2] 13–18, especially 13–14; J. J. Keaney, *AJP* 90 (1969) 406–23, especially 415–17 and n. 20.

Rhodes (pp. 45–6 and n. 219, 86–7, 108–9, 117–18) believes that the inserted piece began with 'his organisation had the following characteristics' (4.1) and ended with 'the injustice he claimed to have suffered' (4.4). But there are several problems with the opening clauses. 'The above is an outline of the earliest constitution' can hardly refer to *Athenaion Politeia* 3 [**1**] in view of the fact that the constitution outlined there is far from the first stage in the development of the constitution in *Athenaion Politeia* 41.2 [**2**]. Moreover, although scholars who accept the chapter as genuine have no difficulty with the term (e.g. F. P. Rizzo, *Memorie dell'Istituto Lombardo – classe di lettere* 27.4 [Milan 1963] 271–308 at 281, 305), the author of the work does not elsewhere use the word *hupographe*, 'outline'. He typically says that so-and-so's constitution had the following *taxis*, 'organisation' (3.1 [**1**], 5.1 [**18**]; cf. 4.1 below) or the arrangements had this *tropos*, 'character' (3.5 [**1**], 7.2 [**42**], 9.1 [**46**], 11.1 [**47**], 12.1 [**24**], 16.1 [**61**]; similarly 26.1, 29.5, 32.2, etc.). Furthermore, there is no clear point of reference for 'not long after these events'; if intended to refer to Kylon's attempted *coup d'état* and its aftermath (as Rhodes p. 109 thinks more likely), it jumps over all the detail of chapters 2 [**17**] and 3 [**1**]. The end of the chapter is also suspect: the last sentence borrows two clauses from *Athenaion Politeia* 2.2 [**17**] with minimal change and was probably created when the 'Drakonian constitution' was inserted in the work. Consequently, it seems best to declare the whole chapter a later interpolation, even though this means the surrender of an otherwise unattested arkhon's name in the second sentence of 4.1.

2 There is no independent evidence for the date of this arkhonship. Later Greeks seem to have agreed in placing Drakon's lawcode twenty-seven years before Solon; if we assume that the reference to Solon is to his arkhonship and not his legislation (cf. note 5 on [**29**]), this would place the codification of the laws in 621/0 BC.

3 *Prutaneis* are executive officers presiding for a limited term; Strategoi are generals, army commanders; Hipparkhoi are cavalry commanders. A document making the qualifications for Strategos higher than those for arkhon suits a late fifth-century context (one suggested period for the invention of this 'constitu-

tion') better than the time of Drakon. But several of the provisions in this document which have parallels in Greek principles or practices have these parallels no earlier than the fourth century BC: see A. Fuks, *The Ancestral Constitution: Four Studies in Athenian Party Politics at the End of the Fifth Century B.C.* (London 1953) 86–95.

4 For an explanation of these terms, see *Athenaion Politeia* 7.3–4 [**42**] with notes.

5 *Athenaion Politeia* 2.2 [**17**].

16 *Plutarch,* Solon *17*

17 First,[1] then, he [Solon] repealed all the laws of Drakon apart from those concerning homicide, because of their harshness and the magnitude of the penalties. (2) For only one punishment was prescribed for virtually all offenders and that was death. Consequently those convicted of idleness were put to death, and those who stole vegetables or fruit were punished in the same way as those who committed sacrilege or murder. (3) Hence the distinction accruing in later times to Demades for his remark[2] that it was in blood, not ink, that Drakon wrote his laws. (4) When Drakon himself, so it is said, was asked why he fixed death as the punishment for the great majority of offences, he answered that he thought the minor offences deserved this punishment and that he did not have any greater punishment left for the major ones.[3]

Notes

1 In *Solon* 16.4–5 [**20**] Plutarch says that the Athenians entrusted everything to Solon. First (this chapter), he repealed all the laws of Drakon. Second (chapters 18–19 [**43**]), Solon enacted various measures to broaden the basis of government. For the repeal of Drakon's laws see also *Athenaion Politeia* 7.1 [**42**].

2 An orator of the late fourth century BC. This is Fragment 13 Sauppe.

3 Even Plutarch, as is indicated by his reservation ('so it is said'), does not endorse this story. All that we can safely say is that Drakon formulated a law concerning homicide (see [**13**]) and that he wrote down (and perhaps formulated) laws on other matters. This chapter, contradicted by the penalty of exile for unintentional homicide (see [**13**] and note 8), shows that Plutarch's biography of Solon must be treated with great scepticism. Plutarch seems in this chapter to have borrowed a statement from the *Athenaion Politeia* (see note 1 above) and then embroidered it liberally.

II

SOLON

The problems confronting Attike

Early in the sixth century a crisis point was reached in Athenian society. Solon, a man who had been arkhon perhaps fifteen to twenty years previously and who commanded respect, was appointed as mediator with power to change the constitution. Our sources generally represent the major problem as a class struggle, with emphasis on the suffering of families under obligation to the rich and of others sold as slaves in Attike or abroad, or even as a dispute over the form of constitution which Athens should have. But these views of the problem do not explain the extraordinary action of the nobles, those with power in Attike, in placing Solon in a position where he could change the rules of the game. What brought the nobles to the point where they were prepared to risk a reduction in their own power? It seems to have been the fear that their lower-class retainers would be swept away from their aristocratic patrons by someone who could use them to establish a tyranny in Athens; and a tyranny would disrupt the structure of politics and destroy the power of the nobles. There are, indeed, references to the dependence of poorer people on the nobles (or at least 'the rich') in our sources.

Also relevant to this section are the passages on the aftermath of the Kylon affair in Chapter I, pp. 17–26. See especially note 11 on [**9**] and note 3 on [**10**].

17 Athenaion Politeia *2*

2 After this there was conflict between the nobles and the common people for an extended period.[1] (2) For the constitution they were under was oligarchic in every respect[2] and especially in that the poor, along with their wives and children, were in slavery to the rich. They were called Pelatai and Hektemoroi.[3] For this was the rent they paid for working the fields belonging to the rich. All the land was in the hands of a few. And if men did not pay their rents, they themselves and their children were liable to be seized as slaves. The security for all loans was the debtor's person up to the time of Solon. He was the first champion of the people. (3) Hence the harshest and bitterest aspect of the constitution for the masses was their enslavement. Furthermore, indeed, they were discontent on other scores. For they had, so to speak, no share in anything.

Notes

1 The author of the *Athenaion Politeia* sees the major problem confronting Attike as a class struggle. Political and economic power was in the hands of a relatively small group of noble families.

Does the picture presented by the ancient sources collected in this section explain the agreement of the nobles to the extraordinary appointment of Solon? Though numerically inferior, the nobles were the ones with power and each noble clan had a 'pyramid' of supporters extending into the lower classes (cf. Forrest 48–50 for this model). What moved the clan leaders to agree to Solon's appointment must have been the fear that one of their number would seek to detach the lower levels of their 'pyramids' of support by a platform of 'Free the debtors!' and 'Redistribute the land!' (For these slogans, compare Plutarch, *Solon* 13.6 and 14.2 [**19**] and *Athenaion Politeia* 11.2 [**47**].) When Kylon had attempted to establish a tyranny, the clients had remained loyal to their aristocratic patrons. (For the political backwardness of Athens see note 6 on [**5**].) But in the crisis before Solon's appointment there was a real threat that noble clans would lose their supporters; that is, that the 'pyramids' on which clan power was based would be disrupted. For this line of argument see J. R. Ellis and G. R. Stanton, *Phoenix* 22 (1968) 95–9.

2 There was an Assembly of Athenian citizens, but the lowest class (the Thetes) were not admitted and its power was effectively limited by the Areopagos, which was composed of ex-arkhons, all of whom were nobles. See *Athenaion Politeia* 3.6 [**1**].

3 Pelatai means 'dependants, clients'. Hektemoroi means 'sixth-parters, sixth-portion men'. The next sentence, 'For this was the rent they paid for working . . .', could be rendered 'For this was the commission they were paid for working . . . .' So we have no clear evidence, apart from Plutarch's interpretation (literally 'paying sixths of their produce to the rich') in *Solon* 13.4 [**19**], that the fraction one-sixth (indicated by the name Hektemoroi) was paid to the patron rather than retained by the dependant. But if the Hektemoroi voluntarily became dependants of noble families (see note 3 on [**19**]), they surely did not hand over five-sixths of their produce. If they were reduced to a form of servitude through inability to repay debts (whether through inefficiency as farmers or a succession of poor seasons) they could not have supported a family on one-sixth of their produce. Hence one-sixth seems to have been the rent which Hektemoroi paid for working land in the hands of the rich. Recently G. Kirk, *Historia* 26 (1977) 369–70, stressing the plural 'sixths' in Plutarch, *Solon* 13.4, has suggested that the landlord's share of the produce may have

varied between one-sixth and five-sixths. But there is no direct evidence for this. For a full discussion see K. von Fritz, *AJP* 61 (1940) 54–61 and 64 (1943) 24–43 = *Schriften zur griechischen und römischen Verfassungsgeschichte und Verfassungstheorie* (Berlin 1976) 110–34.

18 Athenaion Politeia *5.1–2*

5 Since the organisation of the constitution was such as I have described[1] and the many were in slavery to the few, the people rose against the nobles.[2] (2) There was fierce and protracted strife between the opposing factions until finally they agreed to the appointment of Solon as mediator and arkhon, and entrusted the constitution to him.[3] He had composed the elegiac poem which begins:

> I observe, and within my heart there is sadness and deep distress
> As I see the most ancient land in all the Ionian sphere
> Being slain . . . .[4]

In this poem he argues the case of each side in turn against the other and goes on to exhort them to join in putting an end to the quarrel that had arisen.

Notes

1 In chapter 3 [**1**].

2 The author scarcely distinguishes between *hoi polloi* (translated 'the many'), *to plethos* ('the common people') and *ho demos* ('the people'): cf. *Athenaion Politeia* 2.1 [**17**]; 5.1; 9.1 [**46**]; 20.1, 3 [**81**]; 21.1 [**84**]. There is a similar lack of distinction between *hoi gnorimoi* ('the well-known men', i.e. the nobles) and *hoi oligoi* ('the few').

3 Solon was eponymous arkhon of Athens in 594/3 BC (see note 5 on [**19**] below). Although Solon's appointment by common consent as mediator with extraordinary powers (so *Athenaion Politeia* 5.2) or mediator and lawgiver (so Plutarch, *Solon* 14.3 [**19**]) is assigned to his arkhonship by both our sources, there are reasons for believing that his reforms should be dated later than his arkhonship. In particular, he is much more likely to have commanded respect when he had been an ex-arkhon, and member of the Areopagos, for many years. For arguments that Solon's reforms belong to the late 570s see Hignett 316–21; for a different view see French 181–2, A. J. Holladay, *G & R*^{2} 24 (1977) 40–56 at 53–4, and Rhodes 121–2.

4 The final word of the quotation (from *Fragment* 4a) is obscure on the papyrus; it could be *klinomenen* ('made to lean, leaning, tottering') or *kainomenen* ('being slain'). M. L. West in his edition (see note 1 on [**21**]) prefers *klinomenen*, J. D. Thomas (in Rhodes 123) and M. H. Chambers *kainomenen*. For the other fragments in this chapter of the *Athenaion Politeia* see [**23**] below.

19 *Plutarch,* Solon *13.1–14.6*

13 After the Kylonian trouble had ended and the accursed had been expelled, as I have described,[1] Athens was torn by the recurrent conflict about the constitution. The city was divided into as many parties as there were geographical divisions in its territory. (2) For the party of the people of the hills was most in favour of democracy, that of the people of the plain was most in favour of oligarchy, while the third group, the people of the coast, which preferred a mixed form of constitution somewhat between the other two, formed an obstruction and prevented the other groups from gaining control.[2] (3) At this time the inequality of the poor with respect to the rich had, as it were, reached a peak. The city was in an extremely precarious condition and it seemed that only the establishment of a tyranny could restore stability and put an end to the city's disorders. (4) All the common people were bound by ties of obligation to the rich. For either they were farmers, paying one-sixth of their produce to the rich and called Hektemorioi and Thetes, or, contracting debts on the security of their own persons, they were liable to seizure by their creditors, some becoming slaves there, others being sold abroad.[3] (5) Many were forced even to sell their own children – for no law prevented this – and to flee the city because of the harshness of their creditors. (6) But the majority, including the most determined, began to combine and encourage one another not to submit, but to choose a single trustworthy leader, free the debtors, redistribute the land[4] and completely change the constitution.

14 Then the wisest of the Athenians saw that Solon was the only one who was above all reproach and was neither a participant with the rich in their injustices nor involved in the privations of the poor. They asked him to come forward publicly and put an end to the disputes. (2) Yet Phanias of Lesbos records that Solon on his own initiative deceived both sides to save the city, secretly promising the poor a distribution of land and the rich security for their loans. (3) But Solon himself says that it was with reluctance that he first engaged in public affairs, fearing the greed of one group and the arrogant spirit of the other. He was appointed arkhon in succession to Philombrotos,[5] as both mediator and lawgiver. He was accepted readily by the rich because he was a wealthy man and by the poor because he was an honest one. (4) It is also said that there was in circulation before his appointment a saying of his to the effect that equality does not produce war, and this pleased both those with property and those without, the former because they expected him to achieve an equality based on worth and excellence, the latter an equality based on numerical strength. Thus there was great hope on both sides and their leaders urged Solon to let them make him tyrant.[6] They tried to persuade him that, now that he had the city in his power, he might take control of it more boldly. (5) There were also many citizens in a middling position who saw that change by means of debate and law would be laborious and difficult. They did not shrink from putting a single man who was most just and prudent in charge of affairs. (6) Some say that Solon received the following oracle at Delphi:

> Take your seat now in mid-ship; yours is the work
> Of direction; for many in Athens support you.[7]

Notes

1 Plutarch refers back to the murder of the Kylonians and the later banishment of the Alkmeonidai, recounted in chapter 12 [**11**].

2 Plutarch here makes the constitutional squabble, which both he (*Solon* 29.1 [**53**]) and the author of the *Athenaion Politeia* (13.4 [**52**]) say troubled Athens in the period after Solon's reforms, a major part of the conflict leading to Solon's appointment. But such disputes seem anachronistic even shortly after, let alone before, Solon's reforms. See notes on *Athenaion Politeia* 13.5 [**52**]. Whereas the author of the *Athenaion Politeia* uses *staseis*, 'factions' (13.4), Plutarch here uses two words, *meros* ('part') and *genos* ('clan, race'), which I have rendered by 'party'. The groups were not, of course, parties in the modern sense.

3 Section 4 follows the version in *Athenaion Politeia* 2.2 [**17**] closely, with words such as *agogimoi* ('liable to seizure, liable to be led off [as slaves]') used by both sources. But the names given to the farmers in debt, Hektemorioi (not -roi) and Thetes, differ from the Pelatai and Hektemoroi of the *Athenaion Politeia*, with its stress on dependence. It is possible, as P. J. Rhodes has suggested to me, that each author glossed 'Hektemoroi' with a word he expected his readers to know. In that case, the author of the *Athenaion Politeia* gives what is probably a more accurate impression (that Hektemoroi were farmers who had voluntarily or semi-voluntarily [so Rhodes 94] bound themselves to powerful clans in return for economic and physical security) than Plutarch with his explanation 'Thetes' (labourers for another) and less probable spelling 'Hektemorioi'. W. J. Woodhouse, *Solon the Liberator: A Study of the Agrarian Problem in Attika in the Seventh Century* (Oxford 1938), though he believes Hektemoroi paid five-sixths of their produce to their patrons (cf. note 3 on [**17**]), stresses the dependent status of the Hektemoroi (e.g. pp. 29–30).

4 These phrases suggest the slogans in the comment (note 1) on *Athenaion Politeia* 2.1 [**17**] above.

5 M. F. McGregor, in *Polis and Imperium: Studies in Honour of Edward Togo Salmon* (Toronto 1974) 31–4, seeks epigraphical evidence for placing Solon's arkhonship in 594/3 BC (which fits much of the tradition: see T. J. Cadoux, *JHS* 68 [1948] 93–9) rather than in the 570s (as, for example, is done by M. Miller, *Arethusa* 4 [1971] 25–47, especially 45–6) in fragment *a* of Meiggs and Lewis no. 6 (see [**64**] for fragment *c* of this inscription):

[...]N[-----]
[Ky]pselo[s]
[Te]lekle[---]
[Phil]omb[rotos?]

McGregor argues that Kypselos, the father of the elder Miltiades (for the family relationships see note 2 on [**98**]), is the only known Athenian of this name and that he died by 585 BC. He takes the name Philombrotos in line 4 to be certain and restores [Solon] in line 5.

6 On Solon's refusal to become tyrant when he had the opportunity, see in addition to this passage Solon, *Fragment* 32 [**27**], *Athenaion Politeia* 6.3–4 [**33**] and 11.2 [**47**].

7 This Delphic Oracle is no. 90 in the collection of R. Hendess (Halle 1877), no. 15 in the collection of H. W. Parke and D. E. W. Wormell, *The Delphic Oracle* (Oxford 1956) and 'Quasi-Historical' Response 67 in J. Fontenrose, *The Delphic Oracle: Its Responses and Operations* (Berkeley 1978).

20 *Plutarch,* Solon *16.4–5*

(4) . . . However, they soon saw the advantage[1] and laid aside their personal grievances. (5) They both offered a public sacrifice which they called seisakhtheia and declared Solon reformer of the constitution and lawgiver.[2] They did not limit his sphere of action, but entrusted everything equally to him: offices, assemblies, law courts and councils. He could define the property qualifications for each of these bodies, their size and frequency of meeting. He could dissolve or preserve whichever of the currently established institutions he decided.

Notes

1 Of Solon's cancellation of debts and prohibition of loans on the security of a debtor's person (*Solon* 15.2–9 [**34**]).

2 N. G. L. Hammond, *JHS* 60 (1940) 71–83 (= *Studies in Greek History* [Oxford 1973] 145–62, with further remarks at 162–9) bases on this and other passages, notably *Athenaion Politeia* 10.1 [**36**], a division of Solon's public activities into the seisakhtheia, which he dates to 594/3 BC, and the nomothesia ('lawgiving'), which he dates two years later. The phraseology of this passage ('they both

offered a public sacrifice . . . and declared Solon reformer of the constitution and lawgiver, entrusting everything . . .') might suggest a sequence of relief of burdens followed by general legislation. But Plutarch does not make a clear distinction between seisakhtheia (15.2–9 [**34**]) and nomothesia (chapters 17 and following). The grievances mentioned here are not restricted to the cancellation of debts, but refer also to Solon's handling of the whole constitution (16.1–4 [**48**]). In 14.8 [**27**] *nomothesia* refers to Solon's whole legislative activity, for the context concerns the suggestion that Solon become a tyrant, before his cancellation of debts or any other law. In 15.1–2 [**48**] 'the laws' which Solon 'enacted' (*etheto tous nomous*), said by Plutarch not to have made concessions to the powerful nor to have pleased those who had chosen him and allegedly described by Solon as the best the Athenians would accept, is a general term prefacing both the seisakhtheia (whose description begins immediately) and the rest of his legislation. It is preferable to think that Solon had one position which was described by Plutarch as 'both mediator and lawgiver' (*Solon* 14.3 [**19**]), 'mediator, arkhon and lawgiver' (*Moralia* 763e) or simply 'lawgiver' (*Moralia* 805e). *Solon* 14.3, like *Athenaion Politeia* 5.2 [**18**], assigns this position to Solon's arkhonship, but there are reasons for doubting this (see note 3 on [**18**]). For the meaning of 'seisakhtheia' see *Athenaion Politeia* 6.1 [**33**].

Solon: the man and his outlook

What sort of a man was it whom the nobles put in the extraordinary position of being able to change the constitution? For once we have some contemporary evidence, the poems of Solon himself. They tell us relatively little about the political situation which he faced, but they do reveal his values and his highly aristocratic outlook. The fragments of his poems – we do not possess the whole corpus – can be used to check the descriptions of him given by later sources.

21 *Solon,* Fragments *2–3*[1] *in Diogenes Laertios 1.47*

The elegiac verses which most stirred the Athenians were these:

Would that I then change my native land,
From Athens to Pholegandros or Sikinos.[2]
For soon there would arise this saying among men
'This man is an Athenian, one of the Salamis-betrayers.'

And again:

Let us go to Salamis to fight for the island
We desire, and drive away our bitter shame.[3]

Notes

1 The fragments of Solon's poems are numbered according to the edition of M. L. West, *Iambi et elegi Graeci ante Alexandrum cantati* 2 (Oxford 1972), who generally follows the enumeration for Solon's fragments of the fourth edition of T. Bergk, *Poetae lyrici Graeci* 2 (Leipzig 1882). For each fragment I have tried (like West) to give enough of the context to show why the secondary source (in this case Diogenes Laertios) has made the quotation.

2 Two small islands in the Kyklades group, east of Melos.

3 The greater part of the first two verses is preserved also by Plutarch (*Moralia* 813f) and the last two verses are quoted by an ancient commentator on Demosthenes and by an ancient collector of sayings. These fragments presumably belong to the poem 'Salamis', the opening couplet of which is cited in Plutarch, *Solon* 8.2. They illustrate Solon's leadership before his reforms, in the struggle with Megara for control of the island of Salamis.

22 *Solon,* Fragment *4.1–25 in Demosthenes 19* (On the Embassy*). 254–5*

Please take and read these elegiac verses of Solon, so that the jury will see that Solon also detested people like him [Aiskhines]. . . . Go ahead:

Our city will never be ruined by decree of Zeus
Or the purposes of the blessed, immortal gods.
For Pallas Athene, daughter of the mighty one,[1]
Our valiant protector, holds her hands over it.
The citizens themselves it is who, attracted by wealth,
Would fain destroy our great city by imprudence,
And the unjust mind of the people's leaders who surely
Will experience many sufferings for their great arrogance.
They know not how to restrain their greed nor to enjoy
The present banquet festivities in quiet and orderly fashion.[2]
. . . .
They grow rich by yielding to unjust actions.
. . . .
Neither the gods' nor the people's possessions are spared,
They steal and plunder, one from here, one from there.
They do not respect the sacred foundations of Justice,
Who though silent takes cognisance of the present and past
And in time surely comes to exact retribution.
Already this inescapable ulcer comes on the whole city,
She has swiftly fallen into wretched slavery, slavery
Which wakens civil strife and slumbering war,

And war destroys the lovely youth of many.
At the hands of enemies our much-loved city is swiftly
Being consumed in compacts with those who wrong friends.[3]
These are the evils rife among the people; while of the poor
Many, sold and bound with degrading chains,
Are going as slaves to a foreign land.
. . . .[4]

Notes

1 Zeus.

2 Solon made similar comments about the common people (*demos*) and their leaders after his reforms. See *Fragment* 6 [**24**], where again Solon links *koros* (surfeit, greed) with *hubris* (the arrogance or outrage which leads finally to retribution), and *Fragment* 34 [**24**]. Note also that the welfare of the city depends both on gods and men: avaricious men can ruin the city although it has a powerful protector among the gods. Here, again after verse 11 and after verse 25 there are lacunae (gaps) in the preserved text of thirty-nine verses.

3 The reading and the meaning of this couplet are controversial. See the long note by I. M. Linforth, *Solon the Athenian* [University of California Publications in Classical Philology, 6] (Berkeley 1919) 202–4. I accept West's text and take φίλους closely with τοῖς ἀδικέουσι.

4 In the fourteen verses after the lacuna Solon points out how lawlessness (*dusnomia*) brings evil to everyone in the city, while respect for the law (*eunomia*) brings order, checks greed (*koros*), dims arrogance (*hubris*), makes growing infatuation (*ate*) wither and stops acts of civil strife. On the meaning of *eunomia* see A. Andrewes, *CQ* 32 (1938) 89–102, especially 89–91. For a recent analysis of the whole poem see A. W. H. Adkins, *Poetic Craft in the Early Greek Elegists* (Chicago 1985) 110–25, 225–7.

23 *Solon,* Fragments *4a, 4c, 4b in* Athenaion Politeia *5.2–3*

(2) There was fierce and protracted strife between the opposing factions until finally they agreed to the appointment of Solon as mediator and arkhon, and entrusted the constitution to him.[1] He had composed the elegiac poem which begins:

I observe, and within my heart there is sadness and deep distress
As I see the most ancient land in all the Ionian sphere
Being slain . . . .[2]

In this poem he argues the case of each side in turn against the other and goes on to exhort them to join in putting an end to the quarrel that had arisen. (3) By birth and reputation Solon was among the leading men. But it is generally agreed that by wealth and occupation he was in a middling position.[3] He himself testifies to the fact in this same group of poems, where he exhorts the wealthy not to be avaricious:

> Quieten your heart that swells up with ambition,
> You who have soared to a surfeit of good things.
> Moderate your swelling thoughts; for we shall
> Not suffer, nor will that be to your interest.[4]

Indeed he repeatedly attributes the blame for the strife to the rich. Thus at the beginning of the poem he says that he fears 'both greed and an arrogant spirit',[5] implying that the conflict arose through them.

Notes

1 *Athenaion Politeia* 5.1–2 is translated, with notes, above [**18**].

2 See note 4 on [**18**].

3 It is tempting to translate this clause 'by wealth and occupation he belonged to the middle classes'. But the socio-economic models evoked by such terminology are misleading. The author has already made it perfectly clear that Solon was a noble by birth (i.e. a Eupatrid; cf. Plutarch, *Solon* 1.2 [**31**]). Then he implies that Solon was not an owner of large estates. The fact that Solon was a noble, whose appointment was agreed to by noble leaders, must be central to any estimation of Solon's work.

4 As interpreted by the author of the *Athenaion Politeia*, this would be one fragment of Solon's poetry where he aligns himself with the poorer people against the rich ('you' versus 'we'). But elsewhere, in *Fragment* 6 [**24**], the idea of ambitious minds gaining a surfeit of wealth refers to the poorer people; Solon there associates himself with the powerful and advises them on how to handle the common people. So it seems that here also Solon identifies himself with the powerful in Athens. They will not suffer at the hands of people whose minds are not fit to deal with a sudden increase in wealth, nor would the latter benefit from such suffering by the rich. How could the author of the *Athenaion Politeia* have misinterpreted these two couplets? A key word, *peisometha*, is the future of both the verbs 'to suffer' and 'to obey'. The author may not have seen the point of 'we shall not suffer' and hence may have taken the verb to mean 'we shall not obey', that is, we poorer people shall not be subject to you. It seems clear that the fourth-century author also misinterpreted the brief fragment 4c below, for he refers both terms to the rich, whereas Plutarch in *Solon* 14.3 [**19**] interprets 'greed' as applying to the poor and 'an arrogant spirit' as applying to the rich.

5 One of the two nouns in this quotation, *philarguria* ('love of wealth, greed') cannot be read on the papyrus. However, a word like *philarguria*, *philokhrematia* or *philoploutia* may be conjectured on the basis of Plutarch, *Solon* 14.3 [**19**], where *philokhrematia* is used. The reconstruction translated here was made by J. B. Mayor and H. Jackson, *CR* 5 (1891) 107.

24 *Solon,* Fragments *5, 6 and 34 in* Athenaion Politeia *12.1–3*

12 That this was how it happened[1] is universally agreed and is borne out by his own references in his poems. For example:

I gave to the people such status as is sufficient,
I did not deprive them of honour, nor offer them too much.
But those who were powerful, distinguished because of their wealth,
I tried to ensure that nothing unseemly befall.
Both factions I strove to surround with a strong shield,
I did not permit an unjust victory to either's demands.[2]

(2) The following lines make clear his view of how the common people should be treated:

The people will follow their leaders best,
When not left too free nor with violence repressed.
For surfeit begets pride,[3] when great wealth
Attends men whose minds are not prudent.

(3) Again, in another place he refers to those who wanted a redistribution of land:

They came with a mind to plunder, their hopes were not restrained,
They expected, each of them, to find a fortune immense
And me with a coaxing tongue to publish a radical plan.
Vain were their purposes then, but now they look askance
And air their anger toward me, as though I an enemy were.
Unjustly; with the help of the gods my promises I did fulfil,
And my further efforts were not in vain. No pleasure I take
In what is achieved by a tyrant's force, nor in the noble and base
Having an equal share in the wealth of my native land.[4]

Notes

1 In chapter 11 [**47**] the author of the *Athenaion Politeia* states the attitude of the nobles (*hoi gnorimoi*) and of the common people (*demos*) to Solon after his reforms. Then he concludes: 'Solon had resisted both factions, and . . . he chose to incur the hostility of both by saving his country and legislating in its best interests.'

2 These six verses are quoted also by Plutarch (*Solon* 18.5 [**43**]) who reads 'power' (*kratos*) instead of 'status' (*geras*) in the first verse. The fragment shows

that Solon claimed to have done something for the *demos*, while ensuring that the nobles suffered no loss or even indignity. The conservative nature of Solon's reforms is stressed by Aristotle, *Politics* 1273b–1274a [**45**]. Verse 5 is taken by C. Rogge, *Philologische Wochenschrift* 44 (1924) 794–9 at 798, to mean that Solon used his shield to ward off both factions, but verses 1–4 indicate that Solon adopted a protective stance towards both.

3 For *koros* ('surfeit, greed') linked with *hubris* ('pride, arrogance') see also *Fragment* 4.8–9 [**22**] with note 2.

4 The previous fragments of Solon's poetry have all been elegiac couplets. The metre of this fragment, as of *Fragment* 32 [**27**], is the trochaic tetrameter. The manner in which Solon here refers to the two groups has moral overtones: the *esthloi* are assumed to be noble in character as well as by birth, in contrast to the *kakoi*, the 'bad, vile, base'. Compare the neuter usage of *esthlos* and *kakos* in *Fragment* 13.63–4:

> Destiny brings noble and base estate to mortals,
> And the gifts of the immortal gods cannot be declined.

See also H. Lloyd-Jones, *The Justice of Zeus* [Sather Classical Lectures, 41] (Berkeley 1971) 43–4, 46–7. The moral connotations of 'noble' (*agathos*) and 'base' (*kakos*) are also linked to social position in *Fragment* 15, quoted in Plutarch, *Solon* 3.3 [**31**]. For further discussion of *esthlos*, *kakos* and their synonyms, stressing their use as status indicators, see A. W. H. Adkins, *Merit and Responsibility: A Study in Greek Values* (Oxford 1960) 30–40, 75–9 and *Moral Values and Political Behaviour in Ancient Greece* (London 1972) 12–15, 23–30, 35–57.

While our sources, the *Athenaion Politeia* [**23**] and Plutarch [**31**], interpret some fragments so as to align Solon with the poor rather than the rich (see notes on [**23**] and [**31**]), there is no doubt that in *Fragment* 6 above (*Athenaion Politeia* 12.2) he identifies himself with the nobles in stating how the *demos* is best handled. In this passage (*Fragment* 34), written after his reforms, Solon unambiguously declares his opposition to a redistribution of land so that the lower classes would have an equal share (*isomoiria*) with the nobles. He is opposed also to tyranny for himself. Plutarch (*Solon* 14.7–9; cf. [**27**]) tells the story of Solon rejecting the advice of his close friends that he become a tyrant.

25 *Solon,* Fragment *9 in the Vatican Excerpts from Diodoros of Sicily (Diodoros 9.20.2)*

Solon is said also to have predicted to the Athenians in elegiac verses the tyranny that was imminent:

> From a cloud issues the might of snow and hail,
> Thunder comes from a bright flash of lightning.
> From powerful men comes ruin for a city, the people
> Through ignorance fall into slavery under one lord.[1]
> It is not easy later to restrain a man you exalted
> Too far; now must all noble plans be made.[2]

Notes

1 These verses are, of course, quoted in the belief that Solon was warning the Athenians against the tyranny of Peisistratos (see Chapter III, pp. 100–1). But verses 3–4 alone reveal that Solon could give to *monarkhos*, the single ruler, similar negative connotations to those later attached to *tyrannos*, tyrant. (See A. Andrewes, *The Greek Tyrants* [London 1956] 26–7.) Indeed, when verses 3–4 are quoted in Diodoros 19.1.4 *monarkhos* is changed to *tyrannos*. Here, in what seems to be the earliest appearance of the word, the *monarkhos* reduces the *demos* to slavery.

2 L. Dindorf adds οὐ ('not') in verse 5, M. L. West καλά ('noble, good') in verse 6 to the text preserved, with some metrical deficiencies, in the Vatican manuscript. These seem the best supplements so far proposed, even though the second produces a pattern of short words which is not paralleled elsewhere in the second half of Solon's pentameter verses (Gentili and Prato 1.110–11). Books 6–10 and 21–40 of Diodoros have not survived intact, but extensive fragments can be found in such collections as this compilation of historical excerpts made at the direction of the Byzantine emperor Constantine VII Porphyrogenitus (AD 913–59).

26 *Solon,* Fragment *13 in Stobaios 3.9.23*[1]

Glorious children of Memory and Olympian Zeus,
Muses of Pieria, hear me as I pray.
Grant that I may receive prosperity from the blessed gods
And always enjoy fair glory among all men;
Thus to be sweet to my friends, bitter to my enemies,
Respected by the first, a fearful sight to the others.[2]
Riches I desire to have, but I wish not to possess them
Unjustly. Justice assuredly comes later.
Wealth granted by the gods remains with a man,
Solid and secure from lowest foundation to the top.
Wealth prized by men in a spirit of arrogance comes
Unnaturally; constrained by unjust deeds it follows
Against its will and with infatuation is swiftly embroiled.

. . . .

71 There is no set limit of wealth for men.
For those of us who now have the greatest fortune
Double our efforts. What wealth will satisfy all men?
Gains, surely, are bestowed on mortals by immortals,
But from gains emerges infatuation which, when sent
By Zeus for retribution, inflicts now one, now another.[3]

Notes

1 Only the beginning and end are translated here of what is apparently a

complete poem of thirty-eight elegiac couplets given as the twenty-third item in an anthology of sixty-four quotations on *dikaiosune* ('justice, righteousness'). A full analysis of the poem is given by I. M. Linforth, *Solon the Athenian* [University of California Publications in Classical Philology, 6] (Berkeley 1919) 104–13, 227–43. The last six verses are also preserved, in a different form, as verses 227–32 of Theognis, a poet from Megara.

2 Solon, as a poet (compare the beginning of the *Iliad*, the *Odyssey* or Hesiod's poems), addresses the Muses. But he asks them for material resources, which, he seems to recognise, come from other gods. Note the value attached to *doxa* ('glory, prestige') which, along with material resources, will not only gain him the respect of his political allies (*philoi*) but also enable him to help them and harm his enemies.

3 Solon unashamedly desires wealth, the enduring wealth which the gods bestow and men gain by just courses of action. Wealth which derives from *hubris* (vs 11, 16), the arrogant presumption that one can override the laws of the gods, comes contrary to the natural order of things (*kosmos*, v. 11) and rapidly involves its possessor in *ate* (vs 13, 68, 75), the blind infatuation which leads to ruin. The justice (*dike*, v. 8) or retribution (the noun *tisis* in v. 25, the verb *tino* in vs 29, 31, 76) of Zeus, though it may be slow (even delayed until later generations, vs 31–2), is certain. On *ate* see R. D. Dawe, *HSCP* 72 (1968) 89–123, especially 95–101, and R. E. Doyle, *῎ATH, its Use and Meaning: A Study in the Greek Poetic Tradition from Homer to Euripides* (New York 1984), especially 26–7, 37, 41–2, 44; on *dike* see H. Lloyd-Jones, *The Justice of Zeus* [Sather Classical Lectures, 41] (Berkeley 1971), especially 43–5, and E. A. Havelock, *The Greek Concept of Justice from its Shadow in Homer to its Substance in Plato* (Cambridge, Mass. 1978), especially 252–62. C. C. Chiasson, *GRBS* 27 (1986) 249–62, points out that Herodotos, in his account of what Solon said to Kroisos (for the meeting, see [**29**] below), goes beyond the moral view in this poem that only ill-gotten gains are short-lived and asserts that the acquisition of great wealth is itself likely to provoke a jealous divinity.

27 *Solon,* Fragment *32 in Plutarch,* Solon *14.7–8*

(7) Especially did his close associates reproach him for declining monarchy because of the name,[1] as if it would not immediately be transformed into kingship by the excellence of the one who held it. This, they said, had happened earlier for the Euboians when they chose Tynnondas as tyrant and in their age for the Mitylenaians when they chose Pittakos. (8) None of these arrangements shook Solon from his resolve. To his friends he is reported to have said that tyranny was a noble position, but there was no way down from it. To Phokos he wrote in his poems:

If I spared my land,
My native land, and withheld my hand from tyranny

And relentless force, which would taint and disgrace my good repute,
I am not ashamed. Rather I think I shall thus surpass the more
All other men.[2]

From this it is clear that he had great glory even before his legislation.[3]

Notes

1 The context, in which leaders of both sides and many in between press Solon to become tyrant, is given above [**19**].

2 As in *Fragment* 34 [**24**] the use of force characteristic of a tyranny (*tyrannis*) is explicitly rejected by Solon for himself.

3 Note the importance of glory (*doxa*), indicated also by Plutarch in *Solon* 2.6 and 11.1 [**103**], and Solon's fear in the fragment that he might pollute his high reputation (*kleos*). Solon makes explicit the value he places on glory in *Fragment* 13.4 ([**26**] with note 2). On the idea of pollution of a reputation, see R. Parker, *Miasma: Pollution and Purification in Early Greek Religion* (Oxford 1983) 3–4 and n. 8.

28 *Solon,* Fragment *37 in* Athenaion Politeia *12.5*

(5) Again, he rebukes both factions for their subsequent complaints against him:

If I must publicly rebuke, I say:
That what the people now possess are things
Of which they never would have dreamed. . . .[1]
While men of higher rank and greater power
Would praise me and treat me as a friend.

For if anyone else, he says, had obtained this exalted post,

He'd not have held the people back, nor stopped
Until he'd stirred the milk and lost the cream.[2]
But I took up my post in No-Man's Land,
Just like a boundary-stone.[3]

Notes

1 The metre of this fragment, as of *Fragment* 36 (quoted in *Athenaion Politeia* 12.4 [**32**]), is iambic trimeter. About half of verse 3 is missing, and it is likely that verse 4 did not follow immediately after verse 3. In the part omitted from the quotation there was presumably an unfulfilled condition. For example, Solon may have said to the common people (*demos*) that if he had not

supported their interests in the way that he did, they would never have seen in their dreams what they now possess. Again, there is presumably an omitted conditional clause with verses 4–5 along the following lines: if the nobles were to realise that anyone else in Solon's position would not have held the *demos* in check, they would sing Solon's praises and treat him as their political ally (*philos*).

2 The metaphor of verse 8 has been the subject of much debate. The usual interpretation is that someone else would not have stopped 'until he'd churned the milk and snatched the fat'. But the only fat which is obtained by stirring milk is butter, for the use of which there is very little evidence in ancient Greece. T. C. W. Stinton (*JHS* 96 [1976] 159–61) suggests that the hypothetical other man would have deprived the milk of its cream by stirring up the milk. Solon is pointing out to the nobles that they, the cream of society, would have been dissipated and lost in society as a whole if someone else had obtained Solon's position and, quite possibly, gone on to make himself a tyrant.

3 Solon uses the same word, *horos*, as he uses for 'mortgage pillar' in *Fragment* 36.6 [**32**]. Clearly the word could be used in a neutral sense when it referred to a boundary-marker.

29 *Herodotos 1.29.1–1.30.1*

29 When Kroisos had conquered these peoples[1] and was adding their territory to the Lydian realm, all the wise men of Greece who were alive at that time came one after another to Sardis, then at the height of its wealth, for various purposes. Among them, in particular, came Solon the Athenian,[2] who had made laws for the Athenians at their request and was living abroad for ten years. He had sailed away with the declared aim of travel, but in fact his purpose was not to be compelled to repeal any of the laws which he had enacted. (2) The Athenians themselves were not able to do this, for they were bound by solemn oaths to retain for ten years whatever laws Solon would enact for them.[3] *30* For this reason in particular, as well as to travel,[4] Solon lived abroad and visited Amasis in Egypt and Kroisos in Sardis.[5]

Notes

1 Herodotos has just stated, in effect, that Kroisos subdued most of the western half of Asia Minor.

2 Herodotos tells a story about Solon's wisdom in his encounter with Kroisos (1.30.1–1.34.1; cf. 1.86). Many scholars reject the story of Solon's visit to Kroisos on chronological grounds. Kroisos came to the throne c. 560 BC or later, whereas Solon's legislation is usually dated with his arkhonship in 594/3 BC. Plutarch (*Solon* 27.1) says the fame of the story and its consistency with Solon's character override chronological difficulties. The historicity of the visit can be more satisfactorily defended by separating Solon's legislation from

his arkhonship by twenty years and placing Solon's travels in the 560s. If he did not return to Athens when the ten years had finished, he might conceivably have met Kroisos in the 550s.

3 'Ten years' is a more sober figure than the '100 years' of *Athenaion Politeia* 7.2 [**42**] and Plutarch, *Solon* 25.1 [**50**].

4 While Herodotos says nothing about trade as a motive, *Athenaion Politeia* 11.1 [**47**] gives Solon's reasons as 'trade together with travel'. But the trade may merely have been sufficient to finance his travel in a world without coinage (let alone credit cards): see note 2 on [**47**]. For Solon's travels to the east see also Herodotos 2.177.2 [**30**], 5.113.2 (note 5 below) and Plutarch, *Solon* 25.6–28.6 (25.6 in [**50**]). The travels are mentioned by many writers later than Herodotos, Plato (see note 1 on [**30**]) and the *Athenaion Politeia*: examples are the third-century writer Euphorion of Chalkis (*Fragment* 1 Scheidweiler = *Fragment* 1 in J. U. Powell, *Collectanea Alexandrina* [Oxford 1925] 29) and the first-century historian Poseidonios of Apameia (*FGrH* 87 F 28 = Strabon 2.3.6 [102C]). There is even a fragment of papyrus of the third century AD recording an unknown author who wrote:

> [is sai]d to have [l]eft Attike [after binding] the Atheni[a]ns [with] a sol[emn oath to retain the] l[aws] enacted [b]y him [until he] returned [to th]em, and [taken up residence] in th[is] Soloi. [But so]me [others say it wa]s [Sol]oi in Cyp[rus] . . . .

The subject is undoubtedly Solon, whose name was restored in line 4 of the fragment (as the subject of 'is said' at the beginning of the quotation) by W. Crönert, *Kolotes und Menedemos* [Studien zur Palaeographie und Papyruskunde, hrsg. C. Wessely, 6] (Leipzig 1906) 194. See on this papyrus B. P. Grenfell and A. S. Hunt, *The Oxyrhynchus Papyri* 4 (London 1904) 127–30 – referred to as *POxy* 680 – and I. Gallo, *Frammenti biografici da papiri* 1 [Testi e Commenti, 1] (Rome 1975) 185–201. It is conceivable that Solon used his travels to improve Athenian penetration of markets in the east.

5 Here and in *Athenaion Politeia* 11.1 [**47**] Solon's travels are placed immediately after his legislation. Herodotos elsewhere mentions Solon's visit to Philokypros 'whom Solon the Athenian praised in a poem above all other tyrants when he came to Cyprus' (Herodotos 5.113.2; cf. Plutarch, *Solon* 26.2–4). The context for this allusion is a list of the notable men killed when the Persians defeated the Cyprians at Salamis in 498/7 BC. One of them was the son of Philokypros. Hence Philokypros is not likely to have been ruler of Soloi earlier than the 570s; the 560s are preferable. Hignett (p. 320) uses this record of Solon's visit to press the case for dating Solon's legislation late in the 570s. S. S. Markianos, *Historia* 23 (1974) 1–20, points out that other sources link Solon's visit to Cyprus with his visits to Egypt and Sardis (p. 16 and n. 70); he argues that the chronological indications in Herodotos allow a dating of Solon's *apodemia* (period abroad) to the 560s and concludes that Solon's legislative activities took place in the 570s. See also his article in *Hellenika* 28 (1975) 5–28, with English summary at 239. For a recent attempt to dismiss the visits to Amasis and Kroisos as historical and to dispute the link with the ten-year *apodemia*, see R. W. Wallace, *AJAH* 8 (1983 [1986]) 81–95, especially 86–9.

30 *Herodotos 2.177.2*

(2) It is Amasis who established among the Egyptians the law that each year every Egyptian must declare to the ruler of the province his source of livelihood and that, if he fails to do so or does not show legitimate means of livelihood, he should be punished by death. Solon the Athenian took this law from Egypt and enacted it for the Athenians. They observe it still, for it is a faultless law.[1]

Note

1 On Solon's alleged contact with Amasis see also Herodotos 1.30.1 [**29**]. Hignett (p. 320) points out that others attributed this law to Peisistratos and that Herodotos may have been misled by the Athenian tendency to attribute to Solon all the laws of the fifth-century code. Plato (*Timaios* 21e) also says that Solon visited Egypt.

31 *Plutarch,* Solon *1.1–5, 2.1, 3.1–4*

1 Didymos the grammarian, in his reply to Asklepiades on the tablets of Solon,[1] quotes a certain Philokles who declares that Solon's father was Euphorion, but that is contradicted by the opinion of all other writers on Solon. (2) They all agree that his father was Exekestides, a man of moderate wealth and influence, so they say, among the citizens of his day, but from a family of the first rank, since he was descended from Kodros.[2] (3) Solon's mother, according to Herakleides of Pontos, was a cousin of Peisistratos's mother. (4) The two men had at first a strong friendship,[3] based partly on their kinship and partly on the youthful attractiveness of Peisistratos whom, some say, Solon welcomed as a lover. (5) That seems to be the reason why, when they later adopted opposing stances in politics, their enmity did not produce any bitter or uncontrolled feelings, but their former relationship lingered in their hearts and preserved 'embers smouldering with the flame of Zeus' fire still aglow',[4] the grateful memory of their love . . . .

2 When his father had reduced his estate, as Hermippos says, by various acts of generosity and kindness, Solon did not lack friends willing to help him, but he was ashamed to receive support from others because he came from a family accustomed to helping others. So, while he was still a young man, he launched into commerce. Yet some say that Solon travelled to enrich his experience and extend his knowledge rather than to make money.[5] . . .

3 Solon's extravagant and luxurious way of life, and the fact that in his poems he discusses pleasure in a popular rather than a philosophical way,[6] are generally ascribed to his career in commerce; having taken many risks he sought in return various luxuries and enjoyments. (2) But that he aligned himself with the poor rather than with the rich is clear from the following verses:

(3) Many a base man is rich, while the noble are poor.
But we shall never exchange our excellence
For their wealth. For our possession endures,
While riches change owners time after time.[7]

(4) He seems at first to have used his poetry not for any serious purpose, but for his amusement and enjoyment in his leisure time. But later he began to put philosophical tenets into verse and he wove many political ideas into his poems, not for the historical record so much as to provide justifications for his actions[8] and sometimes exhortations, warnings and rebukes for the Athenians.

Notes

1 The *axones* were revolving wooden slabs on which the laws of Solon were inscribed. See also *Solon* 24.2 [**39**], 25.1–2 [**50**] and *Athenaion Politeia* 7.1 [**42**] with notes. Despite the extensive examination by R. S. Stroud, *The Axones and Kyrbeis of Drakon and Solon* [University of California Publications: Classical Studies, 19] (Berkeley 1979), concluding that the *kurbeis* referred to in *Athenaion Politeia* 7.1 [**42**] and some fragments of other writers were more permanent records of bronze or perhaps stone, the *kurbeis* were probably identical to the *axones*. See E. Ruschenbusch, *Σόλωνος νόμοι: Die Fragmente des solonischen Gesetzeswerkes mit einer Text- und Überlieferungsgeschichte* [Historia Einzelschriften, 9] (Wiesbaden 1966) 14–22 and A. Andrewes in D. W. Bradeen and M. F. McGregor (eds), *Φόρος: Tribute to B. D. Meritt* (Locust Valley, NY 1974) 21–8. The *axones* seem to have survived the Persian sack of Athens in 480 BC and to have been available for perusal later: as late as the beginning of the second century BC they were seen by Polemon of Ilion (Eratosthenes, *FGrH* 241 F 37c), while by Plutarch's time only small fragments survived (*Solon* 25.1 [**50**]). See E. Ruschenbusch, op. cit. 1–14, 31–2 and R. S. Stroud in W. A. P. Childs (ed.), *Athens Comes of Age: From Solon to Salamis* (Princeton 1978) 20–42, especially 24–7 and 36. A diagram illustrating the *kurbeis* as man-sized, rectangular pillars revolving on axles is provided in P. J. Rhodes (trans.), *Aristotle: The Athenian Constitution* (Harmondsworth 1984) 123.

2 Kodros was traditionally one of the ancient kings of Attike.

3 *Philia* often refers to political friendship, and kinship by blood (*sungeneia*)

would certainly strengthen it. But Plutarch appears to be stressing the moderating effect which the memory of an earlier homosexual relationship had on the political differences between Solon and Peisistratos. I have not discovered any references to a homosexual relationship developing into political *philia*, but one would expect that if either partner was involved in politics, *philia* would manifest itself there also. The abusive epithet *euruproktos* ('wide-arsed') applied to politicians in Old Comedy implies that the process of anal dilation began early. It is surely with a touch of irony that Plato in the *Sumposion* (191e–192a) makes Aristophanes the comic poet say that those who actively engage in homosexuality in boyhood are the only ones who, when grown to maturity, prove to be men in political life. Plato makes Pausanias condemn capitulation by the subordinate partner for the sake of money or political gain (ibid. 184a–b); this suggests that political assistance could be used as a form of erotic inducement. See further K. J. Dover, *JHS* 86 (1966) 45, *Greek Popular Morality in the Time of Plato and Aristotle* (Oxford 1974) 33. The author of the *Athenaion Politeia* (17.2 [**61**]) argues that the story that Peisistratos as a young man was a favourite (*eromenos*) of Solon is chronologically impossible. However, what is known of their likely birth dates (see Davies, *APF* 323–4, 445) makes the relationship possible.

4 Plutarch quotes Euripides, *Bakkhai* 8. In the original context the neuter plural participle 'smouldering' refers to the ruins of the house of Semele, who was consumed by the fire of Zeus's thunderbolt when he visited her and she gave birth prematurely to Dionysos.

5 Probably Plutarch reflects a debate closer to his own time than to Solon's as to whether Solon was a philosopher or a trader. For the view that Solon traded only so far as was needed to finance his travels, see note 2 on *Athenaion Politeia* 11.1 [**47**].

6 For Solon's commonsense view that happiness is vulnerable to chance and for Aristotle's agreement with part only of that view, see T. H. Irwin in *Oxford Studies in Ancient Philosophy* 3 (1985) 89–124.

7 *Fragment* 15. I have tried to keep the same connotations for *kakoi* ('base') and *agathoi* ('noble') and hence for *arete* ('excellence'), as can be seen in *kakoi* and *esthloi* in *Fragment* 34 [**24**]. It might be thought that the distinction here is primarily one of righteousness, in which case the wicked (*kakoi*) are contrasted with the good (*agathoi*), who will not exchange their virtue (*arete*) for the wealth of the wicked. Certainly the idea of the wicked prospering while the righteous suffer had wide circulation: compare, for example, Job 21 and Psalm 73.2–12 in the Old Testament, or Menander, *Dyskolos* 797–804. These four verses are themselves attributed to Theognis of Megara as well as to Solon, though with little justification, and are repeatedly quoted by Plutarch (as Solon's) with a moral rather than a social interpretation (*Moralia* 78c, 92e, 472d–e). However, Solon is intent on making the point that it is personal qualities that endure. *Arete* is, indeed, a characteristic of nobles and they retain this excellence even if they are poor (cf. A. W. H. Adkins, *Merit and Responsibility: A Study in Greek Values* [Oxford 1960] 77–8). On the testimony of this fragment some nobles, some *agathoi*, in Athens of Solon's day were poor (not destitute, for which the usual designation is *ptokhoi*, 'beggars'), while many people of the lower classes, many *kakoi*, had gained riches.

Plutarch, then, misinterpreted the fragment when he tried to use it to show that Solon 'aligned himself with the poor rather than with the rich'. Basil, bishop of Caesarea in Cappadocia in the fourth century AD, believed that Solon was addressing the rich in this fragment (*On the Value of Greek Literature* 5.46–54 Boulenger). It may rather be the case that Solon is addressing not the rich but the nobles, those who had grown poor as well as those who retained the wealth expected of nobles. *Fragment* 4c [**23**], with which the present fragment was associated by E. Diehl, *Anthologia lyrica Graeca*, 3rd edn (Leipzig 1949) [as *Fragment* 4.5–8 and 4.9–12 on his numbering] was, however, addressed to the ambitious members of the lower classes (see note 4 on [**23**]). The reading ἔμπεδον αἰεί, printed by West at the end of the third verse of *Fragment* 15, is slightly preferable to ἔμπεδόν ἐστιν, printed by K. Ziegler in his text of Plutarch; see B. A. van Groningen, *Théognis: le premier livre* [Verhandelingen der Koninklijke Nederlandse Akademie van Wetenschappen, afd. Letterkunde, n.r. 72.1] (Amsterdam 1966) 128.

8 Hence Solon's intentions have generally to be deduced from poems in which he tries to justify his actions after his reforms. See, for example, *Fragments* 5, 34 and 37 in *Athenaion Politeia* 12.1, 3, 5 above ([**24**], [**28**]) and *Fragment* 36 in *Athenaion Politeia* 12.4 below [**32**].

Solon's relief measures

Solon's actions for the immediate relief of the situation in Attike – for which we have his own claims after the event (passage [**32**]) – were to tear up the pillars which indicated land worked by those under some form of obligation to the nobles, to encourage the return of debtors who had fled abroad, to free slaves in Attike and (in some way) to restore to Athens those sold abroad as slaves. Other sources (passages [**33**] and [**34**]) indicate that Solon forbade the securing of loans on a debtor's person. This removed the only security which many families could offer. Moreover, none of these measures enabled families released from vassalage to feed themselves. The only measure taken by Solon to alleviate this problem was the prohibition on the export of all agricultural produce apart from the produce of the olive (passage [**35**]). This must have induced an immediate drop in the price of grain in Attike. However, those with no resources to offer in exchange for grain must still have been beholden to noble patrons.

32 *Solon,* Fragment *36 in* Athenaion Politeia *12.4*

(4) Again, about the cancellation of debts and about the former slaves who were freed owing to the seisakhtheia, he says:[1]

The people I assembled with these aims;[2]
Did I abandon any unfulfilled?

Thou, my best witness in the court of Time,
Thou mighty mother of Olympian gods,
Black Earth, do testify that from thy breast
I tore the pillars[3] planted everywhere
And set thee free, who then had been a slave.
How many men to Athens I restored
(Their native city, founded by the gods),
Who had been sold for just or unjust cause;
And others, exiled by the pressing need
That follows debtors, who no longer spoke
The Attic tongue – so wide their wanderings.
To those at home in shameful slavery
Who trembled at their masters' every mood,
I gave their freedom.[4] These things I achieved,
Combining force and justice by strong law,[5]
And carried out what I had promised thus.
I drew up laws for bad and good alike,[6]
And set straight justice over each.
Yet had another held the goad as I,
A man of bad intent and filled with greed,
Would he, like me, have held the people back?[7]
Had I supported what then pleased their foes
Or even what their own extremists planned,
Athens had been bereaved of many men.
Therefore I warded off from every side,
A wolf at bay among the packs of hounds.

Notes

1 Because the author of the *Athenaion Politeia* quoted the following passage we have Solon's own claims about his relief measures. For the other quotations from Solon's poetry in *Athenaion Politeia* 12 see **[24]** and **[28]** above. As with *Fragment* 37 **[28]**, the metre of this fragment is iambic trimeter.

2 Here *demos* seems to refer to the whole people (despite the use of *demos* for the lower classes in verse 23). The verse probably indicates that Solon convened a meeting of the Athenian Assembly (Ekklesia).

3 Solon invokes an image of himself being judged in the court of Khronos (Time). (E. A. Havelock, *The Greek Concept of Justice from its Shadow in Homer to its Substance in Plato* [Cambridge, Mass. 1978] 254, however, denies that 'time' should be capitalised; he translates 'during a just procedure carried out in the course of time'. But see K. Ziegler, in *Miscellanea di studi alessandrini in memoria di Augusto Rostagni* [Torino 1963] 647–53 on Khronos in Solon's poetry.) He calls as his chief witness Ge (Earth), for she has experienced at first hand Solon's removal of the *horoi*, the pillars set up on the

land of farmers who were in some way dependent on noble clans (whether they had voluntarily bound themselves to a patron – see note 3 on [**19**] – or had mortgaged their land to a creditor). The *horoi* were presumably made of wood; none survive from Solon's time. Later *horoi*, made of stone, are studied by J. V. A. Fine, *Horoi: Studies in Mortgage, Real Security, and Land Tenure in Ancient Athens* [Hesperia Supplements, 9] (Princeton 1951), M. I. Finley, *Studies in Land and Credit in Ancient Athens, 500–200 B.C.: the Horos-Inscriptions* (New Brunswick, NJ 1952) and P. Millett, *Opus* 1 (1982) 219–49.

4 Solon distinguishes four categories of families that he helped: those with *horoi* on their land, whether these indicated mortgaged land or land one-sixth of whose produce went to a powerful clan in return for protection (verses 5–7); those sold as slaves abroad, some justly, others unjustly (8–10); those who had been enslaved at home (14–16); and those who had been unable to repay their loans, and who had fled abroad (11–13). All that the text of Solon says with respect to the last group is 'by dire necessity' or 'by pressing need', but Plutarch in citing verses 12–14 in *Solon* 15.6 [**34**] identifies the group as those liable to be seized as slaves (*agogimoi*, the same word as in *Athenaion Politeia* 2.2 [**17**] and Plutarch, *Solon* 13.4 [**19**]). Buying back slaves sold abroad must have required some kind of expenditure by the state, unless the foreign owners could be persuaded to part with their Athenian slaves on humanitarian grounds (surely very unlikely).

5 Rhodes (p. 176) finds κράτει νόμου meaning 'by force of law' very hard to accept, apparently on the ground that *nomos* was only adopted by the Athenians as the term for decrees on the initiative of Kleisthenes, who retained the word *thesmos* for the enactments of Solon (ibid. 177, referring to M. Ostwald, *Nomos and the Beginnings of the Athenian Democracy* [Oxford 1969] 158–73). Certainly Solon below (verse 19) uses *thesmoi* of his laws, and the fragment as quoted by Plutarch, *Solon* 15.1 [**48**] and by Aelius Aristides, *Oration* 28.138–40 (2.185–6 Keil) reads ὁμοῦ, 'together', not νόμου, 'of law'. However, the scribe of the London papyrus of the *Athenaion Politeia* obviously thought the reading was κράτει νόμου. Moreover, the oath which the arkhons took that they would observe Solon's laws uses the word *nomos*, according to *Athenaion Politeia* 7.1 [**42**]. This version is preferable to Plutarch's in *Solon* 25.3 [**50**], where *thesmos* is used, because Plutarch or his source adds two details in order to make the penalty conform with a promise in Plato, *Phaidros* 235d (cf. Rhodes 135; for a contrary view, M. Ostwald, op. cit. 4 and n. 1).

6 As with 'noble' and 'base' in *Fragment* 34 [**24**], the words 'good' (*agathos*) and 'bad' (*kakos*) in this passage connote a class distinction, as well as implying a value judgment. After Solon's time these words developed a strong moral sense. The English words 'noble' and 'villain' have a parallel semantic development.

7 The first half of the verse is identical with *Fragment* 37.7 [**28**]: 'he would not have held the *demos* back'.

33 Athenaion Politeia *6*

6 On gaining control of affairs Solon set the people free both in the present and for the future by prohibiting loans on the security of a debtor's person. He also enacted laws and cancelled debts, both private and public.[1] This cancellation is known as the seisakhtheia[2] since the Athenians thus shook off their load. (2) Some people use the seisakhtheia in an attempt to blacken Solon's reputation. For when he was about to enact it, he happened to tell some of the nobles in advance. In the sequel, according to the democrats, he was outmanoeuvred by his friends; but those who wish to denigrate his character assert that he himself had a share in the fraud. These friends raised loans and bought up a great deal of land, and when, not long afterwards, the cancellation of debts was effected, they became rich (this is said to be the origin of those families which later were reputed to have been wealthy since ancient times).[3] (3) However, the version of the democrats is by far the more credible. For such a man is not likely to have defiled himself by such a petty and unworthy fraud – a man who in other respects was so moderate and impartial that he incurred the hatred of both factions and valued his honour and the city's welfare above his personal aggrandisement at a time when he had the power to make his fellow citizens his subjects and become tyrant of Athens. (4) That he had this power is universally agreed: it is indicated by the unhealthy state of the country as well as by repeated references by Solon himself in his poems. One must therefore consider the accusation false.[4]

Notes

1 The opening of the chapter is rather clumsy, especially the intrusion of 'and he enacted laws' into what is otherwise an economic account. It is possible, as Rhodes (pp. 41, 127–8) suggests, that, as in chapter 2 [**17**], the author of the *Athenaion Politeia* here announces both political and economic themes, and proceeds to deal with the economic aspects before (in chapters 7–8 [**42**]) moving on to more extensive treatment of political matters. When the author proceeds in chapter 9 [**46**] to identify the most democratic of Solon's measures, he mentions again the prohibition of loans on the security of a debtor's person. This measure, of course, took away the only security which many families could offer. So they had little choice but to become retainers of noble clans which would provide physical support in return for political adherence. Solon perhaps intended this to happen for the good of Athens' economy; but more likely he saw noble patronage of the poor as natural. He presumably did intend to

prevent a recurrence of the Hektemoroi system, but the end result of poorer families tied to the patronage of noble clans (though freed from the sixth-part obligation) was not very different in terms of political structure from the situation before the *horoi* were uprooted.

2 Literally 'shaking-off of burdens', 'disburdenment'.

3 The author's interest in origins (cf. *Athenaion Politeia* 3.5–6 [**1**], 7.1, 7.4 [**42**], etc.) here interrupts the debate.

4 The whole story must be doubted as a later invention, not because the version in Plutarch, *Solon* 15.7–9 [**34**] names men whose descendants some Athenians might have liked to blacken in the later fifth century (as some have suggested), but because it must have been difficult to borrow large amounts and acquire land at short notice in a society where land changed hands with difficulty and where there was no coinage (see note 4 on [**36**]). Cf. Rhodes 128–9.

34 *Plutarch,* Solon *15.2–9*[1]

(2) . . . More recent writers observe that the Athenians urbanely gloss over the unpleasant aspect of things by disguising their nature with auspicious and charitable names. Thus they call prostitutes 'female companions', tribute payments 'contributions', garrisons of cities 'guards', and the prison a 'facility'. Solon, it seems, was the first to employ this device, when he named the cancellation of debts 'seisakhtheia'.[2] For his first public measure was to enact that existing debts be annulled and that in future no one might make loans on the security of a debtor's person.[3] (3) Yet some writers, Androtion among them, recorded that the poor were relieved not by a cancellation of debts but by a reduction of the interest on them and that in their delight they bestowed the name 'seisakhtheia' on this act of kindness and on the increase in the measures and in the value of money which Solon brought about at the same time.[4] (4) For he made the mina equivalent to 100 drakhmai, whereas formerly it had been worth 73. The result was that the amount paid was the same, but the value of the repayment was less, so the debtors in liquidating their loan derived great benefits while the creditors were not at all harmed. (5) But most writers agree that the seisakhtheia was a cancellation of debt contracts, and they are supported more by the poems. (6) For in these Solon boasts that from the mortgaged land

> He tore the pillars planted everywhere
> And set thee free, who then had been a slave.[5]

And with respect to those citizens who had been seized for debt, some he brought back from abroad

who no longer spoke
The Attic tongue – so wide their wanderings.
Those here at home in shameful slavery

he says he set free.

(7) This action is said to have involved him in the most distressing experience of his life. For when he had determined to cancel debts and was seeking suitable words to justify it and a fitting occasion, he communicated to those political friends with whom he was especially linked and whom he especially trusted – Konon, Kleinias, Hipponikos[6] and their associates – that he was not about to redistribute the land, but had decided to make a cancellation of debts. (8) But they acted immediately and anticipated his action; they borrowed much money from the rich and bought up large tracts of land. Then when the decree was proclaimed they enjoyed possession of the properties and did not give back the money to the lenders, thus rendering Solon the object of strong accusations and calumny, as if he were not an injured party but a collaborator in injustice. (9) But this charge was immediately removed by Solon's famous loss of 5 talents. For such a large sum Solon was found to have lent, and he was the first to remit it in accordance with the law. Some, Polyzelos of Rhodes among them, state that the amount was 15 talents. At any rate, his friends continued to be known as 'khreokopidai'.[7]

Notes

1 For the context (*Solon* 15.1 and 16.1) see [**48**].

2 See *Athenaion Politeia* 6.1 [**33**] and note 2 above.

3 Plutarch thus closely links the four actions mentioned by Solon in *Fragment 36* [**32**] – the removal of the pillars, the freeing of debt slaves in Attike, the return of families sold abroad as slaves, and the inducement to return of those who had fled – with the measure to prohibit loans in future on the security of a debtor's person.

4 For this interpretation – surely mistaken – of Solon's change to the weights and measures, see the notes on this passage [**37**] and on *Athenaion Politeia* 10 [**36**], pp. 61–4 below. Even if it were accurate, it would still be economic nonsense to say, as Plutarch does below (15.4), that the creditors did not lose.

5 Plutarch quotes verses 6–7 from *Fragment* 36 [**32**], changing Solon's verb from first person to third person, and quotes verses 12–14 below.

6 These, the only named *philoi* (political allies or partners) of Solon, seem to have been members of noble clans, as P. J. Bicknell has pointed out (see

Phoenix 22 [1968] 101 n. 25). However, J. K. Davies (*APF* 12, 255, 506) doubts the historicity of these figures; cf. note 4 on [**33**].

7 People who cut off debt repayments or deprive lenders of loans.

35 *Plutarch,* Solon *24.1–2*

24 The only agricultural produce which Solon permitted to be sold abroad was the produce of the olive. He prohibited export of the rest.[1] He decreed that the arkhon should pronounce a curse on offending exporters, or else himself pay a fine of 100 drakhmai into the public treasury. (2) It is the first axon which contains this law.[2]

Notes

1 The immediate effect of this embargo must have been to reduce the price of grain, since grain formerly sold at high prices in foreign markets now had to be sold in Attike. Presumably demand had previously exceeded supply, but this law reversed that situation. Consequently, poorer families experienced the relief of immediately reduced grain prices (but nothing approaching free distribution of grain); they must, however, in many cases have had to rely on the generosity of noble patrons in order to obtain food. (For the long-term effect of this law, see note 1 on [**39**].)

2 Plutarch or his source here claims that the original authority for the embargo on the export of agricultural produce was the first of the *axones* or wooden tablets on which the laws of Solon were inscribed. Drakon's laws also were arranged by *axones* (cf. the republished law on homicide: [**13**]). See also note 1 on [**31**].

Solon's stimulation of the economy

The only way in which Solon could give poorer families a degree of independence from noble patronage was to create employment, and that would have to be in secondary industry and trade. But even with the large resources available to modern governments, the creation of employment takes time. Families that had been dependent on aristocratic clans after the cancellation of debts (pp. 57–8 above) may well have continued to be retainers of such clans after new opportunities for employment were created in the city or its port. However, Solon did enact laws which provided long-term economic benefits for Athens: he placed Athenian weights and measures on the same scale as the more economically advanced cities of Euboia and Korinth (passages [**36**] and [**37**]); he encouraged fathers to teach their sons a trade (passage [**38**]); he encouraged skilled craftsmen to settle in Athens with their families in order to practise a trade (passage [**39**]); and the ban on the export of most primary produce encouraged those with capital to invest, if they did not invest in olive trees, in secondary industry and trade.

36 Athenaion Politeia *10*

10 These seem to be the democratic features of Solon's laws.[1] The cancellation of debts preceded the legislation while an increase both in measures and weights and in the coinage followed it.[2] (2) For under his administration the measures were made larger than those of Pheidon; and the mina which previously had a weight of 70 drakhmai was advanced to the full 100. (The standard coin in early times was the 2-drakhme piece.)[3] He also established weights corresponding to the coinage; he made the talent equivalent to 63 minas and distributed the additional 3 minas proportionately among the stater and the other units of weight.[4]

Notes

1 The author gives what seems to be a concluding assessment of Solon in chapter 9 [**46**], then inserts his view of the reform of measures of capacity, weights and coinage – perhaps in opposition to Androtion's interpretation reported in Plutarch, *Solon* 15.2–5 [**34**] – before offering in chapter 11 [**47**] a second assessment of Solon.

2 This chronological distinction is unjustified: see note 2 on Plutarch, *Solon* 16.5 [**20**]. It may have developed mistakenly from a logical distinction.

3 This statement is supported by the coins discovered: the earliest series of Athenian coins, the *Wappenmünzen* (so called because they bear various devices previously thought to be the badges of noble clans; but see R. J. Hopper, *CQ* n.s. 10 [1960] 242–7), have a didrachm as the standard coin, whereas the standard coin in the 'Owl' series which followed was the tetradrachm. Cf. C. M. Kraay, *Archaic and Classical Greek Coins* (Berkeley 1976) 57–8, 60. But the statement tells us nothing about Solon, since the *Wappenmünzen* appeared after his reforms (see next note).

4 Despite widespread acceptance of the view that Solon reformed the coinage of Athens, recent numismatic studies make it very unlikely that Athens had any coinage at the time of Solon's reforms or, indeed, until c. 560 BC. The debate can be followed in the pages of *The Numismatic Chronicle*: series 6, 10 (1950) 177–204 (W. L. Brown); 16 (1956) 1–8 (E. S. G. Robinson), 43–68 (C. M. Kraay); series 7, 2 (1962) 23–42 (W. P. Wallace), 417–23 (Kraay); 15 (1975) 1–11 (P. J. Rhodes); 17 (1977) 152 (Rhodes), 195–8 (Kraay). A further downdating of Athenian coinage, placing the introduction of the *Wappenmünzen* c. 545 or later and the Owls c. 510–506, has been put forward by M. J. Price and N. M. Waggoner, *Archaic Greek Coinage: the Asyut Hoard* (London 1975) 64–8, 122–4. A more extreme position is taken by M. Vickers, *The Numismatic Chronicle* 145 (1985) 1–44: he removes the perceived discrepancy between archaic Athenian coins now dated later and Greek art dated earlier by moving down the sculpture and vase-painting to a later date (for a counter-argument to his dating of the art see J. Boardman, *Archäologischer Anzeiger* [1988] 423–5 and to his dating of the Owls after 480 BC see M. C. Root, *The*

Numismatic Chronicle 148 [1988] 1–12). But he surely goes too far in attributing the alleged coinage reform of Solon to Ephialtes (c. 462 BC); there are too many coin dies attested for all Athenian coins to belong after 500 BC.

The tendency to downdate the coinage has recently been challenged by D. Kagan, *AJA* 86 (1982) 343–60, who argues that the crucial deposit of coins, presumably Lydian, in the foundation of the earliest Temple of Artemis at Ephesos in Asia Minor was closed no later than c. 645 BC (Vickers's date [op. cit. 15], by contrast, is c. 520 BC) and that consequently the literary evidence associating Pheidon tyrant of Argos with early Aiginetan coinage and Solon with a change in Athenian coinage should be accepted. There is clearly room for debate over the literary evidence associating a Kimmerian leader known to the Greeks as Lygdamis with the burning of a temple of Artemis (the first explicit statement comes from the fifth century AD) and over the date of the objects found with the coins. But even if the Lydians had coinage by the middle of the seventh century, all we have is a *terminus post quem* for Greek coinage. Any Greek city, and especially an economic backwater such as Athens was before Solon's reforms, may have taken many decades to adopt coinage. In their rejoinder to Kagan, J. H. Kroll and N. M. Waggoner, *AJA* 88 (1984) 325–40, point out that Athenian coinage is independent of the earliest Ionian and Lydian coinage; they argue that technical and typological analysis and the evidence of hoards converge to establish the relative chronology of Athenian coins and that the number of coin dies expended points to a date for the earliest Owls in the last quarter of the sixth century and for the earliest *Wappenmünzen* soon after the middle of the century.

It is possible that the attribution to Solon of a coinage reform stemmed from confusion over terms which later referred to coinage on the one hand and to weights and measures on the other (coins being named after the weights of silver which they represented; a reform of weights but not coinage is accepted, for example, by F. Creatini, *Studi classici e orientali* 34 [1984] 127–32 at 128). In that case, Solon may indeed have changed Athens from the old Aiginetan system of weights and measures (attributed to Pheidon and hence called 'Pheidonian measures' in *Athenaion Politeia* 10.2) to the Euboian system. This would facilitate trade not only with Euboia and Korinth but even more so with the Western Mediterranean, particularly the Greek settlements in southern Italy and Sicily.

The relative values of Athenian denominations in classical times were:

1 talent = 60 minas
1 mina = 100 drakhmai
1 mina = 50 staters

Precisely what our author was trying to say, and what changes were made by Solon have both been the subject of much debate. For a more extended but still truncated discussion see Rhodes 165–9. One possible explanation of what the author says in this chapter is as follows:

	old coinage		*new coinage*
	1 Aiginetan mina	=	0.7 Euboian mina
or	100 Aiginetan drakhmai	=	70 Euboian drakhmai

The old mina, the writer says, was only equivalent to 70 Euboian drakhmai, but on revaluation the mina became equivalent to 100 Euboian drakhmai. In other words, one-seventieth part of the old mina was equivalent to one-hundredth part of the new mina.

	old weights		*new weights*
	1.05 old talents	=	1 new talent
or	63 old minas	=	60 new minas

Thus the new talent equalled 63 old minas. With this 5 per cent increase in the talent came a corresponding increase in the value of the stater and the other units (this increase the writer expresses by saying that the additional 3 minas were distributed among the lesser values).

In this explanation the increase in the value of the coinage appears to be far greater than the increase in the value of the weights and measures. Rhodes (p. 167), on the other hand, explains the last sentence of 10.2 as meaning that Solon made 63 minas' worth of coins equivalent to the talent weight. In the author's own day, 63 minas' worth of coins were struck from 60 minas' (1 talent's) weight of silver, and the author may be wrongly assigning this practice to Solon. There are difficulties in all explanations because we do not have complete information. Of course, if one accepts only a reform of weights and measures as a stimulation of trade and secondary industry, the relation which the author postulated between that reform and a non-existent coinage reform is not important for historical reconstruction.

37 *Androtion,* FGrH *324 F 34 in Plutarch,* Solon *15.2–5*[1]

(2) . . . For his first public measure was to enact that existing debts be annulled and that in future no one might make loans on the security of a debtor's person. (3) Yet some writers, Androtion among them, recorded that the poor were relieved not by a cancellation of debts but by a reduction of the interest on them and that in their delight they bestowed the name 'seisakhtheia' on this act of kindness and on the increase in the measures and in the value of money which Solon brought about at the same time. (4) For he made the mina equivalent to 100 drakhmai, whereas formerly it had been worth 73.[2] The result was that the amount paid was the same, but the value of the repayment was less, so the debtors in liquidating their loan derived great benefits while the creditors were not at all harmed. (5) But most writers agree that the seisakhtheia was a cancellation of debt contracts, and they are supported more by the poems.

Notes

1 Historians whose work is not preserved *in extenso* have had the excerpts quoted

by other writers collected by modern scholars. Androtion is historian no. 324 in the standard collection of fragments, that by F. Jacoby (*Die Fragmente der griechischen Historiker* [Berlin 1923–30; Leiden 1940–58], abbreviated as here to *FGrH*). Plutarch mentions the reform of the measures in the context of Solon's relief measures (see [**34**]) because Androtion used that reform to explain the seisakhtheia. Precisely where Androtion's own words begin is open to debate; Jacoby suggests in printing the fragment that 15.3–4 represents Androtion.

2 Surely the account of the *Athenaion Politeia* [**36**] is more likely to be correct about the increase in weights: the new mina was in the relation 100:70 to the old. Some have emended Plutarch's text to read 'whereas formerly it had weighed 70' (so Rhodes 164 with n. 16); but confusion by Plutarch or his source with what the *Athenaion Politeia* says (10.2) about 63 minas is possible.

38 *Plutarch,* Solon *22.1, 22.3*

22 Solon observed that the city was filling up with people who were constantly streaming in from everywhere to find security in Attike; also that most of the land was unproductive and poor, while those who plied the sea[1] were not in the habit of bringing resources in to those who have nothing to exchange. So he turned the citizens to skilled trades and enacted a law whereby there was no obligation on a son to support a father who had not had him taught a trade.[2] . . .[3]

(3) But Solon, adapting his laws to the circumstances rather than the circumstances to the laws, observed that the nature of the land was such that it was scarcely capable of maintaining the farmers and could not support an idle and leisured mob, so he invested the trades with prestige and instructed the Council of the Areopagos to enquire into the source of each man's livelihood and to punish the idle.[4]

Notes

1 Perhaps an allusion to an ancient poem, as E. Will, *Deuxième conférence internationale d'histoire économique, Aix-en-Provence 1962* (Paris 1965) 77 n. 6, suggested. Plutarch's observation is not as banal as it seemed to M. I. Finley (*The Ancient Economy* [London 1973] 132). It recognises the need of a state which is not self-sufficient agriculturally to rise above consumption-oriented thinking and create a surplus (so Piccirilli 238), whether in an agricultural product such as olive oil or in manufactured goods.

2 Either one rejects as unenforceable this law absolving a son from the duty of supporting a father who had not had him taught a trade, or one must see it as an encouragement to secondary industry.

3 In 22.2 Plutarch points out that the problems faced by the Spartans (he says Lykourgos) were completely different, with no pressure from refugees and no shortage of land, but a great mass of Helots in their territory. So it was

appropriate for the Spartans to learn and practise just one occupation, the military.

4 This law also is seen by Plutarch as stimulating secondary industry and trade. It is, however, attributed to Drakon or to Peisistratos by other sources (cf. Hignett 307–8).

39 *Plutarch,* Solon *24.1–2, 24.4*

24 The only agricultural produce which Solon permitted to be sold abroad was the produce of the olive. He prohibited export of the rest.[1] He decreed that the arkhon should pronounce a curse on offending exporters, or else himself pay a fine of 100 drakhmai into the public treasury. (2) It is the first *axon* which contains this law.[2] . . .

(4) His law concerning naturalised citizens is a puzzling one, since it grants citizenship only to those who had been permanently exiled from their own city or who had taken up residence in Athens with their whole family to practise a trade. His purpose in doing this is said to have been not to discourage other immigrants but to invite to Athens immigrants in these categories on the assurance that they could acquire Athenian citizenship. At the same time he thought that one could trust those who had been forced to leave their own city and those who had left with a definite purpose.[3]

Notes

1 While this law would have achieved an immediate reduction in grain prices, as farmers were left with local surpluses they could not sell overseas, in succeeding seasons farmers would presumably grow less grain and try to keep prices high. The long-term effect of this law must have been to encourage producers with capital to invest in olive trees, which produce no crop for six years and take about forty years to reach maximum production (an inscription from Roman Africa indicates that tax rebates for land turned over to olive planting could last for ten years: see K. D. White, *Roman Farming* [London 1970] 519–20 n. 19). Grain could still have been grown between the olive trees as it is today (so Burn, *Lyric Age* 294–5). Solon was stimulating the only primary produce for which Attike was well suited to compete with overseas markets. Oil was used for cooking, producing artificial light and washing. The embargo must also have encouraged men with capital to invest in secondary industry.

It is sometimes suggested that wine was exported in defiance of this law. But both the literary sources and the archaeological evidence (stamped amphoras from other cities found in Athens, but no amphoras from Athens found elsewhere) indicate that Athens imported and did not export wine. See S. Isager and M. H. Hansen, *Aspects of Athenian Society in the Fourth Century B.C.* [Odense University Classical Studies, 5] (Odense 1975) 35–6.

2 See note 2 on [**35**].

3 Athens would become a more attractive city for skilled tradesmen if they could obtain the rights of Athenian citizenship. The enfranchisement of aliens who practised trades in Athens, combined with the law on teaching sons a trade (Plutarch, *Solon* 22.1; cf. 22.3 [**38**]) and the embargo on the export of nearly all primary produce (Plutarch, *Solon* 24.1), constituted a considerable stimulation to the secondary industry and thus to the general economic growth of Athens.

Solon's broadening of the basis of government

Solon formalised four property classes, based on the produce which could be expected from a certain amount of land. He removed aristocratic birth as a qualification for high office in Athens, and distributed the various offices among the classes based on landed wealth. Because an arkhon no longer had to be of aristocratic birth (as well as wealthy), the composition of the Areopagos – into which arkhons passed at the end of their year of office – must have changed over time. Gradually non-nobles would have become members of this body, though they must have been in a minority at least until Peisistratos became tyrant.

Solon also (it may be argued) admitted the lowest class, the Thetes, to the Assembly of all Athenian citizens. An important aspect of this new right was that the Assembly (Ekklesia) seems to have met as a law court (Heliaia) in order to adjudicate cases. Thus the gains of the lower classes, such as the cancellation of debts or the right to attend the Assembly, were protected by a jury which contained a healthy seasoning of lower-class members. The fear that an influx of inexperienced voters into the Assembly would cause instability seems to have been met by the institution of a new steering committee, the Council of Four Hundred, which perhaps vetted the agenda before it went to the Assembly. While Solon took steps which were later seen as basic to democracy, his own inclination was to keep a rein on the political activity of non-nobles. The admission of Thetes to the Assembly and the introduction of the Council of Four Hundred by Solon have been doubted by modern scholars, but the testimony of the ancient sources on these points may be accepted.

40 *Aristotle,* Politics *1273b 35–1274a 3, 1274a 15–21*

Some people think that Solon was an excellent lawgiver who broke the over-exclusive nature of the oligarchy, ended the slavery of the common people and established the ancient democracy with a well-balanced constitution. For they regard the Council of the Areopagos as oligarchic, the elected offices as aristocratic and the law courts as democratic. It seems, however, [*1274a*] that Solon did not put an end to the Council and election to offices, institutions which existed previously, but that he established the democracy by forming the juries in the courts from all citizens . . . .[1] Solon seems to have given the common people no more power than was absolutely essential, that of electing the officials and calling them to account (for without this control the common people are enslaved and hostile),[2] but he assigned all the offices to the noble and wealthy,[3] that is, to the Pentakosiomedimnoi, the Zeugitai and the third class of so-called Hippeis.[4] The fourth class, the Thetes, had no share in any office.

Notes

1 For the portion omitted here see [**45**].

2 Aristotle is here implying that Solon admitted the lowest class, the Thetes, to the Ekklesia (Assembly). He has said above that all citizens had a right to participate in the law courts. These points are supported by the *Athenaion Politeia* (7.3 [**42**] below) and by Plutarch (*Solon* 18.2 [**43**]). Both of them state that Solon gave to the Thetes a share in the Ekklesia and the law courts only. Hignett (pp. 117–18), however, rejects this consensus because he regards the admission of the Thetes to the Ekklesia as too bold a step for Solon. Yet Solon himself claimed to have given the *demos* some status (*Fragment* 5 in *Athenaion Politeia* 12.1 [**24**]). Admission of the Thetes to the Ekklesia would fit this claim admirably. Indeed, U. von Wilamowitz-Möllendorff, *Aristoteles und Athen* (Berlin 1893) 1.71 n. 43 suggests that Aristotle had that fragment in mind when he wrote this sentence. M. Zambelli, in *Miscellanea greca e romana* 4 [Studi pubblicati dall'Istituto Italiano per la storia antica, 23] (Rome 1975) 108, sees in the success of Aristion's motion to grant a bodyguard to Peisistratos (*Athenaion Politeia* 14.1 [**55**] with note 2) an indication that the Ekklesia had a large number of Thetes in it.

The Heliaia was probably the Ekklesia (normally a representative proportion of it) sitting as a court: see note 1 on [**45**]. It seems that Solon instituted this court as a means of safeguarding the gains of the poor against attempts by the nobles to recoup their losses by force. For this court contained a majority of citizens (including Thetes) who were vitally interested in maintaining their gains.

3 It seems undeniable from a comparison of *Athenaion Politeia* 7.3 [**42**] with 3.1 and 3.6 [**1**] that Solon removed birth as a qualification for office in Athens. Aristotle seems to recognise this by listing wealth classifications in this sentence. Yet he refers to the nobles (*gnorimoi*; cf. *Athenaion Politeia* 5.1 [**18**] and note 2) and the wealthy as holding all the offices. Rather than translate *gnorimoi* as 'well-known, notable' (which is its original meaning), it seems better to assume that in Aristotle's view the offices continued to be filled by nobles (who had, of course, to meet the property qualifications for office).

4 Aristotle has the second and third classes reversed: see *Athenaion Politeia* 7.3–4 below [**42**].

41 *Aristotle,* Politics *1266b 5–7, 14–20*

(5) Plato in *Laws*[1] held that, while accumulation of property should be allowed up to a certain point, it should not be possible for any citizen to acquire more than five times the minimum qualification . . . . That the (15) equalisation of property has some influence on the political community, some of the early lawgivers clearly recognised, such as Solon and others who enacted laws preventing anyone acquiring as much land as he might wish.[2] Similarly there are laws preventing the sale of property . . . .

Notes

1 *Laws* 5.744e.

2 While the verb κτᾶσθαι might be rendered 'possess, hold' in line 7 and here in line 18, it is easier to stop the acquisition of more than a certain amount of property than it is to force wealthy landowners to sell off some of their property. Hence Burn (*Lyric Age* 294) is probably correct in his belief that Solon enacted a law limiting the acquisition, not the holding, of property beyond a certain amount. This law is apparently in addition to the cancellation of debts, which would have reduced some large estates. Aristotle himself sees that movement towards equalisation of property influences the political structure of a community.

42 Athenaion Politeia *7–8*

7 Solon established a constitution and enacted other laws; the ordinances of Drakon, with the exception of those relating to homicide, were superseded. The laws were inscribed on the wooden pillars[1] and set up in the Stoa of the Basileus;[2] everyone swore to observe them.[3] The nine arkhons took their oath on the stone, declaring that they would dedicate a golden statue if they should violate any of the laws.[4] This is the origin of the oath to that effect still taken by the arkhons at the present time.

(2) Solon secured the laws against change for 100 years[5] and organised the constitution along the following lines. (3) He divided the population by an assessment of property into four classes, as it had also been divided previously: Pentakosiomedimnoi, Hippeis, Zeugitai and Thetes.[6] He distributed the major offices – the nine arkhons, the treasurers, the *poletai*, the Eleven and the *kolakretai*[7] – among the Pentakosiomedimnoi, Hippeis and Zeugitai, assigning offices to each class in accordance with the value of their assessable property. To those who

were classified among the Thetes he gave a share in the Assembly and the law courts only.[8]

(4) All those who made from their own estate 500 measures, dry and liquid produce combined, were classified as Pentakosiomedimnoi. Hippeis were those who made 300 measures. But some assert that they were those who were able to maintain a horse. In support of this definition they cite as evidence the name of the class, which is assumed to be derived from this circumstance, and also some ancient votive offerings. For there stands on the Akropolis a statue[9] which bears this inscription:

Anthemion, son of Diphilos, offers this horse to the gods
As thanks for his rise from the Thetes to rank as a Hippeus.

And a horse stands beside him, implying that this was the meaning of the rank of Hippeus. Nevertheless, it is more reasonable to assume that Hippeis were defined in terms of measures, just as the Pentakosiomedimnoi were. Those who made 200 measures in both kinds were classified as Zeugitai. The rest ranked as Thetes, and were not eligible for any office. That is why even now,[10] when a candidate for allotment to some office is asked to what class he belongs, no one would say he belonged to the Thetes.

8 Solon enacted that election to the various offices should be by lot, from candidates selected previously by each of the tribes. For the nine arkhons, each tribe made a preliminary selection of ten men and the lot was cast among these.[11] Hence the practice still in existence, of each tribe selecting ten candidates by lot and of a subsequent choice being made among these by lot. Proof that Solon regulated the offices filled by lot according to property qualifications is contained in the law on the treasurers, which continues in use to the present day. It demands that they be selected by lot from the Pentakosiomedimnoi.[12] (2) Such was Solon's legislation concerning the nine arkhons. For in ancient times the Council of the Areopagos summoned those who, in its own judgment, were suitable for each of the offices and appointed them for the year. (3) There were four tribes, as previously, and four tribe-kings. Each tribe was divided into three trittyes and into twelve naukraries. Over the naukraries were officers called Naukraroi, who were assigned to the supervision of current receipts and expenditure.[13] That is why, among the obsolete laws of Solon, it is repeatedly written that 'the Naukraroi are to levy . . .' and 'are to spend out of the Naukraric fund'.

(4) Solon also instituted a Council of Four Hundred, 100 from each tribe;[14] but he assigned to the Council of the Areopagos the task of superintending the laws, acting as guardian of the constitution, as previously. It supervised the largest and most important part of the state's affairs, called offenders to account and had authority to inflict personal punishment and fines.[15] Revenue from fines it deposited on the Akropolis, without recording the reason for which they were paid. It also tried cases of conspiracy against the people and for this purpose Solon established a legal process of impeachment.[16] (5) He also perceived that, although the city was often torn by internal strife, some of the citizens were content through sheer indifference to accept whatever result eventuated. He therefore enacted a law, directed at these people, that whoever in time of civil disturbance did not place his arms at the disposal of either faction should lose his civil rights and be deprived of any share in the state.[17]

Notes

1 The use of the word *kurbeis* here apparently provoked the discussion in Plutarch, *Solon* 25.1–2 [**50**]. On the *axones* and *kurbeis*, probably two terms for the same set of objects, see note 1 on Plutarch, *Solon* 1.1 [**31**].

2 The portico named after the arkhon called Basileus ('king'). Drakon's law on homicide, when republished in 409/8 BC [**13**], was to be placed in front of this Stoa. The portico was discovered in 1970; it is the first building on the right as one enters the Agora from the direction of the Kerameikos at the north-west corner (see note 5 on [**13**]). Since the building probably does not go back to Solon's time (see Rhodes 134–5), the *axones* must have been housed elsewhere originally. But the fact that in 409/8 BC the recorders of the law were to obtain a copy of Drakon's law from the Basileus and to place the newly engraved copy in front of the Stoa of the Basileus shows that that portico had become the home of the *axones* by the end of the fifth century BC.

3 Our author seems to imply that the oath was taken after Solon had published his laws, but the indefinite clause in Herodotos 1.29.2 [**29**] ('they were bound by solemn oaths to retain for ten years whatever laws Solon would enact for them') more plausibly implies an oath in advance of the legislation.

4 The *lithos* in the Agora at or on which the arkhons stand to take the oath is also mentioned in *Athenaion Politeia* 55.5 and in Plutarch, *Solon* 25.3 [**50**]. In the former passage the acceptance of bribes is specifically mentioned as the offence in connection with the performance of the duties of arkhon for which the dedication of a golden statue is required. The *lithos* itself has been identified in front of the Stoa of the Basileus: see T. L. Shear Jr, *Hesperia* 40

(1971) 259–60; H. A. Thompson, *The Athenian Agora: A Guide to the Excavation and Museum*, 3rd edn (Athens 1976) 85 (cf. 315); J. McK. Camp II, *The Athenian Agora: Excavations in the Heart of Classical Athens* (London 1986) 101–2, with photograph in fig. 75.

5 The version of Herodotos (see note 3), according to which the Athenians swore to retain Solon's laws for ten years, is more credible.

6 These names, according to our author, were in use already, but Solon formalised the qualifications in terms of landed wealth (the number of measures which one's land could be expected to produce: *Athenaion Politeia* 7.4) and assigned various offices to the first three classes. Pentakosiomedimnoi seems to have been a popular term referring to those with an income of 500 measures (*medimnoi*) or more (cf. the English word 'millionaires'). Hippeis (often translated 'knights') is the word for cavalry. Zeugitai also is more likely to have had a military connotation (men yoked together as hoplites in a phalanx) than an economic one (men who owned a yoke, or pair, of oxen). Thetes were men who laboured for another. They may have been obliged to follow their patrons to war, though poorly armed or unarmed. Solon took these military and economic descriptions and gave them a political significance, so that (for example) Thetes referred to everyone who did not own land sufficient to produce 200 measures of liquid and/or dry produce. For a different view see G. R. Bugh, *The Horsemen of Athens* (Princeton 1988) 20–34.

7 *Poletai* ('sellers') let public contracts, including the collection of taxes, and sold confiscated property (cf. *Athenaion Politeia* 47.2–3); the Eleven were superintendents of the state prison and executioners (cf. *Athenaion Politeia* 52.1); *kolakretai* were the paying officials of the state treasury. Most editors prefer a supplement for the damaged text of the papyrus which means 'the other offices', as distinct from membership of the Assembly and the Heliaia. But such membership is scarcely an office, so the supplement of von Fritz and Kapp (155 n. 18), meaning 'the major (με[γάλ]ας) offices', is preferable; this word was subsequently read on the papyrus by M. H. Chambers (*TAPA* 96 [1965] 31–9 at 34) and J. D. Thomas (Rhodes 139).

8 By making the qualification for the arkhonship landed wealth instead of birth and wealth, Solon was not only breaking the Eupatrid monopoly of the arkhonship but was also broadening the most powerful institution in Athens, the Areopagos. For arkhons passed into the Areopagos after their year of office. On the admission of the Thetes to the Ekklesia and the law courts see Aristotle, *Politics* 1274a 15–18 [**40**] with note 2.

9 The papyrus adds 'of Diphilos', which is the first word of the two pentameter verses quoted from the inscription. Since, as A. S. Murray pointed out (*CR* 5 [1891] 108), the quotation loses its point if Diphilos belonged to the class of Hippeis as well as his son Anthemion, it is best to omit the word 'of Diphilos' as an interpolation from the inscription (so E. S. Thompson, *CR* 5 [1891] 225).

10 That is, at the time of writing, c. 330 BC.

11 It is questionable whether lot was employed in the selection of arkhons, even if the forty men among whom the lot was supposedly cast had been elected by vote. For arkhons continued to be capable men, hence no doubt elected, until the early fifth century BC. Compare Aristotle, *Politics* 1273b 39–1274a 3, 1274a 15–18 [**40**] and *Athenaion Politeia* 22.5 [**91**] with note 5.

12 For a full explanation of the fourth-century method of selecting arkhons, see *Athenaion Politeia* 55.1; of selecting the treasurers of Athene, 47.1. Treasurers of Athene, apparently two from each tribe, are attested in the mid-sixth century: see G. R. Stanton, *Chiron* 14 (1984) 14.

13 'Trittys' is the singular, 'trittyes' the plural. Naukraries were divisions of the citizens for financial purposes, according to this passage; but further characterisation of them has been much disputed. See note 3 on Herodotos 5.71.2 [**8**].

14 Many scholars deny the existence of a Solonian Council of Four Hundred. Hignett (pp. 92–6) does so partly because the earliest evidence for its existence comes from 411 BC (*Athenaion Politeia* 31.1), but mainly because it looks forward anachronistically to the development of the later democracy. In answer to the first objection one might point out that we have no evidence for Kleisthenes's Council of Five Hundred, which everyone accepts, until 462 BC. Against the second objection it might be argued that the institution of the Council of Four Hundred need not have been a democratic change. If Solon made a real change in the composition of the Ekklesia, by admitting the Thetes (Aristotle, *Politics* 1274a 15–18 [**40**] with note 2), the Council of Four Hundred may have been introduced in order to restrict the agenda of the enlarged Ekklesia. (In a similar vein A. J. Holladay, *G & R*[2] 24 (1977) 56 n. 34 suggests that Solon offset the presence of the Thetes in the Ekklesia by giving control of the agenda to some more responsible group.)

15 The author may have repeated *Athenaion Politeia* 3.6 [**1**] so closely in order to stress that the dominance of the Areopagos continued. The view that Solon instituted the Areopagos, stated and then questioned by Plutarch (*Solon* 19 [**43**]), is a serious error. For the view that Solon extended the competence of the Areopagos see R. W. Wallace, *The Areopagos Council to 307 B.C.* (Baltimore 1989) 55–68.

16 Although some, such as M. H. Hansen, *Eisangelia* [Odense University Classical Studies, 6] (Odense 1975) 17–19 (cf. 56–7), have doubted that this process could have originated with Solon, Solon's known opposition to tyranny for himself (see *Fragments* 34 [**24**] and 32 [**27**], and *Athenaion Politeia* 6.3–4 [**33**] and 11.2 [**47**]) and Kylon's attempt to become tyrant make it conceivable that Solon did enact a law against would-be tyrants.

17 This seems to be curious reasoning. It would be more in accord with Solon's work to discourage citizens from participation in *stasis*. The suggestion made here would fit better the interests of a radical democrat at a time when there was oligarchic pressure for a limited franchise (for example, towards the end of the fifth century). Yet some have defended the authenticity of the law: e.g. J. A. Goldstein, *Historia* 21 (1972) 538–45, R. Develin, *Historia* 26 (1977) 507–8. Of defenders, B. Lavagnini (*RFIC* n.s. 25 [1947] 81–93, especially 88–9) suggests that the law was intended to prevent further movement to the 'left' and hence to prevent a tyranny, V. Bers (*Historia* 24 [1975] 493–8) that it was designed to consolidate support behind Solon himself at the beginning of his reforms. Loss of civil rights, *atimia*, was a serious penalty, since it laid a person open to harm or even death inflicted by members of the community with impunity. See, for example, E. Ruschenbusch, *Untersuchungen zur*

Geschichte des athenischen Strafrechts (Köln 1968) 16–21 or P. J. Rhodes, *CQ* n.s. 28 (1978) 89–90.

43 *Plutarch,* Solon *18–19*

18 Second,[1] Solon wished to leave all the offices as they were, in the hands of the wealthy, but to mix up the rest of the constitution, in which the common people had no share. So he took an assessment of the property of the citizens. He assigned to the first class those who made 500 measures, dry and liquid produce combined, and called them Pentakosiomedimnoi. The second class comprised those able to maintain a horse or to produce 300 measures; these he called 'classified as Hippeis'. Those of the third class, for which the criterion was 200 measures in both kinds, were named Zeugitai. (2) All the rest were called Thetes. He did not make them eligible for any office; they had no share in the constitution except by participating in the Assembly and the law courts.[2] (3) This participation appeared to be worthless at first, but later proved of enormous significance, since the great majority of disputes fell into the hands of the jurors. For in fact, on all the matters which he assigned to the officials to decide, he also gave a right of appeal to the court to anyone who wanted it. (4) He is even said to have increased the power of the courts by framing his laws in a less than clear way and with many points open to objection. For it came about that they were unable to resolve their differences by means of the laws and so were constantly in need of jurors and brought every dispute to them, who were thus in a way sovereign over the laws. (5) Solon himself indicates that he had such an intention in the following way:

> I gave to the people such power as is sufficient,
> I did not deprive them of honour, nor offer them too much.
> But those who were powerful, distinguished because of their wealth,
> I tried to ensure that nothing unseemly befall.
> Both factions I strove to surround with a strong shield,
> I did not permit an unjust victory to either's demands.[3]

(6) However, thinking that it was necessary to provide still further protection to the many in their weakness, he gave to

everyone the right to go to court on behalf of a person who had been wronged. If another person had been assaulted and subjected to violence or injury, it was possible for someone who was willing and able to indict the wrongdoer and prosecute him. The lawgiver was rightly conditioning the citizens, like parts of a single body, to share their feelings and sufferings with one another. (7) A saying of his which is in harmony with this law is recorded. When asked, apparently, which city had the best government, he replied, 'that city in which those who are not being wronged, no less than those who are being wronged, accuse and punish the wrongdoers'.

19 He created the Council of the Areopagos[4] from those who had held the annual office of arkhon, a Council in which he himself also participated through having held the arkhonship. But he saw that the people were swollen with self-assurance through the cancellation of debts. So he established a second Council, selecting[5] 100 men from each tribe (there were four tribes), whom he instructed to deliberate in advance of the people and not to allow any matter to be brought to the Assembly without its having been deliberated on in advance.[6] (2) He appointed the upper Council as guardian of everything and superintendent of the laws, thinking that the city, if it as it were rode at anchor with two councils, would be less affected by the swell and more conducive to tranquillity of the common people.

(3) Now most writers maintain that, as stated, Solon created the Council of the Areopagos and they seem to be supported most by the complete lack of any reference to or naming of Areopagites by Drakon, who always talks about the *ephetai* in connection with homicide cases. (4) On the other hand, the eighth law on the thirteenth *axon* of Solon has been recorded in these very terms:

> Of those without civil rights: all who were deprived of their rights before the arkhonship of Solon are to be in possession of civil rights, except those who were convicted by the Areopagos or the *ephetai* or in the Prytaneion by the Basileus arkhons on charges of homicide or murder or of aiming to establish a tyranny and who were in exile when this ordinance was published.

(5) These provisions prove on the contrary that the Council of

the Areopagos was in existence before the arkhonship and legislation of Solon. For who are those convicted before the time of Solon in the Areopagos if Solon first gave the function of judging to the Council of the Areopagos? Unless, by Zeus, there has come about some obscurity or deficiency in the document, so that in reality those convicted on charges which are now heard by the Areopagites and the *ephetai* and the *prutaneis* are to remain deprived of civil rights, while the rest are to recover possession of civil rights. However, you yourself consider this.

Notes

1 Plutarch says that first (our chapter 17 [**16**]) Solon repealed all the laws of Drakon except those concerning homicide, and second he introduced the measures enumerated in chapters 18 and 19.

2 This negatively framed statement agrees with those of the *Athenaion Politeia* 7.3 [**42**] (whose author perhaps used the same source) and of Aristotle, *Politics* 1274a 15–17, 21 [**40**], and confirms that Solon admitted the Thetes to the Ekklesia and the Heliaia (the law court).

3 Plutarch, though he exaggerates the case by reading 'power' instead of the preferable 'status' in the first verse of this fragment (5; see [**24**] above), links Solon's attitude to the common people with their influence through the courts. Admission of the Thetes to the Assembly and the Heliaia would fit admirably Solon's claim to have given the *demos* some status, while not offering them too much honour.

4 This is certainly wrong, since Aristotle in his critical passage on views of Solon [**40**] states that Solon did not put an end to the Council of the Areopagos, that is, it existed before Solon's reforms. Plutarch himself is aware of evidence against the view he states here, but he finally leaves the matter to the reader's decision (*Solon* 19.5).

5 It is perhaps only loose expression by Plutarch that gives the impression that Solon personally chose the original members of this Council. In fact, we know nothing of the means of selection, apart from the drawing of 100 members from each of the four tribes. Even the function (called 'probouleutic', that is, 'making preliminary decisions' for a more powerful body) which Plutarch attributes to the Council may be a sheer guess based on knowledge of the function of the Council of Five Hundred instituted by Kleisthenes (on which see *Athenaion Politeia* 21.3 [**84**] with notes). In his comparison of Solon and Publicola, Plutarch says that Publicola 'did not create a second Council, as Solon did' (*Publicola* 25.2), but again there is no further information about the Council.

6 Some (see note 14 on *Athenaion Politeia* 8.4 [**42**]) have thought that a Council of Four Hundred could not have been established by Solon because it is anachronistic and more appropriate to a developed democracy. But Plutarch's association of the Council's institution with the sudden confidence of the *demos* may point to Solon's real reason. He may have instituted this probouleutic Council so that it could vet the agenda of the Assembly and not allow any matter to be debated by the Assembly, with its influx of inexperienced voters 

(the Thetes: see *Solon* 18.2 above), without prior consideration by a steering committee.

There was at least one occasion on which a proposal was moved on the floor of the Assembly without prior discussion: Aristion proposed a bodyguard for Peisistratos (*Athenaion Politeia* 14.1 [**55**]). But this may have been regarded as an emergency situation. In general, it was important for the leading families to guide the Assembly (through the Council of Four Hundred) since in theory it was the sovereign body, even though in practice (see *Athenaion Politeia* 8.4 [**42**] with note 15) the Council of the Areopagos seems to have had the upper hand.

Estimates of Solon's achievements

In making their own evaluation of Solon, the ancient sources concentrated on what were perceived to be the democratic features of his constitution. But it was suggested on pp. 40–9 above that Solon cherished aristocratic values and was unlikely to have promoted increased power for the lower classes for its own sake. Rather (pp. 34–40 above), Solon was given his extraordinary commission by the nobles, who wanted him to eliminate the threat that the position of the nobles as a whole would be overthrown. The sequel (Chapter III) shows that Solon failed in this primary purpose. But the measures he took did change – over time – the status and power of the lower classes. And his reforms had beneficial side-effects in the economic sphere.

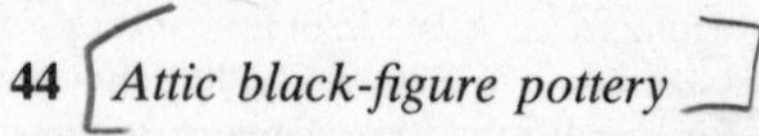

44 *Attic black-figure pottery*

A study of the distribution of exported black-figure ware (the first of the classical Athenian styles of pottery) reveals that during the twenty years from c. 600 to c. 580 BC there was an intensified diffusion of this pottery in Greece and a sudden spread into the Black Sea, to the eastern Aegean and to sites along the trade route to South Italy and Sicily. But during the twenty years from c. 580 to c. 560 BC the diffusion of black-figure pottery in Greece and in both the Eastern and Western Mediterranean was intensified, at the very time when trade in Korinthian pottery began to decline. In particular, Attic ware penetrated inland from the east coast of Asia Minor and reached Italy and Sicily in quantity for the first time. This growth in Athenian secondary industry and trade, and in the export of olive oil, is too early to be attributed to Peisistratos and must be the result of Solon's stimulation of these segments of the Athenian economy. The challenge to Korinthian trade may have been aided by a change in the system of weights and measures to the Korinthian standards (cf. *Athenaion Politeia* 10 [**36**] with note 4) and by a Korinthian tendency in the preceding period to sacrifice quality in the interests of mass production of pottery for export (cf. J. L.

Benson, *Greek Vases in the J. Paul Getty Museum* 2 [1985] 17–18). The evidence for the distribution of Attic black-figure pottery is set out by B. L. Bailey, *JHS* 60 (1940) 60–70. Brief details are given in Burn, *Lyric Age* 296, French 25 and Hammond[2] 165–6.

45 *Aristotle*, Politics *1273b 35–1274a 21*

Some people think that Solon was an excellent lawgiver who broke the over-exclusive nature of the oligarchy, ended the slavery of the common people and established the ancient democracy with a well-balanced constitution. For they regard the Council of the Areopagos as oligarchic, the elected offices as aristocratic and the law courts as democratic. It seems, however, [*1274a*] that Solon did not put an end to the Council and election to offices, institutions which existed previously, but that he established the democracy by forming the juries in the courts from all citizens. For this he is sometimes criticised, on the grounds that he destroyed the other institutions and placed the court, which was filled by lot, in complete control. For when the court[1] grew powerful, politicians showing favour to the somewhat tyrannous common people transformed the constitution into the present democracy. Ephialtes along with Perikles curtailed the Council of the Areopagos, Perikles introduced payment for membership of the courts, and in this way each of the demagogues in turn increased the democratic nature of the constitution until it reached its present form. But it seems that this development took place not in accordance with Solon's purpose, but rather through force of circumstances: the common people who were responsible for naval supremacy in the Persian War grew presumptuous and followed worthless demagogues despite the political opposition of the upper classes. Solon seems to have given the common people no more power than was absolutely essential, that of electing the officials and calling them to account (for without this control the common people would be enslaved and hostile),[2] but he assigned all the offices to the noble and wealthy, that is, to the Pentakosiomedimnoi, the Zeugitai and the third class of so-called Hippeis. The fourth class, the Thetes, had no share in any office.[3]

Notes

1 Aristotle here varies between singular and plural ('courts' in 1274a 3), as does

the author of the *Athenaion Politeia* (singular in 9.1 and 9.2 [**46**], plural in 7.3 [**42**]). But the word used, *dikasterion*, almost certainly belongs to a later time, when there was more than one court. The term in Solon's time was Heliaia (a traditional transliteration, for fifth-century inscriptions indicate there should not be an aspirate). In other Greek cities *aliaia* and other words related to ἡλιαία refer to the assembly of all citizens. Hence, despite the arguments of M. H. Hansen (*GRBS* 19 [1978] 141–3, *C & M* 33 [1981/2] 9–47), the Heliaia seems to have been the Assembly meeting as a court. See Rhodes 160, with more detailed discussion in *JHS* 99 (1979) 103–6, and M. Ostwald, *From Popular Sovereignty to the Sovereignty of the Law: Law, Society, and Politics in Fifth-Century Athens* (Berkeley 1986) 9–12, 35.

2 In the developed democracy the *demos* had this power through the role of the courts in the examination of officials before they took up office and in the scrutiny of the officials after their term of office (see *OCD*[2] s.vv. *dokimasia*, *euthyna*).

3 Aristotle makes a good case for the view that Solon had no intention of becoming the father of Athenian democracy and that the constitution after his reforms was oligarchic in character. For further notes on this passage see [**40**].

46 Athenaion Politeia *9*

9 The above[1] will serve to outline his legislation concerning the offices. These three features of Solon's constitution appear to be particularly democratic:[2] first and most important, the prohibition of loans on the security of a debtor's person; second, the right of anyone who so wished to help injured persons gain redress;[3] third, the institution of appeal to the court.[4] This is said to be the greatest contribution to the later strength of the common people; for when the people are masters of the vote they are also masters of the constitution. (2) Moreover, since the laws were still formulated in an imprecise and obscure way (such as the one concerning inheritances and heiresses), many disputes inevitably arose and the court had to arbitrate in all matters, whether public or private. Indeed some believe that Solon deliberately made the laws obscure, so that the final decision should rest with the people. This is not likely; the reason no doubt lies in the impossibility of securing the best result by means of a general law. For it is not fair to assess Solon's intention from the actual consequences at present[5] but from the tone of the rest of his constitution.

Notes

1 For *Athenaion Politeia* 7–8 see [**42**].

2 This is the kind of view of Solon which Aristotle combats in the previous

passage. E. Ruschenbusch (*Historia* 7 [1958] 398–424, especially 399–408) argues that Solon first came to be regarded as the founder of Athenian democracy about 356 BC. This is too precise, but it is clear that the idea flourished from the 350s on, leading to the debate evidenced by Aristotle's paragraph [**45**] on Solon, and by our author's report of others' views ('this is said to be . . .', 'some believe . . .') in the next few sentences. Of course, much literature has been lost to us, but if we consider such comments on Solon as are available, we must conclude that there is no evidence that Solon was viewed as a democratic reformer for 170 years or more after his reforms. To take an example: a character in Aristophanes's *Clouds* of 423 BC (of which we have a revised version) says that Solon was 'by disposition a friend of the common people' (verse 1187). This merely means that Solon was well-disposed to debtors, since the speaker is explaining a verbal sleight-of-hand to deprive creditors of the money owed to them. Indeed, Solon may be named in this passage simply as the figure to whom all laws, even quite recent ones, were attributed.

3 This provision has not been mentioned at all by the author in his account of Solon, though it is discussed by Plutarch (*Solon* 18.6–7 [**43**]). It was an important safeguard against the informal power of aristocratic patrons. Now, if a poorer citizen was coerced into slavery by one of the nobles, someone else could speak up for him and take his interests to court. And the jury in that court (see note 2 on [**40**] and note 1 on [**45**]) would have a fair smattering of similarly poor citizens.

4 These last two measures may have been designed to take justice out of the hands of the nobles and place it under state control (cf. Peisistratos's use of local judges: *Athenaion Politeia* 16.5 [**61**]). As the next sentence implies, the *demos* (here translated 'the people', to distinguish *ho demos* from *to plethos*, 'the common people', in the previous clause) were eligible to participate in the court. On this point see Aristotle, *Politics* 1274a 2–3 [**45**], *Athenaion Politeia* 7.3 [**42**] and Plutarch, *Solon* 18.2 [**43**]. On the precise significance of the right of appeal see D. M. MacDowell, *The Law in Classical Athens* (London 1978) 29–32.

5 This argument parallels Aristotle's in *Politics* 1274a 5–15. But Aristotle offers some cogent criticisms of the view of the Atthidographers (the local historians of Attike, represented in this case by the *Athenaion Politeia*) that Solon was enacting democratic reforms. The view of the author of the *Athenaion Politeia* is further revealed in 41.2 [**2**], which lists eleven changes in the Athenian constitution: 'the third alteration was that in the time of Solon, after civil conflict; from it arose the beginning of democracy'.

47 Athenaion Politeia *11*

11 When he had organised the constitution along the lines described above,[1] Solon was besieged by people pestering him about his laws, finding fault here and querying there. Since he wished neither to alter what he had done nor to incur odium by staying in Athens, he set out on a journey to Egypt, as both businessman and tourist.[2] He declared he would not return for ten years;[3] there seemed to be no reason for him to stay and interpret his laws; everyone should obey them just as they were written down. (2) Consider his position: many of the nobles had become alienated from him on account of his cancellation of debts and both factions[4] had retracted their support through their disappointment at the state of affairs. For the people expected him to make a complete redistribution of property,[5] while the nobles expected him to make little or no change in the status quo. But Solon had resisted both factions, and though it was possible for him to become tyrant by combining with whichever faction he wished,[6] he chose to incur the hostility of both by saving his country and legislating in its best interests.[7]

Notes

1 This opening certainly does not look back to chapter 10 (on Solon's reform of weights and measures and his alleged reform of coinage [**36**]). Rather it refers to chapters 7–8 [**42**]. The present chapter uses a report of the immediate aftermath of Solon's reforms to reach an assessment of Solon additional to that in chapter 9 [**46**]. Cf. Rhodes 47, 54, 169.

2 L. Braccesi, *Atene e Roma* n.s. 32 (1987) 1–7 argues that tourism in the Greek world was always subordinated to more practical and more remunerative activities. However, it seems that Solon took goods to sell so that he could support himself while he was abroad: see J. Hasebroek, *Trade and Politics in Ancient Greece* (London 1933) 13; the same argument is put forward by G. E. M. de Ste Croix, *The Class Struggle in the Ancient Greek World from the Archaic Age to the Arab Conquests* (London 1981) 129–31, citing a similar phrase as here from Isokrates 17 (*Trapezitikos*).4, where a father finances his son's visit to Athens with two ships of grain as well as cash.

3 It is not easy to date these ten years. Compare Herodotos 1.29.1–1.30.1 [**29**] and 2.177.2 [**30**] with notes.

4 'Faction' rather than 'party' because neither the nobles nor the common people were organised like modern political parties. The word for nobles here, *gnorimoi* ('the well-known ones'), is the same as that used in *Athenaion Politeia* 2.1 [**17**] and 5.1 [**18**]; see note 2 on [**18**].

5 For the demand of the *demos* for a redistribution of land, see also Plutarch, *Solon* 13.6 and 14.2 [**19**] and note 1 on [**17**]; their disappointment, noted here, is mentioned also in Plutarch, *Solon* 16.1 [**48**].

6 As B. D. Farrell has pointed out to me, this claim could only make sense if Solon won over some members of the other faction as well; the scenario seems artificial, like the description of the conflict in *Athenaion Politeia* 2 [**17**] and 5.1–2 [**18**]. It may rather be the case that Solon was tolerated in his office by the nobles; they would have preferred some way of solving their problems other than his extraordinary appointment (cf. note 1 on [**17**]). Although the author of the *Athenaion Politeia* talks about just two factions, the nobles and the common people, the only way in which Solon might have gained a tyranny by alliance

with nobles was by a variation on removal of lower-class support from the 'pyramids' of supporters of noble families (cf. note 1 on [**17**] for this model). 'What their [i.e. the common people's] own extremists planned' (Solon, *Fragment* 36.25 [**32**]) was presumably an alliance by one or two noble families with the poorer people *en masse*. If Solon had supported them, there would have been many deaths (as Solon said, ibid. 36.26) and the rule of a tyrant.

7 The final phrase probably reflects Solon's view of his reforms rather than enthusiastic approval from our author (so Rhodes 171).

48 *Plutarch,* Solon *15.1–2, 16.1, 16.2–4*

15 . . . But although he refused to become tyrant, he did not conduct affairs in a particularly mild manner. He did not enact his laws in weakness, nor in submission to the powerful, nor to please those who had chosen him. Where he approved, he did not apply any remedy or innovation, fearing lest 'by overturning completely and upsetting the state, he might be too weak to establish it again'[1] and reconstitute it for the best. He did only what he hoped to achieve by speaking to the flexible and by compelling the obstinate, as he himself says:

Combining force and justice together.[2]

(2) So, when he was asked later whether he had written the best laws he could for the Athenians, he replied, 'The best they would accept.' . . .[3]

16 He pleased neither side. The rich were aggrieved because he deprived them of their securities, the poor even more so because he did not make a redistribution of land for them as they had hoped, nor establish a strictly uniform and equal way of life as Lykourgos had done. (2) . . . [4] But Solon did not reach these heights with his constitution, being in favour of democracy and in a middling position.[5] He made full use of the power he had, derived solely, as it was, from the approval of the citizens and their trust in him. (3) That he offended the majority who had other expectations, he himself said about them:

Vain were their purposes then, but now they look askance
And air their anger toward me, as though I an enemy were.[6]

(4) And yet he says that if anyone else had had the same power,

He'd not have held the people back, nor stopped
Until he'd stirred the milk and lost the cream.[7]

Notes

1 E. Diehl, *Anthologia lyrica Graeca*, 3rd edn (Leipzig 1949) implies that this is a quotation from Solon (testimonia to his *Fragment* 23.1–12); cf. *Fragment* 33a West.

2 Plutarch, like Aelius Aristeides who quotes verses 3–27 of this fragment (36) at *Oration* 28.138–40 (2.185–6 Keil), reads *homou*, 'together, in harmony'. But the version of the fragment (with all 27 verses) preserved in *Athenaion Politeia* 12.4 [**32**] reads *nomou* and has the sense run on from the previous verse: '[by force] of law'. See note 5 on [**32**].

3 For Solon 15.2–9 see [**34**].

4 Plutarch explains why Lykourgos was able to make radical changes in Sparta.

5 This phrase is an attempt to capture the sense of *mesos*, 'middle, intermediate', as applied to Solon. Compare the description of him in *Athenaion Politeia* 5.3 [**23**] as one of *hoi mesoi*, the men in the middle, with note 3 on that passage; also the reference in Plutarch, *Solon* 14.5 [**19**] to the many citizens *dia mesou* who were happy to entrust sole authority to Solon. *Demotikos*, linked here (16.2) with *mesos*, cannot mean 'one of the common people', for Plutarch knows that Solon was a noble (*Solon* 1.2 [**31**]). It might mean that Solon was chosen by the common people; whereas his position rested on the goodwill and trust of all the citizens (next sentence). But that Solon was chosen by the common people alone contradicts Plutarch's view in *Solon* 14.3 [**19**]. The translation in the text, 'in favour of democracy', is based on the description of Peisistratos in *Athenaion Politeia* 13.4 [**52**] and 14.1 [**55**] as *demotikotatos*. But this interpretation of *demotikos* hardly provides the necessary contrast with Lykourgos of Sparta who ensured, according to Plutarch in the omitted portion of *Solon* 16.2, that 'none of the citizens was either poor or rich'.

6 The verses which surround these two from *Fragment* 34 are preserved in *Athenaion Politeia* 12.3 [**24**].

7 These verses from *Fragment* 37 are quoted in slightly different form in *Athenaion Politeia* 12.5 [**28**]. The author of the *Athenaion Politeia* introduces them with similar words.

49 *Plutarch,* Solon *20.1–2, 20.6*

20 Among his [Solon's] other laws there is a very peculiar and surprising one which decrees that a man who belonged to neither side in a civil conflict be deprived of his civil rights. It seems that he wished that no one should be indifferent or insensitive to the common good or safeguard his private affairs while glorying in the fact that he does not share in his country's sufferings and sickness. Rather he wished every one promptly to attach himself to the side which was acting better and more justly, to share the danger and help rather than await the victory of the stronger side without running any risks.[1]

(2) Another law which seems out of place and ridiculous is that

which permits an heiress to marry one of her husband's next of kin if her lawful husband and master proves to be impotent. Yet some say that this was a good measure against men who, though unable to engage in intercourse, take heiresses in marriage for the sake of wealth and use the law to do violence to nature.[2] . . .

(6) In all other marriages Solon abolished dowries, allowing the bride to bring with her three changes of clothing, household possessions of little value, and nothing else. For his intention was that marriage should not be a mercenary or revenue-producing institution, but that husband and wife should live together[3] for child-bearing, affection and love . . . .[4]

Notes

1 For the law against neutrality, which seems alien to Solon's efforts for peace, see *Athenaion Politeia* 8.5 [**42**] with note 17. Plutarch suggests the motivation of Solon, as he does for the other laws cited in this chapter.

2 The law against neutrality was 'very peculiar and surprising', and this law seems absurd, as Plutarch emphasises by his word order. Although Plutarch begins by citing the opinions of others on this apparently absurd law, he goes on (in 20.3–5) to expound its purpose. The law reported here was not in existence in later times, but if we interpret it in terms of the position of the heiress in the classical period, it would seem that the heiress had virtually no freedom of choice. She was considered a possession and inherited along with the property of which she was called the 'heir' (*epikleros*). See J. E. Karnezis, *The Epikleros (Heiress): A Contribution to the Interpretation of the Attic Orators and to the Study of the Private Life of Classical Athens* (Athens 1972) 206, 232–6 or D. M. Schaps, *Economic Rights of Women in Ancient Greece* (Edinburgh 1979) 25–6. In this light Plutarch's view that the law 'permits' an heiress to marry seems overstated.

3 The same word (*sunoikismos*) is here used of man and wife as is commonly used of the unification of Attike (see [**5**] and note 5).

4 Plutarch proceeds to a short homily on marriage (he wrote an essay of advice to a married couple: *Moralia* 138a–146a).

50 *Plutarch,* Solon *25.1–3, 25.6*

25 He [Solon] gave all his laws validity for 100 years.[1] They were engraved on wooden *axones* which revolved in the rectangular frames which contained them. Even in my time small fragments of them were preserved in the Prytaneion. According to Aristotle,[2] they were termed *kurbeis*. (2) Kratinos the comic poet says somewhere:

> By Solon and Drakon I swear, whose *kurbeis*
> are now used to roast our barley corns.

But some writers say that *kurbeis* properly refers only to the tablets concerned with sacred rites and sacrifices, and the rest are called *axones*.

(3) In any case, the Council[3] swore an oath collectively to establish the laws, while individually each of the Thesmothetai declared by the stone in the Agora that, if he transgressed any of the ordinances, he would dedicate a man-sized golden statue at Delphi . . . .[4]

(6) When his laws had been put into effect, people used to come to Solon every day, commending or criticising, or advising him to insert or delete a certain particular in what had been written. Great numbers came to enquire, to query or to urge him to give further instruction and clarify the meaning of each law and his intention in enacting it. He saw that in this situation he would incur ridicule by not acting and odium by acting, and wished to get out from under the difficulties completely and to escape from the captious and fault-finding behaviour of the citizens – for 'in great affairs it is difficult to please everyone', as he himself says.[5] He made his trading interests as a ship-owner an excuse for travel[6] and sailed away, having asked the Athenians for a period of ten years' absence. For he hoped that in this time they would become accustomed to his laws.[7]

Notes

1 Plutarch mentions below (25.6) that Solon planned to be absent for ten years. Herodotos 1.29 [**29**] is probably correct to link the ten years with the guarantee that the laws would be maintained. We should, then, prefer Herodotos's ten years to the 100 years of *Athenaion Politeia* 7.2 [**42**] and Plutarch.

2 Plutarch accepts the attribution of the *Athenaion Politeia* to Aristotle. The reference is to 7.1 [**42**]. The comic poet Kratinos, whose Fragment 274 Kock is quoted below, wrote in the late fifth century BC. This fragment provides our earliest reference to Drakon, the lawgiver of two centuries earlier. That the joke is not evidence for the destruction of Solon's *kurbeis* is argued by N. D. Robertson, *Historia* 35 (1986) 147–76 at 148–53.

3 This must refer to the Council of the Areopagos. The three senior arkhons and the six Thesmothetai passed into this Council at the end of their year of office (cf. *Athenaion Politeia* 3.6 [**1**]). But any oath to keep Solon's laws in force must have been given before his laws were published, to judge from the hostile reaction after their announcement.

On the oath taken by arkhons 'on the stone' (*Athenaion Politeia* 7.1; cf. 55.5) see note 4 on [**42**].

4 In 25.4–5 Plutarch attributes to Solon the observation of the non-coincidence of the cycles of the sun and the moon, and then traces back to Solon certain features of the Athenian calendar.

5 *Fragment* 7 West.

6 For travel as Solon's primary motive and trade as secondary (as here), see note 2 on [**47**].

7 Compare *Athenaion Politeia* 11.1 [**47**].

III

FROM SOLON TO PEISISTRATOS

Factional conflict after Solon's reforms

If Solon's main aim was to end conflict among the noble clans, as suggested in Chapter II (see p. 34), he failed. On two occasions shortly after his reforms were enacted, the Athenians failed to elect an arkhon. The noble clans could not agree even on conducting amicably the election for that office which each hoped that their own protégé would hold. Moreover, one arkhon would not lay down his office at the end of the year, and was removed by force after two years and two months (passage [**52**]). Finally, Peisistratos after a number of attempts succeeded in establishing himself as tyrant (see pp. 91–102), thus accomplishing the very thing which the nobles as a whole had hoped to avoid when they put Solon in such an extraordinary position. The sources in this section (especially passage [**52**]) suggest that the factions which dominated politics in the period after Solon were factions of landed aristocrats, each based on a particular region of Attike.

51 *Herodotos 1.59.3*

(3) . . . When the Athenians of the coast, headed by Megakles son of Alkmeon, and those from the plain, headed by Lykourgos son of Aristolaïdes, were engaged in factional conflict, Peisistratos raised a third faction with the aim of gaining a tyranny.[1] He assembled his partisans, championed the cause of the people from beyond the hills[2] and contrived the following plan.[3]

Notes

1 The Paraloi, the 'people of the coast', were led by the grandson of the Megakles who was arkhon when Kylon attempted to become tyrant in Athens (Chapter I, pp. 19, 23). He was presumably the most prominent member of

the Alkmeonidai family in his generation. Lykourgos, who led the 'people of the plain' (Pediakoi, to use the term in the *Athenaion Politeia* [**52**]) probably came from the Boutadai family, which regarded itself as so well-born that it adopted the name Eteoboutadai, the 'real Boutadai', after its name was given to a deme under the reform of Kleisthenes (Chapter V, pp. 145–65). See [**108**] with note 1, [**109**] with note 3 and D. M. Lewis, *Historia* 12 (1963) 22–4, 26. Peisistratos also was a noble (for a man of the same name, presumably an ancestor, was arkhon in [traditionally] 669/8 BC: Pausanias 2.24.7), with estates near Brauron on the east coast of Attike ([Plato], *Hipparkhos* 228b 4–5; Plutarch, *Solon* 10.3 [**56**] with note 3).

2 'The people from beyond the hills' seems to be the meaning of Hyperakrioi, which is more specific than the names for this faction in *Athenaion Politeia* 13.4 (below) and Plutarch, *Solon* 29.1 ([**53**]; also *Moralia* 763d and 805d–e). Those names (Diakrioi and Epakrioi) mean simply 'the people of the hills'. Herodotos's early date and his understanding of politics, combined with the fact that the complex name is more likely to be original than the simple one, suggest that we should accept his name for the basis of Peisistratos's faction. 'The people from beyond the hills' (considered from the standpoint of the city) were presumably landed nobles like those who formed the basis of the other two factions. For further discussion see Hignett 110–12; A. French, *G & R*[2] 6 (1959) 46–57 and *The Growth of the Athenian Economy* 26–7; E. Kluwe, *Klio* 54 (1972) 101–24; A. J. Holladay, *G & R*[2] 24 (1977) 40–56; A. Andrewes, in *CAH*[2] 3.3.392–3.

3 For Peisistratos's attempts to become tyrant see Herodotos 1.59.4–1.64.1 [**54**].

52 Athenaion Politeia *13*

13 These, then, were the reasons for which Solon went abroad.[1] After his departure the state was still troubled by dissension. For four years the Athenians lived in peace; but in the fifth year after Solon's arkhonship they elected no arkhon because of the factional strife, and again four years later they failed to elect an arkhon for the same reason.[2] (2) Then, still in the same period,[3] Damasias was elected arkhon; he held office for two years and two months, until he was expelled from the arkhonship by force.[4] Then they decided because of the dissension to elect ten arkhons, five from the nobility, three from the farmers and two from the craftsmen.[5] These held office for the year following Damasias. From this, incidentally, it is clear that the arkhon possessed the greatest power;[6] for it was invariably around this office that dissension seemed to centre. (3) On the whole, however, the Athenians suffered from continual internal disorder. Some found the cause and justification for their discontent in the cancellation of debts (for they had thereby been reduced to poverty); others were dissatisfied with the constitution because of the radical change it had undergone; while some were motivated by personal rivalries among themselves.[7]

(4) There were three factions.[8] First, there was the faction of the coast, which was headed by Megakles son of Alkmeon and which seemed to be striving particularly for a moderate form of government. Then there was the faction of the plain, led by Lykourgos, which aimed at an oligarchy. The third faction was that of the hills, directed by Peisistratos, who had the reputation of being an extreme democrat.[9] (5) Recruits were added to this faction by motives of poverty, incurred by creditors deprived of debt repayments, and by motives of fear, felt by persons of impure descent. That such people did join is shown by the fact that after the overthrow of the tyrants the citizen roll was revised on the ground that many were participating in the franchise who were not entitled to it.[10] The various factions derived their names from the districts in which they had their farms.[11]

Notes

1 See *Athenaion Politeia* 11 [**47**].

2 They created *anarkhia* (the situation of being without an arkhon). Presumably this word appeared in the arkhon list and thus found its way into the *Athenaion Politeia*.

3 It is possible that the author meant to say 'after a similar period had elapsed' (i.e. after another four years), but the result (Solon's arkhonship – four years – *anarkhia* – four years – *anarkhia* – four years – Damasias's arkhonship) would seem to be a schematised tradition and therefore unreliable.

4 This looks like an attempt by Damasias to set himself up as a tyrant (compare Kylon's attempt in the late seventh century: Chapter I, pp. 17–26), since he was expelled from the office by force.

5 The composition and significance of this coalition government is subject to debate. (See, most recently, T. J. Figueira, *Hesperia* 53 [1984] 447–73. He provides a bibliography of other views and argues that the board of ten arkhons was merely a minor aberration achieved by aristocrats, a short-lived diversion from the political development of Athens in the sixth century.) Rhodes (p. 183) suggests that it is virtually impossible to find a role for two occupational classes called Agroikoi ('farmers, landowners') and Demiourgoi ('craftsmen, labourers') in sixth-century Athens; the division of the non-Eupatrid five may have been invented by later theorists. Even if there were three categories represented, it is certainly possible that the five Eupatridai ('well-born' people), three Agroikoi and two Demiourgoi were all members of the highest income class. On such a board, the non-nobles held at most five votes and the nobles held sufficient votes to apply a veto, if they did not have an absolute majority. On other interpretations, of course, control of the board by nobles is also possible. In other Greek states of the archaic period

Demiourgoi ('skilled workers in public things') were high-ranking politicians or officials: see L. H. Jeffery, *Archeologia Classica* 25–6 (1973–4) 319–30. There is no explicit evidence that the term had such an application in Attike, but C. A. Roebuck, for example, suggests that in Attike they were clansmen and landholders, perhaps local officials, and that even the Geomoroi (if these were the same as Agroikoi) were substantial landholders, perhaps descended from the cadet of a clan sent out to establish himself away from the city (*Hesperia* 43 [1974] 485–93, especially 490–3).

6 Compare *Athenaion Politeia* 3.3 [**1**].

7 The first cause of discontent seems to suit Eupatridai who had lost the income of one-sixth from the Hektemoroi (*Athenaion Politeia* 2.2 [**17**] with note 3) – but who presumably retained sufficient land not to be reduced to poverty by the cancellation of debts. The second complaint certainly came from Eupatridai, disappointed at the curtailment (however slight) of their political power. Personal rivalries also may have applied mainly to Eupatridai, but competition between Eupatridai and non-Eupatridai is also conceivable.

8 Hardly parties as we know them in modern politics.

9 Peisistratos was certainly not an extreme democrat; he wanted to be tyrant (though he would use lower-class support to achieve that end).

10 The people who were most likely to be unable to show pure Athenian descent were the children of those skilled tradesmen whom Solon had attracted to Athens with the promise of enfranchisement (cf. Plutarch, *Solon* 24.4 [**39**]). While their own name may have been Athenian, their father's name was likely to have been obviously non-Athenian. Kleisthenes may later have sought the support of those struck off the citizen roll. See *Athenaion Politeia* 21.2, 21.4 [**89**] with notes 2 and 3.

11 This sentence strongly suggests that the three factions were in fact three factions of landed aristocrats. Certainly their leaders came into this category (see note 1 on [**51**]). Some scholars interpret the factions as economic or class groups (Pediakoi, people of the plain = noble landowners; Paralioi, people of the coast = merchants; Diakrioi, people of the hills = poor farmers). Herodotos's name for the third faction (1.59.3 [**51**]) – Hyperakrioi, people from beyond the hills – is to be preferred; it suggests that this faction was based on the nobles whose estates were in the eastern plains of Attike. Even though there may have been some economic divergencies among the factions (but R. J. Hopper, *BSA* 56 [1961] 189–219 at 201–5 reduces the likelihood of distinct differences), each must have derived its cohesion from clan leadership. Other scholars (e.g., B. R. I. Sealey, *Historia* 9 [1960] 162–9) stress the regional basis of the factions. Whether they were economic groups, local groups or noble factions, the alleged division in terms of constitutional policy is not to be believed. As Rhodes (pp. 185–6) points out, talk about a 'moderate' or 'mixed constitution' belongs with the philosophers of the fourth century and later, and is quite out of place in the early sixth century. Moreover, one can hardly be 'an extreme democrat' before democracy is visible somewhere in the Greek world. Since all three factions wanted predominance in either an oligarchic government or a tyranny, the claims in *Athenaion Politeia* 13.4 and in Plutarch, *Solon* 13.2–3 [**19**] (cf. 29.1 [**53**]) about constitutional squabbles should be rejected.

53 *Plutarch,* Solon *29.1–5*

29 While Solon was abroad, the people in the city resumed their factional conflict. The people of the plain were led by Lykourgos, the people of the coast by Megakles son of Alkmaion, and the people of the hills by Peisistratos.[1] The last group included the crowd of Thetes, who had deeply felt grievances against the rich.[2] The result was that although the city still lived under the laws [of Solon], everyone now expected a revolution and longed for another form of government. They did not look for equality, but hoped to gain the advantage in the change and to prevail over their opponents completely.[3] (2) This was the situation when Solon returned to Athens. He was respected and honoured by all, but he was no longer able or willing, because of his old age, to take an active role as before in public debate and affairs. Nevertheless, he met privately with the leaders of the factions and tried to reconcile them and bring them into harmony.[4] Peisistratos especially seemed attentive to him, (3) for he had a disarming and endearing manner in discussion, was ready to help the poor and in his quarrels was reasonable and moderate. (4) The qualities which he did not possess naturally, he simulated and was believed to possess them more than those who actually did. He was regarded as a circumspect and law-abiding man, a great lover of equality and intolerant of any attempt to disturb the present system and grasp at revolution. By these means he deceived the majority. (5) But Solon quickly detected his real character and was the first to study his plans. He did not dislike him, but tried to soften him and influence him with advice. He even told Peisistratos and others that if someone were to eradicate the ambition for primacy from his soul and cure his yearning for tyranny, he would surpass all in natural excellence and good citizenship.[5]

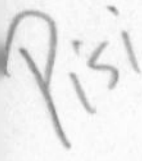

Notes

1 Plutarch calls the three factions (i) Pedieis (here and elsewhere); (ii) Paraloi (here, in *Solon* 13.2 [**19**] and *Moralia* 763d) or Paralioi (*Moralia* 805d–e, as in *Athenaion Politeia* 13.4 [**52**]); (iii) Diakrioi (here, in *Solon* 13.2 and *Moralia* 805d–e) or Epakrioi (*Moralia* 763d).

2 Plutarch thinks that the grievances of the Thetes existed both before (*Solon* 13.4 [**19**]) and after Solon's reforms. By contrast the author of the *Athenaion Politeia* (13.3, 13.5) speaks of the grievances of those who had been reduced to poverty by the cancellation of debts. The latter author may well be mistaken

(see note 7 on [52]). Certainly the Thetes had good reason for resentment, as Plutarch implies. For while Solon had cancelled their debts he had not – in the short or medium term – provided them with a means of supporting themselves.

3 The author of the *Athenaion Politeia* (13.3 [52]) speaks of some who were dissatisfied with the great change which the constitution had undergone, not of people who wanted a revolutionary change of government. Perhaps, however, both sources refer to a desire for a counter-revolution (Plutarch's 'everyone . . . longed for another form of government'), for a return to the old aristocratic rules of politics ('they did not look for equality'). In such a contest the poorer people would again be divided among the noble factions.

4 If one were to accept as authentic the law against neutrality attributed to Solon (see *Athenaion Politeia* 8.5 [42] with note 17), it would seem from this passage that the law also required an equilibrium between opposing factions in order to be effective. Cf. Piccirilli 271.

5 The author of the *Athenaion Politeia* says nothing of Solon's personal attempt to influence Peisistratos, but he does preserve the tradition of Solon's public opposition to the proposal that Peisistratos be granted a bodyguard (14.2–3 [55]; cf. Plutarch, *Solon* 30.1–7 [57]).

Peisistratos's attempts to become tyrant

Peisistratos built up a faction of the traditional kind, but he found that his fortunes rose and fell as the family of the Alkmeonidai, leaders of 'the people of the coast', made or broke alliances. For his final, successful attempt to take over the Athenian state by force, he not only amassed enough riches to pay a mercenary army but also formed a network of alliances (*philiai*) and ties of hospitality (*xeniai*) with noble leaders from other Greek cities. He was practically invincible on this third attempt.

54 *Herodotos 1.59.1, 1.59.3–1.64.1*

59 Kroisos learned that one of these nations,[1] the Athenian, was oppressed and torn apart by Peisistratos son of Hippokrates, who was tyrant of Athens at that time.[2] . . . (3) . . . When the Athenians of the coast, headed by Megakles son of Alkmeon, and those from the plain, headed by Lykourgos son of Aristolaïdes, were engaged in factional conflict, Peisistratos raised a third faction with the aim of gaining a tyranny. He assembled his partisans, championed the cause of the people from beyond the hills and contrived the following plan. (4) He wounded himself and his mules and drove his cart into the Agora, pretending that he had escaped from enemies who wished to murder him as he drove into the country. He asked the people that he might receive from them a guard, having previously distinguished himself in his generalship against Megara, when he captured Nisaia and performed other great deeds.[3] (5) The people of Athens were deceived and gave him a selection of citizens[4] who were not Peisistratos's bodyguard, but his club-bearers. For they carried wooden clubs instead of spears and followed behind him. (6) They joined with Peisistratos in rebellion and occupied the Akropolis.

So Peisistratos was ruler of Athens. He did not upset the existing offices[5] nor change the laws, but governed the city with good administration in accordance with established patterns.

60 Not long afterwards the factions of Megakles and of Lykourgos united and drove him out. Thus Peisistratos was master of Athens for the first time and lost the tyranny before it had taken firm root. But those who expelled Peisistratos came into conflict with one another again. (2) Frustrated in the political struggle, Megakles sent a message to Peisistratos, asking whether he wished to marry his daughter with a view to gaining the tyranny. (3) When Peisistratos received the message and agreed with the terms, they devised for his return by far the silliest trick that I have ever heard of; if, that is, these people did at that time devise the following trick among the Athenians, who are said to be first of the Greeks in wisdom (the Greek race was separated from the barbarian long ago as being more sophisticated and more removed from foolish simple-mindedness). (4) In the deme of Paiania there was a woman named Phye who was three fingers' breadth short of four cubits in height and beautiful in other respects.[6] They dressed this woman in full armour, made her climb into a chariot and showed her the expression which was likely to make her appear most impressive.[7] They drove into the city, sending messengers ahead on foot who, on their arrival in the city, proclaimed the message which they had been instructed to announce:

(5) Athenians, receive favourably Peisistratos, whom Athene herself has honoured most of men by restoring him to her Akropolis.

They went to and fro saying this and immediately the rumour went out to the villages that Athene was restoring Peisistratos. Convinced that the woman was the goddess herself, those in the city prayed to the human and received Peisistratos.

61 Having regained the tyranny by the method described, Peisistratos married Megakles's daughter in accordance with the agreement with Megakles. But since he had children who were already young men and the Alkmeonidai were said to be accursed,[8] he did not want to have children by his newly wed wife and had intercourse with her in an unlawful way. (2) At first the woman kept this secret to herself, but later, whether in answer to a question or not, she told her mother, who told her husband. He was indignant at being slighted by Peisistratos and in his anger he put aside his hostility towards the other faction. When he learned of the combination against him Peisistratos departed from the country altogether.[9] He went to Eretria and there conferred with his sons. (3) Hippias's opinion that they should recover the tyranny prevailed. So they collected contributions from all the cities which had any obligation to them. Though many provided large sums, the Thebans surpassed all in their gift of money. (4) To cut the story short, time passed and all had been prepared by them for their return. For Argive mercenaries arrived from the Peloponnese and a man from Naxos, named Lygdamis, came of his own accord, providing a great deal of support and bringing both money and people.[10] *62* They arrived back in the eleventh year, setting out from Eretria. The first place they gained in Attike was Marathon.[11] While they were encamped in this place their partisans from the city arrived and others flowed in from the villages, preferring tyranny to freedom.[12] (2) So they were mustered. The Athenians in the city paid no attention while Peisistratos collected money and later when he took Marathon. But when they learned that he was marching from Marathon against the city, they went to assist against him. (3) They went with all their forces against the returning exiles, while Peisistratos and his people set out from Marathon and went against the city. They met at the temple of Athene Pallenis[13] and took up positions facing one another. (4) Then by divine guidance Amphilytos of Akarnania, a soothsayer, came and stood by Peisistratos and uttered the following oracle in hexameter metre:

> The cast has been made, the net is spread out,
> The tunny-fish will dart in the moonlit night.

63 After this inspired utterance Peisistratos understood the oracle, said that he accepted the prophecy and led his army to battle.[14] The Athenians from the city had been busy with lunch at that time and after lunch some had turned to dice, others to sleep. Peisistratos and his people attacked the Athenians and put them to flight. (2) As they fled Peisistratos devised a very cunning plan in order that the Athenians might not gather together again but be scattered. He made his sons mount their horses and sent them ahead. When they overtook those who fled they said what Peisistratos had instructed them, bidding them not to be afraid and to go back each to his own home. *64* The Athenians obeyed, and so Peisistratos gained control of Athens for the third time.

Notes

1 Kroisos of Lydia asked two Greek oracles whether he should make war against the Persians and whether he should make an alliance with an army. Having (wrongly) interpreted the oracles' answer to the first question to be affirmative, he took their advice on the second question and enquired which of the Greeks were most powerful, with a view to forming an alliance. His enquiries revealed that the Spartans and the Athenians – the two 'nations' referred to here – were the most prominent of the Greeks (1.53.1–1.56.2).

2 There follows (1.59.1–3) an account of the warning against having a son which was given to Hippokrates at the Olympic festival. Later Peisistratos was born. The Athenians may have been oppressed by Peisistratos's tyranny, but Peisistratos seems to have solved much of the earlier disunity by his absolute control. Perhaps 'torn apart' reflects the propaganda of the Athenians in exile who, under Alkmeonid leadership, overthrew Peisistratos's son Hippias.

3 The war between Athens and Megara is usually placed before the legislation of Solon, on the basis of Plutarch, *Solon* 8–10. If so, Peisistratos may have been too young to have been a general or to have been responsible for the capture of Nisaia, the port of Megara.

4 The above translates the MSS reading καταλέξας ἄνδρας τούτους (so Hude[3] and Rosén). Others, such as J. Berenguer Amenós (Barcelona 1960) and J. E. Powell in his translation (Oxford 1949), adopt the emendations καταλέξασθαι (Legrand) and τριηκοσίους (Naber) and so read 'allowed him to select 300 citizens'.

5 The Council of the Areopagos and the arkhons (also the Council of Four Hundred, if that existed).

6 Height was an important element of beauty for the Greeks. This woman was nearly six feet tall and her name refers to her fine stature. Paiania was a village due east of Athens, but separated from it by Mount Hymettos and hence approached via Pallene (cf. Herodotos 1.62.3 with n. 13 below). Paiania was therefore not far from the main route to the city from the eastern plains where Peisistratos had his estates and many supporters.

7 Although Herodotos seems to be sarcastic here and has expressed his surprise at the whole story in 1.60.3, he accepts the story. Other testimony: *Athenaion*

Politeia 14.4 [**55**] and Kleidemos (*FGrH* 323 F 15), the latter making Phye the wife of Hipparkhos (very unlikely: see Davies, *APF* 452). For possible cultural overtones of this ceremonial procession see W. R. Connor, *JHS* 107 (1987) 40–50, especially 42–7.

8 For an explanation of the labelling of the Alkmeonidai as 'accursed', see Herodotos 5.71 [**8**] with notes. On Peisistratos's measures to avoid the friction that might arise from his having a son by Megakles's daughter when he was tyrant – a son that might have a stronger claim to the 'throne' than his sons by his Argive consort who were born before the tyranny – see J.-P. Vernant, *PP* 28 (1973) 61 and M. B. Hatzopoulos, in *Ancient Macedonia* 4 [Institute of Balkan Studies, 204] (Thessaloniki 1986) 290 and n. 66.

9 This implies that when Peisistratos was removed from the tyranny the first time he simply withdrew from the city and stayed in Attike, presumably on his estates in the eastern plains. Stein (on Herodotos 1.61), presumably believing that the daughter of an Alkmeonid leader such as Megakles would not have put up with being insulted for long, says that the second tyranny could scarcely have continued for a year.

10 To the list of supporters given by Herodotos one can add Thessaly (Herodotos 5.63.3 [**77**]) and the government of Eretria (*Athenaion Politeia* 15.2 below). Peisistratos and Lygdamis had obviously formed an alliance in order to put one in power in Athens and the other in Naxos: see Herodotos 1.64.2 [**60**] and *Athenaion Politeia* 15.3 below. Notice the ties of obligation which are used by Peisistratos. Much giving in Greece was carried out with a return in mind: see A. R. Hands, *Charities and Social Aid in Greece and Rome* (London 1968), chapter 3 and G. Herman, *Ritualised Friendship and the Greek City* (Cambridge 1987), chapter 4 (pp. 90–1 on this particular episode). Peisistratos also made good use of the silver derived from mines on the Strymon (see Herodotos 1.64.1 [**60**] and *Athenaion Politeia* 15.2 [**55**]).

11 No doubt Peisistratos landed at Marathon because his faction was based on the eastern plains. His estates had been on the east coast and it was a noble who probably came from a neighbouring area who moved the motion for the bodyguard which led to Peisistratos's first tyranny (*Athenaion Politeia* 14.1 [**55**] with note 2; Plutarch *Solon* 30.3 [**57**]).

12 Some consider this comment unjust, believing that the Athenians regarded Peisistratos as their deliverer from *stasis*: 'hence the unmolested landing at Marathon, the difficulty the oligarchs had in getting a force together and the ease with which it was dispersed by Peisistratos' (A. H. Sayce on Herodotos 1.62). But Peisistratos's force was virtually irresistible: see Herodotos 1.61.3–4 with note 10 (above) and *Athenaion Politeia* 15.2 [**55**] and 17.3 [**61**] with note 16.

13 Pallene (a deme under Kleisthenes's reorganisation of the tribes [see Chapter V, pp. 145–65, and the map on p. 150]) and the temple of Athene Pallenis lay on the main route to the city from the eastern plains around Marathon and Brauron.

14 Peisistratos interpreted the tunny-fish as his enemies darting helplessly into his net and the moonlit night as the middle of the day. For the association of Peisistratos's family with oracles see also Herodotos 1.64.2 [**60**], 5.90.2 [**95**] and 7.6.3.

55 Athenaion Politeia *14–15*[1]

14 Peisistratos had the reputation of being an extreme democrat and had particularly distinguished himself in the war against Megara. He covered himself with wounds and, on the ground that he had suffered these injuries at the hands of his political opponents, persuaded the people to grant him a bodyguard through a motion proposed by Aristion.[2] With the help of the so-called 'club-bearers' he received, he rebelled against the people and occupied the Akropolis, in the arkhonship of Komeas,[3] the thirty-second year after the enactment of Solon's laws. (2) It is said that,[4] when Peisistratos asked for the bodyguard, Solon opposed the proposal, declaring that he was wiser than some and braver than others; for he was wiser than those who did not realise that Peisistratos was making an attempt at tyranny and braver than those who were aware of it but kept silent. When he failed to convince them, he set up his armour in front of his door and said that he had helped his country as far as he was able (for he was already a very old man) and that he thought the rest should do likewise. (3) On that occasion, then, Solon achieved nothing by his exhortations. Peisistratos took over the government and administered public affairs, constitutionally rather than in the manner of a tyrant.[5] But before his rule had properly taken root, the factions of Megakles and Lykourgos formed a coalition and expelled him in the sixth year after his first seizure of power, in the arkhonship of Hegesias.

(4) But in the twelfth year after this Megakles, being frustrated in the political struggle, sent a proposal to Peisistratos that the latter should marry his daughter, and restored him by a primitive and exceedingly simple trick. He first disseminated the rumour that the goddess Athene was restoring Peisistratos. Then he found a tall and beautiful woman named Phye (according to Herodotos she was from the deme of Paiania;[6] but according to others she was a Thracian garland-seller from the deme of Kollytos), dressed her in imitation of the goddess and brought her into the city with Peisistratos. So Peisistratos drove into the city on a chariot, with the woman standing beside him, and the people there fell down in worship and received him with awe.

15 Such was the manner of his first return. Again he did not hold power for long, for about the seventh year after his return he was expelled a second time. He feared a coalition of the other two factions owing to his refusal to have intercourse with the daughter of Megakles, and withdrew from the country.[7] (2) First he joined in the establishment of a colony in a place called Rhaikelos, near the Thermaic Gulf, and from there he moved on to the district around Mount Pangaion. Here he made money with which he hired mercenaries;[8] not till the eleventh year did he go again to Eretria[9] and attempt, for the first time, to regain control by force. In this enterprise he was supported by many allies, especially the Thebans and Lygdamis of Naxos, and also the Hippeis[10] of Eretria, who controlled the government in their city.

(3) After his victory in the battle at Pallenis,[11] he captured the city and disarmed the people – thus, at last, establishing himself securely as tyrant. He also took Naxos and set up Lygdamis as ruler there.[12] (4) The manner in which he confiscated the people's weapons was as follows. He arranged a military review in full armour in the Theseion[13] and attempted to address the assembled throng. He had not been speaking long when the audience claimed they could not hear him; so he told them to come up to the gateway of the Akropolis, in order that he would be more audible. While he protracted his harangue there, people appointed for the purpose collected the arms and locked them up in the buildings near the Theseion. Then they came and signalled to Peisistratos. (5) When he had finished the rest of his speech he informed them what had happened to their arms; he told them not to be astonished or distressed, but to go home and attend to their private affairs, for in future he would take care of all public affairs.

Notes

1 In this passage the author of the *Athenaion Politeia*, as well as naming Herodotos once as an authority (14.4 – in fact, the only occasion on which he cites another author, apart from Solon), follows that source closely. Note, for example, the echoes of Herodotos in 'particularly distinguished himself in the war against Megara' (14.1; cf. Hdt. 1.59.4 [**54**]: 'previously distinguished himself in his generalship against Megara'), 'he covered himself with wounds and, on the ground that he had suffered these injuries at the hands of his political opponents . . .' (14.1; cf. Hdt. 1.59.4: 'he wounded himself and his mules and drove his cart into the Agora, pretending that he had escaped from enemies'), 'he rebelled against the people and occupied the Akropolis' (14.1; cf. Hdt. 1.59.6: 'they joined with Peisistratos in rebellion and occupied the Akropolis'), and 'the factions of Megakles and Lykourgos formed a coalition and expelled him' (14.3; cf. Hdt. 1.60.1: 'the factions of Megakles and of

Lykourgos united and drove him out'). The additional material in the *Athenaion Politeia* is largely composed of chronological notes, presumably from an *Atthis* (so Rhodes 189, 191).

2 Despite the frequency of the name Aristion (Rhodes 200), this man who was ready to jump up and propose a bodyguard for Peisistratos on the floor of the Assembly may well be identified with an Aristion whose gravestone (*IG* I^2 1024 = I^3 1256) of c. 510 BC was found not far north of Peisistratos's own estates at Brauron: see U. von Wilamowitz-Möllendorff, *Aristoteles und Athen* (Berlin 1893) 1.261; Burn, *Lyric Age* 305; Piccirilli 274; and note 3 on [**56**]. Of course, the term 'write' (the motion) may be anachronistic: C. Mossé, *La tyrannie dans la Grèce antique* (Paris 1969) 63.

3 The most widely accepted date for the arkhonship of Komeas is 561/0 BC. However, the dates of Peisistratos's three attempts at gaining a tyranny are the subject of much dispute. J. G. F. Hind (*CQ* n.s. 24 [1974] 1–18) makes the attractive suggestion that for the first three numerals in *Athenaion Politeia* 14.3–15.2 the correct unit was 'month', not 'year'. Rhodes (191–9, summarising his exposition in *Phoenix* 30 [1976] 219–33) argues that the *Athenaion Politeia* had access to a complete chronology of the tyranny and so we should produce internal consistency with as little violation of the text as possible. However, he has to alter two figures to obtain consistency: 'twelfth' year to 'fifth' in 14.4 and 'forty-nine' years to 'thirty-six' in 19.6 [**79**]. Rhodes further argues that the author's dates are wrong where they conflict with the indications in Herodotos's narrative. For our purposes it is sufficient to note that the dates suggested by Hind and Rhodes, though each is critical of the other's method, are not significantly different. In the following table Hind suggests specific dates in brackets in order to give a clearer idea of the progress of events, and Rhodes brackets particularly doubtful dates.

	Hind	*Rhodes*
First coup (decree of Aristion). Arkhon Komeas	560/59 (Apr. 559?)	561/0?
First expulsion Arkhon Hegesias	559/8 (Sept. 559?) Read 'sixth month' in 14.3	(561/0 or 560/59??)
Second coup (Phye episode)	558/7 (Aug. 558?) Read 'twelfth month' in 14.4	(557/6 or 556/5??)
Second expulsion	558/7 (Mar. 557?) Read 'about the seventh month' in 15.1	556/5?
Third coup (battle of Pallene)	547/6 (Feb./Mar. 546?) Nearly eleven years later	546/5
Death of Peisistratos Arkhon Philoneos	528/7 (First half of 527?)	528/7
Murder of Hipparkhos	514/13 (Aug. 514)	514/13

Expulsion of Hippias Arkhon Harpaktides	511/10 (June/ July 510?)	511/10
Battle of Marathon Arkhon Phainippos	490/89 (Sept. 490)	490/89

For other recent discussions of the chronology of the tyranny see G. V. Sumner, *CQ* n.s. 11 (1961) 31–54 at 37–49, J. S. Ruebel, *GRBS* 14 (1973) 125–36 and C. Reid Rubincam, *Phoenix* 33 (1979) 293–307.

4 This introduction may indicate that the author does not vouch for the story. Rhodes (pp. 201–2) examines the two versions of the story (Plutarch **[57]**, **[62]** preserves the most detail) and concludes that while Solon may have lived to witness Peisistratos's first coup, nearly all other detail is probably invention.

5 This favourable view of Peisistratos's tyranny, seen more fully in chapter 16 **[61]**, is of course at odds with the saying of Solon reported above (14.2), which presumes that tyranny was a bad thing.

6 Herodotos 1.60.4 **[54]**. The alternative version may be an attempt to slur Phye both by making her an alien and by asserting that she lived in an undesirable quarter of the city (to judge from the comment about prostitution in Kollytos in Plutarch, *Demosthenes* 11.5).

7 The daughter of Megakles is unlikely to have tolerated humiliation for long (cf. note 9 on **[54]**). The assumption that the period of the second tyranny should be about six months and not six years (note 3 above) suits the implication of Herodotos's narrative (1.61.1–2 **[54]**) which our author has made explicit in 'he did not hold power for long'.

8 Peisistratos moved from the western side of the Chalkidic peninsula to the Thracian gold- and silver-mining area east of the peninsula. For Peisistratos's activities in both areas, and for the suggestion that Rhaikelos was founded not only from Eretria (cf. Herodotos 1.61.2 **[54]**) but in collaboration with the Eretrians, see J. W. Cole, *G & R*[2] 22 (1975) 42–4 and D. Viviers, *JHS* 107 (1987) 193–5. The mercenaries may well have been hired from Thrace, since Thracian warriors appear on Athenian vases from c. 540 BC: J. G. P. Best, *Thracian Peltasts and their Influence on Greek Warfare* (Groningen 1969) 5–7.

9 Here the author gives away the fact that he is following Herodotos carelessly, because unlike Herodotos (1.61.2 **[54]**) he has not mentioned Peisistratos's first visit to Eretria. Rhodes (p. 208), however, takes the word 'again' not with 'go to Eretria' but with the time phrase: 'ten years later again'.

10 The cavalry class: see note 6 on **[42]** for the formalisation of the Hippeis class at Athens.

11 A rather awkward abbreviation for Herodotos's 'at the temple of Athene Pallenis' (1.62.3 **[54]** with note 13).

12 This alliance between two nobles was obviously formed in order to set both up as tyrants in their respective cities by means of their combined forces. Peisistratos later had the sons of Athenian nobles kept as hostages by Lygdamis on the island of Naxos (Herodotos 1.64.1–2 **[60]**).

13 The Theseion probably did not exist until the time of Kimon, after the Persian Wars (Pausanias 1.17.6). Another source, Polyainos (1.21.2), locates this parade in the Anakeion, an open-air enclosure on the east or north-east side of the Akropolis (for the location of the Anakeion, see G. S. Dontas, *Hesperia* 52 [1983] 48–63 at 60–2).

56 *Plutarch,* Solon *10.3*[1]

(3) . . . One of them settled at Brauron in Attike, the other in Melite;[2] the Athenians have a deme Philaidai, from which Peisistratos came,[3] named after Philaios.

Notes

1 For the context of this excerpt see passage [**100**].

2 Plutarch is speaking of Philaios and Eurysakes, the sons of Aias (Ajax), hero of the island of Salamis. Philaios, the story goes, settled at Brauron, on the east coast of Attike, and Eurysakes in the town itself.

3 Together with [Plato], *Hipparkhos* 228b 4–5, this passage indicates that Peisistratos's family estates were in the vicinity of Brauron, on one of the eastern plains of Attike. He also seems to have had a power base in the plain of Marathon, to the north, since he landed there on his third and successful attempt to become tyrant in Athens (Herodotos 1.62.1 [**54**] with note 11).

57 *Plutarch,* Solon *30.1–7*

30 When Peisistratos had covered himself with wounds and come into the Agora in a chariot, he incited the people with the claim that his enemies had laid an ambush for him because of his political stance, and had many angry supporters clamouring for his cause. Solon approached and, standing beside him, said, 'Son of Hippokrates, it is not for good that you play the part of Homer's Odysseus. For it is to mislead the citizens that you do the same as that man did when he wounded himself, whereas he did it to deceive the enemy.' (2) As a result of this the crowd[1] was ready to take up arms on Peisistratos's behalf, and the people gathered in Assembly. (3) Ariston[2] moved a motion that Peisistratos be granted a bodyguard of fifty club-bearers. Solon stood up and opposed the motion. He covered in detail many points similar to the following sentiments written in his poems:

> For you attend to the tongue and words of a wily man.
> Every one of you walks with the steps of a fox,
> But together there is in you an empty mind.[3]

(4) When he saw that the poor were stirred up to grant the favour to Peisistratos and were shouting in support, while the rich shrank from the danger and were running away, he went away saying that he was wiser than one group and braver than the other. He was wiser than those who did not observe what was being done and braver than those who did observe it but were

afraid to oppose the tyranny. (5) The people passed the resolution, but did not continue to examine closely the number of club-bearers attached to Peisistratos. They overlooked his maintenance of as many as he wanted and his public array of them, until he occupied the Akropolis. (6) When this happened and the city was in turmoil, Megakles immediately fled with the rest of the Alkmaionidai,[4] and Solon, who was now very old and had no supporters, nevertheless came forward in the Agora and reasoned with the citizens. While reproaching them for their lack of judgment and cowardice, he still urged them on and called on them not to betray their freedom. That was the occasion of his memorable statement that recently, while the tyranny was being germinated, it had been easier for them to prevent it, but it is a greater and more illustrious task to cut down and eradicate the tyranny now that it has been already established and taken root. (7) No one paid attention to him because of fear, so he went to his own house, took his arms and placed them in the street in front of his door, saying 'I have done as much as I could to come to the aid of my country and its laws.'

Notes

1 In the first sentence of the chapter Plutarch uses *ho demos* to refer to the common people incited by Peisistratos. Here and in 30.5, however, Plutarch needs *ho demos* to refer to the citizens in their sovereign Assembly, so he uses *to plethos* here to refer to the common people. See note 2 on *Athenaion Politeia* 5.1 [**18**].

2 For the suggestion that Peisistratos was using a supporter from the eastern plain near Brauron, Aristion (the spelling of *Athenaion Politeia* 14.1 is preferable), see note 2 on [**55**].

3 Plutarch has two hexameter verses followed by a pentameter instead of the expected alternation of hexameter and pentameter verses in an elegiac poem. Hence many editors (including West: his Fragment 11.7, 5–6) change the order of the verses and place the first one in Plutarch's text after the other two. The word *khaunos*, 'empty, in vain', is also used by Solon in Fragment 34.4 [**24**].

4 Plutarch is almost alone in using this spelling for the Alkmeonidai.

58 *Plutarch,* Solon *32.3*

(3) Solon survived a long time after Peisistratos became tyrant, as Herakleides of Pontos records, but less than two years, according to Phanias of Eresos. Peisistratos became tyrant in the arkhonship of Komias, but according to Phanias[1] Solon died in the arkhonship of Hegestratos, who was arkhon after Komias.

Note

1 Herakleides of Pontos, Fragment 148 Wehrli[2]; Phainias of Eresos, Fragment 21 Wehrli[2]. Davies, *APF* 323–4 believes that Phainias is transmitting the date of his teacher Aristotle and prefers this version to the vagueness of another student of Aristotle, Herakleides. The spelling Komeas for the name of the arkhon in *Athenaion Politeia* 14.1 [**55**] is more likely to be correct.

IV

THE PEISISTRATID TYRANNY

The tyranny of Peisistratos

In general the tyrants who controlled various cities in Greece in the seventh and sixth centuries BC were remembered as hated despots. Peisistratos, however, received a remarkably favourable press in antiquity. He is even described as 'an extreme democrat' (passage [**55**]) and as ruling 'constitutionally rather than in the manner of a tyrant' (passages [**55**] and [**61**]). Part of the explanation for this good press may lie in the aristocratic sympathies of our fifth- and fourth-century sources. Peisistratos was seen as a noble whose autocratic rule could be admired. Certainly the public works programme he undertook [**59**] provided a glamorous centre for the court with which were associated the nobles who collaborated with Peisistratos. At the same time, of course, the construction of buildings and roads provided employment for poorer citizens. No doubt the latter were also thankful to the tyrant for removing the administration of justice from the hands of the great families in each area and placing it under the control of the state (passage [**61**] and note 5). Other measures of Peisistratos, such as the promotion of festivals which recalled Attike-wide traditions and played down local cults (controlled by the nobles in each area) also served to counteract disunity in Attike.

59 *Archaeological Evidence*

Architectural remains attest a number of building projects undertaken in Athens in the period of Peisistratos's tyranny and presumably initiated by him. A large building of irregular shape, known simply as Building F, constructed at the southern end of the western side of the Agora belongs to the period c. 550–525 BC and must be a candidate for the palace of Peisistratos, if he (like tyrants from other cities) had one: see J. S. Boersma, *Athenian Building Policy from 561/0 to 405/4 B.C.* [Scripta archaeologica Groningana, 4] (Groningen 1970) 16–17, T. L. Shear Jr, in W. A. P. Childs (ed.), *Athens Comes of Age: From Solon to Salamis* (Princeton 1978) 6–7 and J. McK. Camp II, *The Athenian Agora: Excavations in the Heart of Classical Athens* (London 1986) 44–5 with figs 21, 22 and 27. A large open-air enclosure, almost square (27m by 31m), in the south-western corner of the Agora may have been a law court (ibid. 46–7). Literary evidence records Peisistratid concern to improve the water supply, particularly by the provision of a nine-spouted fountain, the Enneakrounos (location unknown), and a fountainhouse in the south-eastern corner of the Agora may go back to Peisistratos (ibid. 42–4 with figs 25–6). Two sanctuaries in the north-western part of the Agora may also belong to the time of Peisistratos, but their date is not precisely known (cf. J. S. Boersma, op. cit. 17, 172, 198, referring to H. A. Thompson, *Hesperia* 6 [1937] 8–10 and 77–84 with fig. 72 on 133). The area around the road ('the Street of the Panathenaia') which passed diagonally through the Agora towards the Akropolis was left free for athletic and equestrian contests which accompanied (for example) the Panathenaia (on which see note 3 on [**7**]), a festival which Peisistratos is reported to have reorganised (Scholion on Aelius Aristeides, *Oration* 13.189.4 [= 1.362 Behr], p. 323 Dindorf). A part of the square was called the *orkhestra*, so dancing, singing and drama also took place in the Agora (J. McK. Camp, op. cit. 45–6). Outside the city wall, which was probably constructed shortly before the tyranny of Peisistratos when the Akropolis ceased being a fort and became a religious centre (E. Vanderpool, in D. W. Bradeen and M. F. McGregor (eds), *Φόρος: Tribute to B.D. Meritt* [Locust Valley, NY 1974] 156–60), attention was paid by Peisistratos – according to Theopompos (*FGrH* 115 F 136) – to the Lykeion, an exercise ground for land forces situated between the Akropolis and the river Ilissos to the east (R. E. Wycherley, *GRBS* 4 [1963] 157–75 at 171–2; J. Travlos, *Pictorial Dictionary of Ancient Athens* [London 1971] 345, 347; M. H. Jameson, Ἀρχαιογνωσία 1 [1980] 213–36, especially 224–7, 233). Further afield, a temple was constructed on the eastern side of Mount Hymettos, a colonnade was added to the temple of Athene at Cape Sounion and, in connection with his purification of Delos (Herodotos 1.64.2 [**60**] and note 4), the temple of Apollon on the island was restored with Athenian building techniques and stone (J. S. Boersma, op. cit. 17–18). On the building programme of the Peisistratid tyranny as a whole see ibid. 11–27 with plans I–II and maps I–II, T. L. Shear, op. cit. 1–19 and J. McK. Camp, op. cit. 39–48.

Attempts to use two other kinds of archaeological evidence, sculpture and vase paintings, to infer Peisistratid propaganda or policy are largely unsuccessful. J. Boardman, in a series of articles (for example, *RA* [1972] 57–72, especially 60–5, *JHS* 95 [1975] 1–12, *RA* [1978] 227–34), has argued that Peisistratos not only made use of the popularity of the mythical hero Herakles, but was actually symbolised in contemporary Athenian art by the figure of Herakles. B. S. Ridgway, in C. G. Boulter (ed.), *Greek Art: Archaic into Classical: A Symposium held at the University of Cincinnati April 2–3, 1982* [Cincinnati Classical Studies, n.s. 5] (Leiden 1985) 4 makes the point that on certain monuments the one myth has been taken to be tyrannical propaganda (Peisistratos = Herakles, indispensable to the divine victory) or to be a statement of the new democracy (gods = Kleisthenes and the Alkmeonidai). J. Bažant, *Eirene* 18 (1982) 21–33, especially 22–3, 25, points out that Athenians continued to buy paintings in which (it is alleged) the propagandist programme of the dethroned dynasty is expressed; Herakles vases were popular at the very time that a statue group honouring the tyrannicides Harmodios and Aristogeiton (see pp. 128–9 below) was being erected.

60 *Herodotos 1.64*[1]

64 . . . Peisistratos gained control of Athens for the third time. He fortified his tyranny with many mercenaries and revenues, derived partly from Attike and partly from the river Strymon.[2] He took as hostages children of those Athenians who stayed and did not immediately flee, putting them on Naxos (2) (Peisistratos had captured the island by war and placed Lygdamis in charge).[3] In addition he purified the island of Delos in accordance with the oracles. The method he used was to dig up the dead from all the land which one can see from the temple and transfer them to another place on Delos.[4] (3) So Peisistratos became tyrant of Athens. Some of the Athenians fell in the battle, others fled from their homeland with the Alkmeonidai.[5]

Notes

1 For Herodotos 1.59.3–1.64.1 see [**54**].

2 For Peisistratos's connection with the Strymon area see also *Athenaion Politeia* 15.2 [**55**].

3 Other references to the tyranny of Lygdamis are given by Jeffery 201 n. 3.

4 The purification of Delos raised the prestige of Athens, showing her pre-eminence in the Ionian world.

5 The departure of noble families apparently allowed Peisistratos to make allotments from their estates for the poor (cf. *Athenaion Politeia* 16.2–3 [**61**] below). The manuscripts have 'with Alkmeonides', that is, with a particular person whose name indicates that he belongs to the Alkmeonidai. But modern scholars are probably right in accepting that Herodotos refers here to the family as a whole.

61 Athenaion Politeia *16–17*

16 Such was the origin and such the vicissitudes of Peisistratos's tyranny.[1] (2) As has been said before,[2] Peisistratos administered the city's affairs in a moderate fashion and constitutionally rather than in the manner of a tyrant. For he was in every respect benevolent and tolerant, and ready to forgive those who committed an offence; he even advanced money to the poor for their husbandry so that they could make a living as farmers.[3] (3) In doing this he had two objectives: first, that they might not stay in the city, but be scattered throughout the country; and second, that they might be reasonably well off and busy with their own affairs, and thus have neither the time nor the inclination to concern themselves with public affairs. (4) At the same time his revenues were increased by the thorough cultivation of the land. For he levied a tax of 10 per cent on agricultural produce.[4] (5) For the same reasons he set up local judges,[5] and he himself frequently made a tour of the country in order to review and settle disputes so that people might not come into the city and neglect their farm work. (6) It was on one of these tours by Peisistratos, so the story goes, that the incident took place of the farmer on Mount Hymettos who was farming the land which was later called 'Tax-Free Farm'. Peisistratos saw a man digging and cultivating what was nothing but stones; being curious, he sent his attendant to ask the farmer what he got out of this piece of ground. 'A lot of aches and pains', he said, 'and of these aches and pains Peisistratos ought to take his 10 per cent.' The man answered without knowing who the questioner was; but Peisistratos was pleased with his frankness and industry, and granted him exemption from all taxes.

(7) In general Peisistratos caused the common people a minimum of trouble throughout his reign, and continually fostered peace in internal and external affairs.[6] For this reason the tyranny of Peisistratos was often referred to as a golden age.[7] For later the rule of his sons, who succeeded him, turned out to be much harsher. (8) But most important of all the qualities mentioned was his democratic and benevolent disposition. In everything he sought to conduct his administration in accordance with the laws[8] and he allowed himself no special privilege. Once, for example, when he was summoned before the Areopagos on a charge of homicide, he went in person to defend himself; but the

prosecutor lost his courage and abandoned the case.[9]

(9) For these reasons he remained in power for a long time and easily retrieved his position each time he was expelled. For he was supported by a majority of both the nobles and the democrats.[10] The former he won over by mixing with them socially, the latter by helping them financially in their private affairs. His personality appealed to both factions. (10) Furthermore, in Athens at that time the laws regarding tyrants were mild, particularly the one referring specifically to the establishment[11] of a tyranny. The law read as follows: 'These are the statutes and ancestral rules of the Athenians: if any persons shall attempt to set themselves up as tyrants, or if any person shall join in establishing a tyranny, he and his whole family shall be outlawed.'[12]

17 Thus Peisistratos grew old in the possession of power and he died of natural causes in the arkhonship of Philoneos.[13] He lived for thirty-three years after the time when he first established himself as tyrant; nineteen years he spent in the possession of power, and the remainder in exile.[14] (2) On this basis it is clear that we may disregard as nonsense the story which asserts that Peisistratos as a young man was a favourite of Solon and that he was a general in the war against Megara for control of Salamis. It is chronologically impossible as anyone can see who calculates the length of their respective lives and the dates of their deaths.[15]

(3) After the death of Peisistratos his sons held on to the government and conducted the administration along the same lines. There were two sons by his legitimate wife, Hippias and Hipparkhos, and two by his Argive consort, Iophon and Hegesistratos, whose alternative name was Thettalos.[16] (4) For Peisistratos married a woman of Argos, Timonassa, the daughter of an Argive named Gorgilos; she had previously been the wife of Arkhinos of Ambrakia, a descendant of Kypselos.[17] This is the origin of Peisistratos's alliance with the Argives, 1,000 of whom were brought by Hegesistratos and fought on his side in the battle at Pallenis.[18] According to some authorities, the marriage with the Argive woman took place during the first exile; according to others, while he was in possession of power.[19]

Notes

1 *Athenaion Politeia* 14–15 [**55**].

2 *Athenaion Politeia* 14.3 [**55**], with reference to Peisistratos's first period of

tyranny. Rhodes (pp. 203, 213) points out that our author employs expressions used by the orator Isokrates in both passages.

3 Rhodes (p. 214) draws attention to the statement by Dion of Prousa (25.3) that Peisistratos ordered Attike to be planted with olives. Solon's measures encouraged families with capital to invest in olive trees and secondary industry. But subsistence farmers needed to feed their families before there was a rise in employment opportunities. Cf. A. J. Holladay, *G & R*^{2} 24 (1977) 40–56. For thinking similar to that in the next sentence see Aristotle, *Politics* 1292b 25–9 and 1318b 9–17 (the lack of leisure of farmers ensures a minimal number of meetings of the Assembly, if they control the state, and contentment with their farm work), 1311a 13–15 (expelling the mob from the city is a common practice of tyrants [and oligarchs]) and 1319a 26–32 (members of the lower classes loitering in the city can easily attend the Assembly, in contrast with farmers scattered throughout the country).

4 Since Peisistratos taxed primary produce, he provided further inducement for men with capital to invest in secondary industry. Peisistratos's taxes are mentioned also by Herodotos (1.64.1 [**60**]). Thucydides (6.54.5 [**69**]) attributes a 5 per cent tax on primary produce to Peisistratos's sons Hippias and Hipparkhos. Perhaps the economic boom which Athens experienced enabled a reduction in taxation.

5 Or 'provided judges in the various demes', that is, in the villages or local districts of Attike. The purpose was undoubtedly to remove the administration of justice from the local noble family and place it in the hands of the state. Apparently the practice fell into disuse later, for it was revived in 453/2 BC and modified after 404/3 (*Athenaion Politeia* 26.3 and 53.1–3 with Rhodes 215, 257, 331, 588).

6 Thucydides 6.54.5 [**69**] says that his sons, the 'Peisistratidai', brought their wars to a successful conclusion.

7 Literally, 'life in the time of Kronos' – as we might refer to 'life in the Garden of Eden'.

8 He 'did not upset the existing offices nor change the laws' (Herodotos 1.59.6 [**54**]), but he ensured that those who filled the offices would not act contrary to his interests. Compare the comment by Thucydides on Peisistratos's sons (6.54.6 [**69**] with note 3). On Peisistratos's need to govern through officials chosen by his family see R. J. Bonner and G. Smith, *The Administration of Justice from Homer to Aristotle* 1 (Chicago 1930) 183.

9 So Plutarch, *Solon* 31.3 [**62**].

10 The term translated 'the democrats', *hoi demotikoi*, is used also in *Athenaion Politeia* 6.2–3 [**33**] and 18.5 [**75**] and it is contrasted, as here, with *hoi gnorimoi* in *Athenaion Politeia* 34.3.

11 The noun 'establishment' is not in the text and is supplied with some hesitation from the verb 'to join in establishing' in the law quoted.

12 In 'primitive' Athenian law, to say that a clan 'shall be *atimos*' means that it is outlawed, that is, its members may be killed with impunity. But the author of the *Athenaion Politeia* takes the term in its later sense, of loss of citizenship only, and hence calls the law mild. On this law against tyranny see M. Ostwald, *TAPA* 86 (1955) 106–9 and Rhodes 220–3. For argument that the second 'if' clause is original (because the main clause is also expressed in the

singular) and that the prescript and first 'if' clause were added later, possibly towards the end of the fifth century BC, see J. K. Davies, *CR* n.s. 23 (1973) 225–6.

13 528/7 BC. This is a standard method of dating. Compare 17.2 below, where the author bids the reader calculate the respective ages of Solon and Peisistratos and (literally) 'at the time of which arkhon each died'.

14 These figures do not agree completely with those given in *Athenaion Politeia* 14–15 [**55**]. Rhodes prefers to retain the figures here (p. 194; cf. pp. 191–9 for a full discussion of the chronology).

15 Although the author uses unusually strong language to reject the sexual relationship between Solon and Peisistratos, the story is chronologically possible on the basis of the likely birth dates of the two. See Rhodes 223–4 and note 3 on [**31**]. In 14.1 [**55**] our author accepts the participation of Peisistratos in the war against Megara as chronologically possible. Perhaps his expression is merely careless here and what he wants to deny is a generalship against Megara. But in 22.3 [**91**] he has Peisistratos as general on some occasion before he became tyrant.

16 The author is wrong in identifying Thessalos with Hegesistratos. Davies, *APF* 445–50 sets out the case for five sons of Peisistratos: Hippias, Hipparkhos and Thessalos by his Athenian wife and Iophon and Hegesistratos by his Argive wife. The name Thessalos suggests that Peisistratos had links with Thessaly as well; this is confirmed by Herodotos 5.63.3 [**77**]. The alliance (*philia*, the word for 'friendship') with Argos was strengthened by the marriage which produced Hegesistratos. Support from these two areas should be added to that listed for Peisistratos in *Athenaion Politeia* 15.2 [**55**]: Eretria, Thebes, Lygdamis of Naxos and mercenaries hired with money from Thrace. Peisistratos's forces at the battle of Pallene were overwhelming. See also Herodotos 1.61.3–4 [**54**] with note 10.

17 Tyrant of Korinth for thirty years in the second half of the seventh century BC. Kypselos or his successors founded a colony at Ambrakia (Strabon 7.7.6 [325C], 10.2.8 [452C]).

18 For this battle see Herodotos 1.62–3 [**54**] and *Athenaion Politeia* 15.3 [**55**] with note 11.

19 This would have to be Peisistratos's first period of power, since Hegesistratos was old enough to be installed as tyrant of Sigeion by his father (Herodotos 5.94.1 [**95**]): see Davies, *APF* 449–50; Rhodes 199, 227.

62 *Plutarch,* Solon *31.2–5*

(2) Nevertheless, when Peisistratos was in control of affairs he so won over Solon – by honouring him, treating him with affection and sending for him – that Solon actually became his adviser and commended many of his actions. (3) For Peisistratos retained most of Solon's laws,[1] being the first to observe them himself and compelling his supporters to do likewise. Indeed, he was summoned when already tyrant to the Areopagos on a charge of

homicide. He went in person to defend himself with decorum. But his accuser failed to appear.[2]

He himself enacted other laws, including the one which provides that men disabled in war be maintained at public expense. (4) Herakleides[3] says this and that Peisistratos was following the example of Solon, who had earlier had a decree passed in the case of a disabled man named Thersippos. (5) Theophrastos has recorded that even the law on idleness was not enacted by Solon, but by Peisistratos,[4] who thus made the country more productive and the city more peaceful.

Notes

1 If the Stoa of the Basileus (see note 5 on [**13**] and note 4 on [**42**]), who had an important role in the state cults and in the administration of justice, goes back to the time of Peisistratos as its excavator believes (T. L. Shear Jr, *Hesperia* 40 [1971] 249–50; cf. H. A. Thompson and R. E. Wycherley, *The Athenian Agora* 14 [Princeton 1972] 84, T. L. Shear, in W. A. P. Childs [ed.], *Athens Comes of Age: From Solon to Salamis* [Princeton 1978] 7–8, 14 n. 28), this claim would be strengthened.

2 Plutarch in this section follows closely the account in *Athenaion Politeia* 16.8 [**61**].

3 This author is Herakleides of Pontos and the Fragment is no. 149 in Wehrli's second edition (Fragment 148 is cited in *Solon* 32.3 [**58**]). The following citation of Theophrastos is Fragment 99 Wimmer.

4 Plutarch himself (*Solon* 17.2 [**16**]) preserves the tradition that it was Drakon before either Solon or Peisistratos who included a law against idleness.

The tyranny of the Peisistratidai

It was natural for the ambitious Greek aristocrats who seized power in their own cities in the seventh and sixth centuries to seek to hand on their autocratic rule to their sons. However, the second generation of Greek tyrants had a poor track record and was frequently overthrown. In the case of Athens, the transmission of power to the sons of Peisistratos (the 'Peisistratidai') did not mean an immediate change in style. Indeed, some of the public works undertaken may as easily be attributed to the sons as to the father [**63**]. But the tyranny became harsher, according to our sources, particularly after the assassination of one of the tyrants, Hipparkhos (see pp. 119–29 below). It is difficult to decide, however, how far this picture of increased savagery is created by sources wishing to reconcile the generally hostile accounts of tyranny with the positive picture they have painted of Peisistratos.

63 *Archaeological evidence*

It is often difficult to distinguish the public building programme of Peisistratos from that of his sons. It would, for example, be consistent with Peisistratos's interest in counteracting disunity in Attike to improve communications between the city and the rural communities. But as it happens, it is his sons whose connection with such improvements is explicitly attested. Thus Hipparkhos set up *hermai* (stones representing Hermes, the god of wayfarers) which served as milestones along the roads ([Plato], *Hipparkhos* 228d) – one has been found which marked the halfway point between the Agora and the deme Kephale (*IG* I^3 1023; D. M. Lewis, in *CAH*^{2} 4.293 fig. 29). The son of Hippias, Peisistratos the younger, dedicated the altar of the Twelve Gods (cf. [**69**] and note 4) from which all distances were marked, as is indicated by Herodotos 2.7.1 and *IG* II^2 2640. See, for these indications of work on roads, Jeffery 96 and J. McK. Camp II, *The Athenian Agora: Excavations in the Heart of Classical Athens* (London 1986) 40–2. Building work, such as the renovation of the temple of Athene Polias, resumed on the Akropolis: see J. S. Boersma, *Athenian Building Policy from 561/0 to 405/4 B.C.* [Scripta archaeologica Groningana, 4] (Groningen 1970) 20–1, 180–1. The huge Temple of Olympian Zeus south-east of the Akropolis, which was only completed by the Roman emperor Hadrian c. AD 132, is reported by Aristotle (*Politics* 1313b 23) to have been begun by the Peisistratidai nearly 650 years earlier. At Eleusis, the hall of the mysteries, the Telesterion, was replaced by a larger building and the walls of both sanctuary and town were strengthened (G. E. Mylonas, *Eleusis and the Eleusinian Mysteries* [Princeton 1961] 77–88, 91–7). This was surely an activity of the tyrants designed to consolidate feelings of unity in Attike (ibid. 103–5) and, as with the Olympieion, intended to enhance the prestige of the ruling family. Competition for glory with other tyrants and cities (cf. T. L. Shear Jr, in W. A. P. Childs [ed.], *Athens Comes of Age: From Solon to Salamis* [Princeton 1978] 8–11), let alone with rival noble families of Attike, had the convenient side-effect of providing employment for many poorer citizens (cf. J. S. Boersma, op. cit. 24–5, 27).

64 *Meiggs and Lewis no. 6, Fragment* c^1 = IG *I^3 1031* *(c. 425 BC)*

[On]eto[rides]	(527/6 BC)
[H]ippia[s]	(526/5 BC)
[K]leisthen[es]	(525/4 BC)
[M]iltiades	(524/3 BC)

[Ka]lliades	(523/2 BC)
[. . . . .]strat[os]	(522/1 BC)

Note

1 This fragment is one of four thought to belong to a list of the Athenian (eponymous) arkhons which was set up about 425 BC. The names on this fragment can be assigned to the period of the tyranny by the inclusion of Miltiades (one of the generals at Marathon) who is known from literary evidence (Dionysios of Halikarnassos, *Roman Antiquities* 7.3.1) to have been arkhon in 524/3 BC.

The first arkhon on this fragment (his full name is probably Onetorides, although only the third, fourth and fifth letters of it survive on the stone) held office in the year after the sons of Peisistratos (the 'Peisistratidai') succeeded their father in the tyranny. He had probably been nominated for the arkhonship by Peisistratos before his death. But Peisistratos's son Hippias held the eponymous arkhonship in the first available year to show that he was the new head of state.

The most interesting information is derived from the next two names on the inscription: Kleisthenes the Alkmeonid and Miltiades the Philaid (for these families see Chapter VI, pp. 200–6 and pp. 195–200). Evidently Hippias wished to continue the policy of his father (for reconciliation under Peisistratos rather than under Hippias see M. E. White, in J. A. S. Evans [ed.], *Polis and Imperium: Studies in Honour of Edward Togo Salmon* [Toronto 1974] 85–6) of winning over powerful noble families by nominating members of the Alkmeonidai and the Philaidai for the important honour of the eponymous arkhonship immediately after himself. Moreover, these two noble families accepted this degree of collaboration with the tyrants. By contrast the literary evidence had suggested that the Alkmeonidai were in continuous exile from the battle of Pallene to the expulsion of the tyrants (see, especially, Herodotos 1.64.3 [**60**] and 6.123.1 [**102**]).

The name Kalliades was too common in Athens to enable identification of his family. The last name on the fragment can be restored [Peisi]strat[os]. We know that Peisistratos the son of Hippias was arkhon during the tyranny (Thucydides 6.54.6–7 [**69**]), but other Athenian names can be restored in this place (e.g. Kallistratos).

References to detailed discussion are given by Meiggs and Lewis; add (since they wrote) W. H. Plommer, *CR* n.s. 19 (1969) 126–9 and M. E. White, op. cit. 81–95. There are brief discussions of the historical significance of the inscription by Andrewes, *Greek Tyrants* 109–11, Burn, *Lyric Age* 312–13, B. D. Meritt, *Inscriptions from the Athenian Agora* [Excavations of the Athenian Agora: Picture Book no. 10] (Princeton 1966) no. 5 (with photograph) and D. M. Lewis, in *CAH*[2] 4.288–9.

65 *Meiggs and Lewis no. 11* = IG *I*[3] *948 (521–510* BC*)*

This memorial of his arkhonship Peisist[ratos s]on [of Hippias] dedicated in the precinct of Pyth[i]an Apollon.[1]

Note

1 This inscription was engraved on a sculptured marble cornice. Two fragments, providing a fairly complete elegiac couplet, were found in 1877. Thucydides quotes this inscription from the altar in the sanctuary of Pythian Apollon. The finding place of the two fragments, near the Ilissos, helps to locate the sanctuary (see Thucydides 6.54.7 [**69**] with note 4). The altar has been splendidly reconstructed by W. B. Dinsmoor Jr and placed on display by the Epigraphical Museum in Athens. Dinsmoor suggests (1982) that the inscription ran along the shorter end of a rectangular altar and was surmounted by a triangular tympanon (see D. M. Lewis, in *CAH*[2] 4.295 fig. 30). However, while there are clamp holes at three corners of the top of the block, there is no hole for such an upper block above the first two words ('This memorial') of the inscription.

Since the grandson of Peisistratos cannot have been allowed to remain in Athens after the expulsion of his father Hippias, his arkhonship must belong before 510 BC; indeed in Thucydides 6.54.6–7 [**69**] it serves as an example of how the tyrants controlled the offices. The grid-pattern inscription Meiggs and Lewis no. 6, Fragment *c* [**64**] allows, but does not require, the name [Peisi]strat[os] as the arkhon of 522/1 BC. But the lettering of the present inscription has been thought by some scholars to require a date in the fifth century: e.g. A. E. Raubitschek, *DAA* 449–50. It can conveniently be compared with the Hekatompedon inscription (*IG* I[3] 4), precisely dated to 485/4 BC, in J. Kirchner, *Imagines Inscriptionum Atticarum*[2] (Berlin 1948): Meiggs and Lewis no. 11 = no. 12, *IG* I[3] 4 = no. 20. B. D. Meritt, *Hesperia* 8 (1939) 62–5 sought to place the arkhonship of the younger Peisistratos in one of the three years 499/8–497/6 BC for which the arkhons' names were then unknown, but his preferred year, 497/6, is now occupied by Arkhias (cf. D. M. Lewis, *CR* n.s. 12 [1962] 201). W. B. Dinsmoor [senior], in P. W. Long (ed.), *Studies in the History of Culture: The Disciplines of the Humanities* [= Festschrift W. G. Leland] (Menasha, Wisc. 1942) 185–216, while pointing out that architecturally a date c. 520 BC is possible for the cornice (p. 197; cf. J. Boardman, *The Antiquaries Journal* 39 [1959] 206–7 on the leaf and dart ornament), suggested that the inscription was cut later, probably in 496/5 BC, at a time when the Athenians preferred not to be involved in the Persian sphere of influence in the Eastern Aegean (p. 198). But the developed forms of alpha and epsilon, which have caused scholars to look for a fifth-century occasion for the inscription, can be paralleled on vase paintings of the late sixth century (L. H. Jeffery, *The Local Scripts of Archaic Greece* [Oxford 1961] 75; cf. A. J. Graham, in *Acta of the Fifth International Congress of Greek and Latin Epigraphy: Cambridge 1967* [Oxford 1971] 13). The letters theta and chi show early forms (commentary on Meiggs and Lewis no. 11, p. 20). And the same mason cut another fine inscription, on the base of a dedication by Hipparkhos at the sanctuary of Apollon Ptoïos in Boiotia (L. Bizard, *BCH* 44 [1920] 237–41). If we assume that an advanced mason who performed fine work was employed by the same tyrant family for the Ptoïon inscription, that inscription must belong before Hipparkhos's death in 514 BC. So an arkhonship for Peisistratos son of Hippias between 522/1 and 512/11 BC is likely.

66 *Herodotos 6.39.1*[1]

39 After Stesagoras's death in this manner[2] Miltiades, the son of Kimon and brother of the dead Stesagoras, was sent with a trireme to take charge of affairs in the Chersonese by the Peisistratidai, who had treated him well at Athens,[3] as though they were not responsible for his father's death. How that happened I shall tell in another place.[4]

Notes

1 Herodotos 6.38.1–6.39.2 is translated at [**98**].

2 Herodotos has told of the capture of the cities of the Thracian Chersonese, across the Hellespont from Persian territory, by the Phoenician navy (6.33). Previously these cities had been under the tyranny of Miltiades son of Kimon, the son of another Stesagoras (6.34.1 [**98**]) – the Miltiades who was to become famous as a general at Marathon. Miltiades son of Kypselos, who was prominent in the days when Peisistratos held all power in Athens, took the opportunity offered by some natives of Thrace to become a tyrant in the Chersonese, 'for he disliked the rule of Peisistratos and wished to be out of the way' (6.34.1–6.36.1 [**98**]; quotation from 6.35.3). He died childless and left his power to his nephew, Stesagoras son of Kimon. Stesagoras also died childless (6.38.2 [**98**]) and the Peisistratidai sent the famous Miltiades to replace him, about 515 BC. It seems that the tyrant family recognised the right of rival dynasts to take up a private inheritance and retain a major source of wealth.

3 They allowed Miltiades to hold the eponymous arkhonship shortly after Hippias himself: see Meiggs and Lewis no. 6, Fragment *c* above [**64**].

4 See Herodotos 6.103.1–3 [**67**] below.

67 *Herodotos 6.103.1–3*

103 When the Athenians heard this,[1] they also went to Marathon. They were led by ten Strategoi,[2] one of whom was Miltiades. This man's father, Kimon son of Stesagoras, had been banished from Athens by Peisistratos son of Hippokrates. (2) During his exile he won a victory at Olympia with a four-horse chariot . . . . At the next Olympic festival he won with the same mares, but allowed Peisistratos to be proclaimed victor. (3) Having ceded the victory to Peisistratos, he was brought home with a guarantee of safety. He won yet a third Olympic victory with the same mares,[3] but after the death of Peisistratos he died at the hands of Peisistratos's sons, who set men in ambush for him at night near the Prytaneion.[4]

Notes

1 That the Persians had landed at Marathon (490 BC).

2 Note that the new army organisation, with ten Strategoi (generals), is in use at Marathon in 490 BC, though the Athenian charge is still led by the Polemarkhos, Kallimakhos, on the right wing (Herodotos 6.111.1). Compare *Athenaion Politeia* 22.1–3 [**90**] with notes.

3 Probably the three victories belong to the Olympic Games of 536, 532 and 528 BC. Racing with four-horse chariots showed that families such as the Philaidai belonged in the top echelon of society.

4 For Herodotos 6.103.3–6.104.1 see [**99**]. If the Peisistratidai were responsible for the death of Kimon, they concealed the fact from Miltiades, who collaborated with them (Meiggs and Lewis no. 6, Fragment *c* [**64**] and Herodotos 6.39.1 [**66**]). Other inscriptional evidence for the presence of noble families in Athens during the tyranny of the Peisistratidai is discussed by A. E. Raubitschek, *DAA* 10–12 and 457 (cf. [**105**]–[**106**] with notes). The view that the Peisistratid tyrants allowed officials in charge of the mint who were responsible for the coins known as *Wappenmünzen* (see note 3 on [**36**]) to strike coins with private devices of their own choosing, has been recently restated by J. H. Kroll, *ANSMN* 26 (1981) 1–32, especially 3, 7–10.

68 *Thucydides 1.20.1–2*

20 Such is the character of earlier events I found, though it is difficult to rely on every inference drawn from the evidence.[1] For men accept from one another reports of past events – even when they happened in their own locality – with a similar lack of critical questioning. (2) The majority of Athenians, for example, think that Hipparkhos was tyrant when he was killed by Harmodios and Aristogeiton. They do not know that Hippias, as the eldest of the sons of Peisistratos, was ruler, whereas Hipparkhos and Thessalos were merely his brothers.[2]

Notes

1 In the first 23 chapters of his book, Thucydides compares the Peloponnesian War about which he writes with earlier wars and explains why they were not as great. This introduction includes a section on the principles of writing history (1.20–2), the transition to which is made here.

2 This does not, perhaps, contradict the statement of *Athenaion Politeia* 17.3 [**61**] that Hipparkhos and Thessalos were half-brothers. But Thucydides's later treatment [**69**] of the Athenians' misunderstanding does indicate that Thessalos was, like Hippias and Hipparkhos, a legitimate son. This testimony should be preferred to the confused version of the *Athenaion Politeia*. See note 16 on [**61**].

69 *Thucydides 6.54.5–6.55.4*

(5) Indeed, in other respects their government was not offensive

to the majority; they established it without creating hostility.[1] More than any other tyrants these men exercised virtue and intelligence. Although they imposed on the Athenians a mere 5 per cent tax on agricultural produce,[2] they adorned their city beautifully, they brought their wars to a successful conclusion and they offered sacrifices at the sanctuaries. (6) In all other respects the city was left free to observe the laws previously enacted, except in so far as they always took care that one of themselves held the offices.[3] Among those who thus held the annual arkhonship at Athens was Peisistratos, the son of Hippias who became tyrant. He was named after his grandfather. While arkhon he dedicated the altar of the Twelve Gods in the Agora and the altar of Apollon in the sanctuary of Pythian Apollon.[4] (7) The people of Athens later extended the altar in the Agora in length and thus obscured the inscription. But the inscription on the altar in the sanctuary of Pythian Apollon is clear even now. It reads in faded letters:

> This memorial of his arkhonship Peisistratos son of Hippias
> dedicated in the precinct of Pythian Apollon.[5]

55 As for the fact that Hippias as the eldest son was the ruler, I maintain it firmly both because I have learned it from more accurate reports than others and because one can deduce it from the following evidence. Hippias alone of the legitimate sons of Peisistratos, it seems, had children, as is indicated both by the altar and by the free-standing inscription mentioning the wrongs of the tyrants which stands on the Akropolis in Athens.[6] On the latter neither Thessalos nor Hipparkhos is said to have a child, but Hippias has five, borne to him by Myrrhine, daughter of Kallias son of Hyperokhides.[7] Now it is likely that the eldest was the first to marry. (2) And on the same inscription Hippias is listed first after his father, not unnaturally as he was the eldest after Peisistratos and the one who became tyrant. (3) Again, I do not believe that Hippias would ever have seized the tyranny easily at a moment's notice if Hipparkhos had been in power when he was killed and Hippias had tried to establish himself on that very day. Rather it was through his existing custom of making the citizens afraid and paying assiduous attention to his mercenaries[8] that he retained control with a considerable margin of safety. He was far from being the younger brother, at a loss what to do at a time when he had not been familiar before with the constant exercise of power. (4) It fell to Hipparkhos because of the misfortune of his assassination to become famous and thus to acquire with later generations the reputation of having been tyrant.

Notes

1 For the digression of which this is part, see Thucydides 6.53.3–6.54.5 [**74**]. I have accepted C. Hude's emendation of this sentence from singular to plural (the vague 'their', 'they' referring to the Peisistratidai in general). While one might accept a statement that 'his (Hipparkhos's) government was not offensive', it is intolerable that Thucydides should say that 'he (Hipparkhos) established his government' when the major point of the digression is that Hippias, not Hipparkhos, was tyrant (especially 6.54.2 [**74**]). See K. J. Dover, *Thucydides: Book VI* (Oxford 1965) 62–3.

2 Unless we understand the 10 per cent tax in *Athenaion Politeia* 16.4 [**61**] as a generic term (like 'tithe') – unlikely because there is a precise parallel in the 10 per cent tax attributed to Kypselos tyrant of Korinth by [Aristotle], *Oikonomika* 2.2.1 (H. W. Pleket, *Talanta* 1 [1969] 46 n. 95) – we must conclude that a tax of 10 per cent under Peisistratos was subsequently halved by him or his sons.

3 Thucydides apparently means that the Peisistratidai (and, similarly, Peisistratos) always had a member of their own family in each office. But the clan cannot have been so numerous as to fill more than the crucial offices (those of eponymous arkhon and Polemarkhos, for example) and the fragmentary arkhon list [**64**] shows that, at least as far as Peisistratos's sons were concerned, the tyrant family used the cadets of other prominent families on whom they could rely. The implication of this sentence, with its clause 'except in so far as', is that the Peisistratid tyrants violated the constitutional procedures in filling the offices with their own political supporters and associates.

4 The altar of the Twelve Gods, dated purely on archaeological grounds to the second half of the sixth century, has been excavated on the north side of the Agora, adjoining the Panathenaic Way. Together with its enclosure, it was rebuilt about a century later (cf. 54.7 below). See M. Crosby, in *Commemorative Studies in Honor of Theodore Leslie Shear* [Hesperia Supplements, 8] (Princeton 1949) 82–103; H. A. Thompson, *Hesperia* 21 (1952) 47–82, especially 52–3, 71; H. A. Thompson and R. E. Wycherley, *The Athenian Agora* 14 (Princeton 1972) 20–1, 129–36. The sanctuary of Apollon Pythios, on the basis of relevant finds (including the two fragments of Meiggs and Lewis no. 11 [**65**]), was in the south-east of the city, perhaps outside the walls: see R. E. Wycherley, *AJA* 67 (1963) 75–9, *GRBS* 4 (1963) 166–7; J. Travlos, *Pictorial Dictionary of Ancient Athens* (London 1971) 100–3.

5 For the inscription bearing this elegiac couplet (partially restored from the text of Thucydides) see [**65**]. Since the letters are distinctly cut, Thucydides's comment about 'faint letters' probably refers to the disappearance of red paint which originally filled the deeply cut letters (so W. B. Dinsmoor, in P. W. Long

[ed.], *Studies in the History of Culture: The Disciplines of the Humanities* [Menasha, Wisc. 1942] 196); indeed, traces of red paint may be seen in some of the grooves today.

6 Since, as K. J. Dover (*Thucydides: Book VI* [Oxford 1965] 65) points out, no examples of narrative inscriptions survive from archaic or classical Greece, this *stele* ('free-standing inscription') presumably outlawed the surviving Peisistratidai and their descendants. The inscription on the altar, of course, merely confirms that Hippias had a son, not that his brothers had no children.

7 Thucydides evidently regards Hippias, Thessalos and Hipparkhos as the only sons of Peisistratos by his Athenian wife (though sons of non-Athenian mothers were in fact legitimate until the middle of the fifth century BC). Another wife of Hippias, the daughter of Kharmos, is attested by Kleidemos, *FGrH* 323 F 15. Perhaps she died before bearing Hippias any children and was followed by Myrrhine. Thucydides is trying to give the impression that Hipparkhos and Thessalos were too young to have children, but the impression is false since Hipparkhos was about fifty when he was murdered a few years before the expulsion of the tyrant family (so K. J. Beloch, *Griechische Geschichte*[2] [Strassburg 1913] 1.2.295).

8 The mercenaries of Peisistratos are mentioned by Herodotos (1.64.1 [**60**]).

70 Athenaion Politeia *18.1*

18 Hipparkhos and Hippias took over control of affairs through their prestige and their age. But Hippias, being the elder and a naturally shrewd politician was effectively in charge of the government. Hipparkhos was a playboy, constantly engaged in love affairs and fond of music and poetry (it was he who invited Anakreon, Simonides and other poets to Athens).[1]

Note

1 Hipparkhos reorganised the musical contests at the Panathenaia: see J. A. Davison, *JHS* 78 (1958) 38–41 = *From Archilochus to Pindar* (London 1968) 58–64. [Plato], *Hipparkhos* clearly has the family structure wrong in stating that 'the son of Peisistratos of Philaidai, Hipparkhos . . . was the eldest and wisest of the sons of Peisistratos' (228b); so we should treat that author with caution when he goes on to say that Hipparkhos, 'among the many other fine demonstrations of his wisdom, first brought the epics of Homer to this land, and compelled the rhapsodes to recite them at the Panathenaia in relays, each taking up where the last left off, just as they do still at the present time. He sent a fifty-oared ship for Anakreon of Teos and brought him to the city; Simonides of Keos he had always by his side, winning him over with large commissions and gifts' (228b–c). For the *hermai* (cf. [**63**]) bearing edifying verses which this author says (228d–229b) were set up by Hipparkhos along the roads [**63**], see J. F. Crome, *AM* 60–1 (1935–6) 300–13, especially 305–8, and B. M. W. Knox, in W. A. P. Childs (ed.), *Athens Comes of Age: From Solon to Salamis* (Princeton 1978) 43–52 at 48–9.

The murder of Hipparkhos

One of the most notable events of the tyranny of the Peisistratidai was the assassination of Hipparkhos. Thucydides ([**73**]–[**74**]), especially, was intent on arguing that the motive was a personal one. But the older of the two lovers who formulated the plot may have had political motives as well, and the fact that a number of people were involved in the conspiracy points to a political movement. In addition to the exercise of trying to determine what actually happened in the incident, the sources challenge the reader to discern what traditions existed in the fifth century. There are the drinking songs [**71**] which give a rather superficial assessment of the effectiveness of the assassins' action; there are the accounts of Herodotos [**72**] and Thucydides; and the argumentative points made by these two writers reveal contrary views, some of which are not otherwise attested, while others are preserved for us only in fourth-century writings (especially in the *Athenaion Politeia* [**75**]).

71 *Drinking songs (late sixth or early fifth century BC)*[1]

In a branch of myrtle I shall carry my sword,
As did Harmodios and Aristogeiton,
The day they slew the tyrant and made
Athens a city of equal laws.[2]

Dearest Harmodios, you are yet alive.
You dwell, they say, in the Isles of the Blessed
Where also are fleet-footed Akhilleus and, they say,
The son of Tydeus, noble Diomedes.

In a branch of myrtle I shall carry my sword,
As did Harmodios and Aristogeiton,
The day when they killed a tyrant man,
Hipparkhos, at the sacrifice to Athene.[3]

Your fame will be everlasting on earth,
Dearest Harmodios and Aristogeiton –
Because they slew the tyrant and made
Athens a city of equal laws.[4]

Notes

1 These four aristocratic drinking songs (*skolia*) preserved by Athenaios 15.50 p. 695a–b, though probably composed impromptu at symposia (note the availability of beginnings and ends of stanzas for use by the singer and the

change of subject within the fourth stanza), indicate the heroic stature assigned to the assassins of Hipparkhos. They are discussed by C. M. Bowra, *Greek Lyric Poetry*² (Oxford 1961) 391–6, M. Ostwald, *Nomos and the Beginnings of the Athenian Democracy* (Oxford 1969) 121–36, C. W. Fornara, *Philologus* 114 (1970) 155–80 and M. W. Taylor, *The Tyrant Slayers: The Heroic Image in Fifth Century B.C., Athenian Art and Politics* (New York 1981) 51–77.

2 The epithet *isonomos* ('having equal laws', i.e. 'where there are equal rights') applied to Athens might be thought to suggest a date for the first and fourth stanzas when Athens had a developed democracy and 'equality of laws' was valued. But *isonomia* may mean 'equality of laws' primarily in the sense of the reinstatement of the existing laws after the overthrow of tyrannical rule: compare H. W. Pleket, *Talanta* 4 (1972) 63–81 at 64–8. Kleisthenes the Alkmeonid (Chapter V) may have used *isonomia* as a slogan to promote his reforms after the tyranny, but if so it cannot have connoted genuine implementation of 'the principle of political equality' (M. Ostwald, op. cit. 97) since Kleisthenes did nothing to remove the graded qualifications for political office instituted by Solon (*Athenaion Politeia* 7.3 [**42**]); the hierarchical distribution of offices remained in force. In these drinking songs *isonomia* is clearly contrasted with tyranny (and not with oligarchy as well). Moreover, M. H. Hansen has recently argued (*LCM* 11 [1986] 35–6) that the word which democrats used for their preferred form of government, as early as c. 470 BC, was *demokratia*. The claim that Harmodios and Aristogeiton 'made Athens a city of equal laws' may well have been made by the opponents of the Alkmeonidai, people who also set up the statues of the tyrannicides (see note 2 on [**76**]) about the same time (so H. W. Pleket, op. cit. 75–7).

3 This stanza provides at an early date an association of the assassination with the festival of the Panathenaia (see Herodotos 5.56.1 [**72**], Thucydides 6.56.2 [**74**] with note 6 and *Athenaion Politeia* 18.3 [**75**]).

4 While one may accept C. W. Fornara's point (*Historia* 17 [1968] 405 and n. 19) that Herodotos and Thucydides were capable of making inferences themselves, it remains true that the clan of the Gephyraioi, to which Harmodios and Aristogeiton belonged (Herodotos 5.55.1, 5.57.1 [**72**]), were the major beneficiaries of the glorification of the tyrannicides, whereas the Alkmeonidai benefited from the main thrust of the accounts by Herodotos and Thucydides of the overthrow of the tyranny. M. Ostwald, noting that it is difficult to identify anti-Alkmeonids in the period before 480 BC, suggests that the Alkmeonid Kleisthenes (Chapter V) sponsored the cult of Harmodios and Aristogeiton (op. cit. 130–1, 134–6). But members and connections of the Alkmeonid family were successfully expelled from Attike by ostracism in the 480s, when our information becomes more plentiful again; it is difficult to name politicians of any persuasion in the period from Kleisthenes's reforms to 480 BC. The statue group of the tyrannicides ([**76**] and note 2), as well as these drinking songs, may well constitute early attempts to take away credit from the Alkmeonidai (see note 2 above).

72 *Herodotos 5.55–5.57.1*

55 Driven from Sparta, Aristagoras went to Athens, which had recently been freed from tyrants – in the following way.[1] Hipparkhos son of Peisistratos, the brother of the tyrant Hippias,[2] although he saw a brilliant vision [of his own fate][3] in his sleep, was killed by Aristogeiton and Harmodios, who were descended in time past from the clan Gephyraioi. After this murder the Athenians endured tyranny no less for four more years;[4] indeed it was harsher than before. *56* The vision which Hipparkhos saw in his sleep was as follows. On the night before the Panathenaia Hipparkhos thought he saw a tall, attractive man standing beside him and speaking this riddle in epic verse:

> Endure, o lion, the unendurable with enduring spirit;
> No man who wrongs you will fail to pay recompense.

(2) He was seen disclosing this dream to the interpreters as soon as day broke. But he then rejected the vision and took part in the procession, during which he died.

57 The Gephyraioi, to whom the murderers of Hipparkhos belonged, came according to their own account from Eretria originally, but as I have discovered by enquiry they were Phoenicians . . . .[5]

Notes

1 Aristagoras of Miletos, having failed to win the support of the Spartan king Kleomenes for the revolt of the Greek cities in Ionia from the Persian king, comes to Athens. Herodotos launches into a long account (5.55–5.96) of recently liberated Athens with the ostensible reason of explaining why the Athenians of 499 BC were disposed to support the Ionian revolt.

2 Herodotos thus corrects the assumption expressed in the first drinking song [**71**] that Hipparkhos was 'the tyrant' at the time of his assassination.

3 These words are thought to be an insertion in the text of Herodotos.

4 The murder of Hipparkhos can be dated on this basis to 514/13 BC. See also note 3 on [**55**], note 6 on [**75**] and Rhodes 191–8.

5 Herodotos does not get past the murder of Hipparkhos – a mere preliminary, in his view (cf. 6.123.2 [**102**]), to the liberation of the Athenians from the tyrants – before he is distracted into telling the descent of the Gephyraioi, the family from which both Harmodios and Aristogeiton came. For Herodotos's account of the overthrow of the tyranny, see 5.62.1–5.65.5 [**77**].

73 *Thucydides 1.20.2*

(2) The majority of Athenians, for example,[1] think that

Hipparkhos was tyrant when he was killed by Harmodios and Aristogeiton. They do not know that Hippias, as the eldest of the sons of Peisistratos, was ruler, whereas Hipparkhos and Thessalos were merely his brothers. On the very day and at the last moment Harmodios and Aristogeiton suspected that some of their accomplices had passed information to Hippias. They kept away from him on the assumption that he had been forewarned, but wishing to take a risk and achieve something before their arrest, they came upon Hipparkhos as he was marshalling the Panathenaic procession near what is called the Leokoreion[2] and killed him.[3]

Notes

1 For the context, see 1.20.1 [**68**] and note 1.

2 A sanctuary which is suitable for identification as the one remembering the daughters of the hero Leos (who in mythology were sacrificed to save the city: Ailianos, *Historical Miscellanies* 12.28; for the legend see E. A. M. E. O'Connor-Visser, *Aspects of Human Sacrifice in the Tragedies of Euripides* [Amsterdam 1983] 223) was found in 1971–2 in the north-western corner of the Agora, in front of the Stoa of the Basileus (for which see note 5 on [**13**] and note 2 on [**42**]) and beside the Panathenaic Way. For the excavation reports, see T. L. Shear Jr, *Hesperia* 42 (1973) 121–79 at 126–34, 359–407 at 360–9 (without accepting the identification as the Leokoreion). A poros parapet was built late in the fifth century BC to enclose a natural rock used as a sacred stone on which donors shattered their votive gifts. The lack of offerings which can be dated before the middle of the fifth century may be thought an obstacle to the identification of the sanctuary as the Leokoreion near which Hipparkhos was marshalling the Panathenaic procession. But there are parallels for a similar lack of offerings at two other shrines, the Tritopatreion just outside the Sacred Gate and the triangular sanctuary south-west of the Agora (H. A. Thompson, *Hesperia* 37 [1968] 58–60; G. V. Lalonde, ibid. 123–33), in periods when they must have been in use. So we can picture Hipparkhos marshalling a part of the procession (Thucydides 6.57.3 [**74**] below is non-committal on what Hipparkhos was doing) just as the Panathenaic Way enters the north-western corner of the Agora on its way to the Akropolis, while Hippias does likewise outside the wall. I am grateful to H. A. Thompson for information and discussion about the sanctuary in the north-western corner of the Agora; for his tentative identification of it as the Leokoreion, see his addendum of August 1971 in *The Athenian Agora* 14 (Princeton 1972) 121–3 at 123 and, for his more confident acceptance despite the hesitation of others (for example, R. E. Wycherley, *The Stones of Athens* [Princeton 1978] 63–4, 98 and S. I. Rotroff, *Hesperia* 47 [1978] 206–7 and n. 53), see his paper in W. A. P. Childs (ed.), *Athens Comes of Age: From Solon to Salamis* (Princeton 1978) 96–108 at 101–2 with n. 36.

3 The two extended accounts of Thucydides ([**74**], [**78**]) and the *Athenaion Politeia* ([**75**], [**79**]) agree on several points: the attack on Hipparkhos resulted from a love affair involving Harmodios; there were repeated attempts to seduce

Harmodios away from Aristogeiton; Harmodios's sister was insulted by being invited to be a basket-carrier in a procession; Harmodios and Aristogeiton believed that Hippias had been warned of the impending attack; they assassinated Hipparkhos near the Leokoreion because they could not risk being arrested while attempting to assassinate Hippias; Harmodios was killed immediately whereas Aristogeiton died no easy death; and the tyranny became harsher after the assassination of Hipparkhos.

74 *Thucydides 6.53.3–6.54.5, 6.56.1–6.59.1, 6.60.1*

(3) For the common people had been taught that the tyranny of Peisistratos and his sons had become harsh in its final stages and moreover that it was not they and Harmodios who had overthrown it, but the Spartans. Hence they were constantly afraid and treated anything with suspicion.[1]

54 Now the daring attempt of Aristogeiton and Harmodios was undertaken as a result of a love affair, which I shall relate at some length in order to show that the Athenians themselves give a completely inaccurate account of their own tyrants and of the incident, and so do other people.[2] (2) For when Peisistratos died, having remained tyrant into old age, it was not Hipparkhos, as most people think, but Hippias as the eldest who held office. Harmodios was a startlingly attractive youth who was loved and possessed by Aristogeiton, a private citizen but a moderately wealthy one. (3) Harmodios was solicited by Hipparkhos, son of Peisistratos, but not successfully, and reported the approach to Aristogeiton. In emotional torment and afraid that Hipparkhos might use his power to obtain Harmodios for himself by force, Aristogeiton immediately plotted, as far as a man of his standing could, the overthrow of the tyranny.[3] (4) Meanwhile Hipparkhos made another attempt to seduce Harmodios, but was no more successful. Far from wanting to do anything violent, he set about devising some means of insulting Harmodios which would not suggest to the public that this affair was the motive.

(5) Indeed, in other respects, their government was not offensive to the majority. . . .[4]

56 After Harmodios firmly rejected his approach, Hipparkhos insulted him just as he planned. First they invited his young sister to come and carry a basket in a certain religious procession, then they drove her away, saying that they had not invited her to the position because she was not worthy. (2) Harmodios was greatly upset[5] and Aristogeiton even more annoyed on his behalf. They had now completed their preparations with those who were going to join them in the conspiracy, but they were waiting for the Great Panathenaia.[6] On that day alone it did not engender suspicion for those citizens who were about to take part in the procession to be together in a body while armed. The plan was that Harmodios and Aristogeiton would begin the attack and the armed men would immediately come to their aid as the bodyguards reacted. (3) For security's sake there were not many in the conspiracy; they hoped that those who were not privy to it would on the spur of the moment use their weapons to join in freeing themselves, however few took the risk.

57 When the day of the festival came, Hippias was with his bodyguards outside the city wall in the place called the Kerameikos, arranging the way in which each segment of the procession must go ahead. Harmodios and Aristogeiton for their part, already wearing daggers, were advancing to attack (2) when they saw one of their fellow conspirators conversing in a friendly fashion with Hippias (who was readily accessible to all). They were alarmed and thought that they had been betrayed and were now on the point of being arrested. (3) At this juncture they determined first, if possible, to avenge themselves on the man who had outraged them and was the cause of their terrible risk. They rushed inside the gates just as they were and found Hipparkhos near what is called the Leokoreion.[7] They immediately fell upon him without further thought, driven by the anger of a wounded lover in one case and of an insulted citizen in the other. They struck him repeatedly and killed him. (4) One of them – Aristogeiton – briefly escaped the bodyguards as the crowd converged on the scene, but was later captured and harshly treated. Harmodios was killed on the spot.

58 When the news was brought to Hippias in the Kerameikos, he did not approach the incident but went immediately to the participants in the procession who were fully armed before they, being some distance away, realised what had happened. Revealing by his facial expression nothing of the disaster which had befallen him, he bade them move to a certain spot, which he indicated, without their weapons. (2) The men withdrew, expecting that he was about to say something to them,[8] but he gave instructions to his mercenaries to collect the weapons and immediately singled out those whom he blamed and all who were found in possession of a dagger. For the custom was to participate in the procession with shield and spear only.

59 Such was the way in which the conspiracy of Harmodios and Aristogeiton had its origin in a lover's resentment and the reckless act of daring sprang from a moment of panic. . . .[9]

60 The common people of Athens took these events to heart and were mindful of all the reports which they knew about them. They were now harsh and suspicious towards those who had been blamed in connection with the mysteries. Everything seemed to them to have been done in the interests of an oligarchic and tyrannical conspiracy.[10]

Notes

1 In his account of the Athenian expedition to Sicily during the Peloponnesian War, Thucydides explains why the state ship had arrived (July 415 BC) to take Alkibiades back for trial, although he had been allowed to sail with the fleet after the desecration of the mysteries and the mutilation of the *hermai* (statuettes of the god Hermes). Alkibiades, indeed, had played a decisive part in the determination of Athenian strategy in Sicily (6.46.5–6.50.1). Thucydides reports that highly respectable citizens were arrested and imprisoned, though the informer might be a rogue, as a result of the desire of the Athenians to discover the truth about the crimes committed just before the expedition sailed (June 415 BC). Nevertheless, Thucydides seems to give this account of the Peisistratidai for its own sake.

2 The 'other people' besides the Athenians who give an inaccurate account of the tyranny probably include a historian of repute, Hellanikos of Lesbos: see K. J. Dover in Gomme, *HCT* 4.321–2.

3 This broad aim, as well as Thucydides's attention to Aristogeiton's lack of political standing, diminishes the bald opening claim that the murder of Hipparkhos was the result of a love affair. Thucydides strengthens this latter view by claiming (6.56.3 below) that there were not many in the conspiracy and that people at the festival would spontaneously join in the violence; but the author of the *Athenaion Politeia* (18.2 [**75**]) says that many men were involved in the conspiracy.

4 For Thucydides 6.54.5–6.55.4, see [**69**] above.

5 It is possible that the implication of the tyrants was that Harmodios's sister was not a virgin, since it seems clear that at the Panathenaia, at least, girls who carried the sacred baskets had to be virgins (see Menander, *Epitrepontes* 438–41, with the commentary by A. W. Gomme and F. H. Sandbach [Oxford 1973] 329). Such a view has recently been put forward by B. M. Lavelle, *AJP* 107 (1986) 318–31, with parallels from modern Greek rural communities. But 'not to be ἄξιος (worthy)' should refer to the standing or prestige (ἀξίωμα) of the girl. Philokhoros, *FGrH* 328 F 8 states that unmarried girls 'of standing' (ἐν ἀξιώματι) carried the baskets of the goddess, and Hesykhios (s.v. *kanephoroi* [basket-carriers]) makes it clear that not all

unmarried girls were 'of standing'. Late authors (Scholion to Aristophanes, *Akharnians* 242, Photios s.v. *kanephoroi*) clearly take good birth to be a prerequisite. Harmodios was upset not merely on his sister's behalf but because a judgment that the girl was not of sufficient status to carry a basket in the procession was an insult to the standing of his family (in 6.57.3 Harmodios is the one insulted; compare also the reference to the standing [ἀξίωσις] of Aristogeiton in 6.54.3).

6 The Panathenaia was celebrated each year in summer, with the major festivities on 28 Hekatombaion. Thucydides's epithet here ('the Great Panathenaia') indicates the more magnificent festival celebrated every fourth year from 566/5 BC and, in conjunction with the interval of time indicated in 6.59.4 [**78**], enables us to date the murder of Hipparkhos to 514 BC.

7 A sanctuary which can be plausibly identified with the Leokoreion has been discovered: see note 2 on Thucydides 1.20.2 [**73**] above.

8 In *Athenaion Politeia* 15.4–5 [**55**] a similar ruse is made the means by which Peisistratos disarmed the people. If Thucydides has confused the two tyrants on this ruse, his view that arms were carried in the procession (6.56.2, 6.58) should give way to the contrary view of *Athenaion Politeia* 18.4 [**75**]. See further note 7 on [**75**].

9 Although (in 6.59.2–4 [**78**]) Thucydides speaks of the more oppressive tyranny after the murder of Hipparkhos, he seems to have told the story of the murder for its own sake and at much greater length than was needed to explain the attitude of the Athenian *demos* in 415 BC.

10 The establishment of either oligarchy or tyranny would entail the overthrow of the democracy.

75 Athenaion Politeia *18*

18 Hipparkhos and Hippias[1] took over the control of affairs through their rank and their age. But Hippias, being the elder and a naturally shrewd politician, was effectively in charge of the government. Hipparkhos was a playboy, constantly engaged in love affairs and fond of music and poetry (it was he who invited Anakreon, Simonides and other poets to Athens). (2) Thettalos was much younger, reckless and arrogant in his behaviour; he was the source of all the family's troubles.[2] He fell in love with Harmodios and, failing to win any reciprocal affection, he gave vent to his ungovernable rage. He showed his bitterness in many ways; and finally, when the sister of Harmodios was going to carry the sacred basket in the Panathenaian procession, he prevented her, slandering Harmodios as being effeminate.[3] This incited Harmodios and Aristogeiton, with many accomplices, to perpetrate their famous deed. (3) As they were lying in wait for Hippias on the Akropolis during the Panathenaia (he was awaiting the arrival of the procession, while Hipparkhos was supervising its departure),[4] they noticed one of their fellow conspirators talking amicably with Hippias. Since they supposed he was betraying the plot and wished to achieve something before they were arrested, they ran down and made their move before the priests began.[5] They killed Hipparkhos near the Leokoreion as he was marshalling the procession, but spoiled their plan as a whole.[6]

(4) Of the two leaders, Harmodios was killed immediately by the bodyguards and Aristogeiton later, after he was arrested and subjected to a long period of torture. Under torture he accused many persons who were members of distinguished families and also supporters of the tyrants. At first the investigators could find no trace of the conspiracy. We may dismiss as untrue the generally accepted story that Hippias made the men who were participating in the procession put down their arms and had them searched for daggers. For at that time arms were not carried in the procession, this being a practice adopted later by a decree of the people. (5) Democratic writers maintain that Aristogeiton accused the supporters of the tyrants with the deliberate intention that they would both commit an impious act and weaken themselves by killing their own innocent supporters; others say that he did not fabricate a false story but betrayed his actual accomplices. (6) Finally, when he was unable, despite all his efforts, to obtain relief through death, he declared that he would inform against many others and persuaded Hippias to give him his right hand as a token of good faith. As soon as he had hold of it he reviled him for having given his right hand to his brother's murderer. Thus he provoked Hippias to such a fit of rage that, unable to control himself, he pulled out his dagger and slew Aristogeiton.[7]

Notes

1 Hipparkhos is no doubt mentioned first because his assassination is the subject of this chapter. The author does recognise (next sentence) that Hippias was effectively in command.

2 Thucydides (6.54.2–4, 56.1 [**74**]) is surely to be preferred (n. 7 below) in his view that it was Hipparkhos who was in love with Harmodios but failed to lure him away from Aristogeiton. Our author has outlined characteristics of Hipparkhos which suit Thucydides's version, but he leaves that characterisation in the air, and abruptly and awkwardly attributes the love affair to Thettalos (cf. Davies, *APF* 448–9).

3 Presumably when Harmodios refused Thettalos's advances, the latter taunted

him with being homosexually passive (*malakos*, 'soft, effeminate' could imply this; for taunts of such a kind see K. J. Dover, *Greek Homosexuality* [London 1978] 103–5, 143–6). Thucydides 6.56.1 [**74**] makes the slight an insult to Harmodios and his family, but clearly thinks that the procession involved preceded the Panathenaia.

4 Thucydides (6.57.1, 6.58.1 [**74**]) provides a consistent picture of Hippias remaining outside the city gates (cf. 6.57.3), while our author seems open to the allegation that he has simply made a logical reconstruction; but there is no easy way of deciding between the two versions.

5 This is the apparent meaning of the text as read by Chambers (τῶν ἱ̣ερ‹έ›ω̣ν). Others generally assume the papyrus is illegible at this point and follow Kenyon in printing τῶν [ἄλλω]ν. The clause would then mean 'they ran down and made their move without waiting for the others'. However, there are traces in this position which are not compatible with [ἄλλω].

6 514/13 BC (cf. Herodotos 5.55 [**72**], Thucydides 6.59.4 [**78**] and *Athenaion Politeia* 19.2 [**79**]). 'They killed Hipparkhos near the Leokoreion as he was marshalling the procession' is one of the few verbal reminiscences of Thucydides (1.20.2 [**73**]; but 6.57.1 [**74**] has Hippias marshalling the procession).

7 This account should be compared with those of Herodotos [**72**] and Thucydides ([**73**], [**74**]). Thucydides corrects a traditional account, but it seems that the author of the *Athenaion Politeia* set out to correct Thucydides at several points. Thucydides says that Hippias and not Hipparkhos succeeded Peisistratos, although he allows Hipparkhos some share in the rule (6.54.3, 6.56.1). Our author makes Hippias and Hipparkhos joint rulers (*Athenaion Politeia* 18.1). Thucydides says that Hipparkhos was the Peisistratid who quarrelled with Harmodios (6.54.2–5); the fact that Hipparkhos was the one killed supports Thucydides against our author, who makes the cause of the trouble Thettalos's approaches to Harmodios (*Athenaion Politeia* 18.2). Thucydides says that the conspirators chose the Panathenaia for their attack since they could carry arms without arousing suspicion on that occasion (6.56.2). Our author may be correct in his assertion that in the time of the Peisistratidai no weapons were carried in the procession (*Athenaion Politeia* 18.4). But that does not disprove the whole story of the search for daggers (Thucydides 6.58). For recent discussion of the murder of Hipparkhos and the traditions about it, see M. Lang, *Historia* 3 (1954/5) 395–407, T. R. Fitzgerald, *Historia* 6 (1957) 275–86, A. J. Podlecki, *Historia* 15 (1966) 129–41 and C. W. Fornara, *Historia* 17 (1968) 400–24.

76 *Pausanias 1.8.5*

(5) Not far away[1] stand Harmodios and Aristogeiton who killed Hipparkhos. The nature of their motive and the way the deed was done have been described by others. One set of statues is the work of Kritios; the older set was made by Antenor. Xerxes took it away as spoils of war when he occupied Athens, after the city

had been evacuated by the Athenians. But Antiokhos later sent it back to the Athenians.[2]

Notes

1 Pausanias is describing a walk through the Agora of Athens. Not far from the statues described in 1.8.4 stand not one but two versions of the pair of tyrant-slayers.

2 The earlier statue group was made by Antenor in bronze (Valerius Maximus 2.10, ext. 1). It was set up, according to Pliny the Elder (*Natural History* 34.17), in 509 BC. While Pliny's synchronism of the Athenian with the Roman liberation from tyranny must be treated with caution, as pointed out by S. Brunnsåker, *The Tyrant-Slayers of Kritios and Nesiotes* [Skrifter Utgivna av Svenska Institutet i Athen, 4° 17] (Stockholm 1955) 40–1, 43, the erection of the statue group may be evidence that the Alkmeonid claim to fame as the overthrowers of the tyranny was subject at an early date to competition from other noble families. When the earlier statue group was taken in 480 BC by Xerxes in his sack of Athens, it was quickly replaced (by 477/6 BC: *The Parian Marble*, *FGrH* 239 A 54) with a statue group by Kritios or (Loukianos, *Philopseudeis* 18) Kritios and Nesiotes, of which part of the base has been found, inscribed with two elegiac couplets (B. D. Meritt, *Hesperia* 5 [1936] 355–8; for a recent speculative attempt to restore the verses from a stone in Chios see J. W. Day, in *The Greek Historians: Literature and History: Papers Presented to A.E. Raubitschek* [Stanford 1985] 25–46). If the Leokoreion has been correctly identified in the north-west corner of the Agora (see note 2 on [**73**]), it is possible that the statues stood near the site of the murder, as was observed by M. W. Taylor, *The Tyrant Slayers: The Heroic Image in Fifth Century B.C., Athenian Art and Politics* (New York 1981) 33–50 at 42 (but cf. 45–6). The earlier group was returned to Athens by Alexander (Pliny, *Natural History* 34.69–70 and Arrian 3.16.7, 7.19.2), Seleukos I (Valerius Maximus) or Antiokhos I (Pausanias in this passage). On the attention of the Athenians of the fifth century BC to the cult of Harmodios and Aristogeiton, see S. Brunnsåker, op. cit., especially 120–4, C. W. Fornara, *Philologus* 114 (1970) 155–80, I. Calabi Limentani, *Acme* 29 (1976) 9–27 and M. W. Taylor, op. cit. 18 [page 19 should follow 15], 20–7. Not only was the statue group rapidly replaced (see above) – the new version having a striking effect on vase-painting in the next decade – but the oldest living descendants of Harmodios and Aristogeiton were granted public maintenance in the Prytaneion (*IG* I^3 131, with the supplement in line 7 proposed by M. Ostwald, *AJP* 72 (1951) 24–46 at 32–5), the tyrannicides were honoured with a tomb in the Kerameikos (Pausanias 1.29.15) and annual sacrifices were offered to them by the Polemarkhos (*Athenaion Politeia* 58.1). But the Alkmeonidai, who could point to an effective removal of Hippias in 511/10 (see the following section), can hardly have been pleased with these honours for the unsuccessful tyrant-slayers: see A. J. Podlecki, *Historia* 15 (1966) 129–41 (but the idea that, of all the politicians active in the 470s, Themistokles was the instigator of the tribute to the tyrannicides, is quite unsupported by any evidence).

The expulsion of the Peisistratidai

The assassination of Hipparkhos did not end the tyranny. Rather, according to our sources, the tyranny of Hippias understandably became more oppressive. The effective ejector of the tyrants in Athens was the Spartan army. But one must ask the question, why did the Spartans abandon their ties of hospitality with the Peisistratidai and expel them by force from Athens? The answer given by the ancient sources ([**77**], [**79**]) is that they were persuaded to liberate Athens by the Delphic oracle, and that the oracle in turn was persuaded to give this injunction repeatedly to the Spartans by an Athenian noble family, the Alkmeonidai. Again conflict between noble factions – one led by the tyrant family and another by that family, the Alkmeonidai, which alternately opposed and collaborated with the Peisistratids – seems to be at the base of political action.

77 *Herodotos 5.62.1–5.65.5*

62 I have related the vision which Hipparkhos had in his sleep and the origin of the Gephyraioi, among whom were the murderers of Hipparkhos. In addition, I must resume the story, which I originally set out to tell,[1] of Athens' liberation from the tyrants. (2) When Hippias was tyrant and was embittered towards the Athenians because of the death of Hipparkhos, the Alkmeonidai, an Athenian family who had fled from the Peisistratidai,[2] did not succeed in their full-scale attempt with the other Athenians in exile, but met with disaster when they made a serious attempt to return home and free Athens by fortifying Leipsydrion in the country above Paionia.[3] Subsequently the Alkmeonidai tried every device against the Peisistratidai, gaining from the Amphiktyonic Council the contract to build the temple which now stands at Delphi, but did not then exist.[4] (3) They had been wealthy and distinguished men for a long time, and they constructed the temple more handsomely than the plans specified, in particular by using Parian marble in the completion of the front, whereas the contract specified limestone for the construction of the temple. *63* According to the Athenians, these men resident in Delphi persuaded the Pythia with their wealth to put pressure on any Spartan citizens, whether on a private or on a public mission to the oracle, to free Athens.[5] (2) Since the same message was always being declared to the Spartans, they sent Ankhimolios son of Aster, who was renowned among his fellow-citizens, with an army to drive the Peisistratidai out of Athens, although they had particularly close ties of hospitality with the Peisistratidai – they gave the affairs of the god more weight than those of men. The expedition was sent by sea. (3) Ankhimolios brought his ships into Phaleron and disembarked his army. The Peisistratidai had learnt of this in advance and summoned an auxiliary force from Thessaly, which had an alliance with them.[6] The Thessalians agreed on joint action and despatched to them on request 1,000 cavalry and their own king, Kineas of Kondaia. Since the Peisistratidai had these allied troops, they devised the following strategem. (4) They cut down the trees on the plain of Phaleron and made this area suitable for horses, then launched their cavalry against the army. They fell on and destroyed Ankhimolios himself and many other Spartans, and drove the survivors back to their ships. That was the end of the first expedition from Sparta. The burial place of Ankhimolios in Attike is at Alopeke,[7] near the temple of Herakles in Kynosarges.

64 Later the Spartans prepared a larger force and sent it not by sea this time but overland against Athens. They appointed king Kleomenes, son of Anaxandrides, general of the army.[8] (2) The Thessalian cavalry made the first contact with the invaders of Attike, but fled after a brief engagement. They lost more than forty men and those remaining alive withdrew by as direct a route as they could for Thessaly. Kleomenes arrived in the city with those Athenians who wished to be free and began to besiege the tyrants, who were confined within the Pelargic wall.[9] *65* Since they had not expected to be making a siege and the Peisistratidai were well stocked with food and drink, the Spartans would not have taken the Peisistratidai and would have departed for Sparta after besieging them for a few days. But at this point an accident occurred which was disastrous for one side and beneficial to the other. The children of the Peisistratidai were captured as they were being secretly moved to safety outside the country.[10] (2) When this happened all the plans of the Peisistratidai were thrown into confusion and they surrendered in return for their children on the Athenians' terms, namely that they would depart from Attike within five days. (3) Then they departed for Sigeion on the Skamander,[11] having ruled Athens for thirty-six years.[12] By origin they were Pylians, descendants of Neleus, being of the same family as Kodros and Melanthos, who had been kings of

Athens in earlier times, although they were foreigners. (4) This origin explains why Hippokrates gave his son the name Peisistratos, in memory of Nestor's son Peisistratos. (5) In this way Athens was liberated from the tyrants.[13]

Notes

1 Back in chapter 55 [**72**].

2 For the leadership of the Alkmeonidai among the exiles see Herodotos 1.64.3 [**60**] and 6.123–4 [**102**]. The stress on the native Athenian standing of the Alkmeonidai may be to counteract a tradition that they came from the Peloponnese (Pausanias 2.18.9) or to contrast them with the Peisistratidai, who were proud of their Peloponnesian origin (see 5.65.3–4 below).

3 Herodotos presumably means the deme Paionidai, south of Parnes; in that case, 'above Paionidai' is an accurate description of Leipsydrion.

4 The temple of Apollon at Delphi had been burnt down in 548/7 BC and its replacement was financed by subscriptions collected from all areas of Greece and even from Egypt (see Herodotos 2.180). Philokhoros (*FGrH* 328 F 115) asserts that the Alkmeonidai did not complete the temple until after their return to Athens and the archaeological evidence is not inconsistent with this. The Amphiktyonic League, whose Council is referred to here, was a powerful religious association controlling particularly the temple of Demeter near Thermopylai and later the temple of Apollon at Delphi: see J. A. O. Larsen, *OCD*[2] s.v. Amphictionies.

5 *Athenaion Politeia* 19.4 [**79**] does not mention bribery, but attributes the Alkmeonid influence to their generosity. Plutarch (*Moralia* 860c–d) denies Herodotos's charge of bribery. Apparently the Alkmeonidai made a lot of money out of the building contract at Delphi (*Athenaion Politeia* 19.4). The temple at Delphi received some large gifts in this period. The Athenians, according to Herodotos, later believed that the Pythia was bribed by the Alkmeonidai. But the close connection with the priests over the rebuilding is sufficient to explain the influence of the Alkmeonidai. In gratitude the Alkmeonidai gave the temple a marble pediment in front instead of the limestone one specified in the contract. This chronology is disputed by W. G. Forrest, *GRBS* 10 (1969) 277–86, who believes that the new temple was well advanced before the overthrow of the tyrants in 511/10 BC. He also accepts (pp. 280–1) Schweighäuser's emendation of the opening phrase of chapter 63 from 'According to the Athenians' to 'According to the Spartans'. However, the intensity of conflict between the Alkmeonidai and their factional rivals is sufficient to explain a dominant Athenian tradition, faithfully recorded by Herodotos, that the Alkmeonidai had bribed the priestess at Delphi. (For further criticism of the change from 'Athenians' to 'Spartans' see K. H. Kinzl, *RhM* 118 [1975] 193–204 at 194–5 n. 8 and R. Develin, in J. W. Eadie and J. Ober [eds], *The Craft of the Ancient Historian: Essays in Honor of Chester G. Starr* [Lanham, Maryland 1985] 125–39 at 127–8.)

The Pythia was an old woman of Delphi who gave ecstatic prophecies to the temple's clients under the inspiration of Apollon and in his name. She was available for the high-class service of ecstatic prophecy on only nine days of the year. The enquirer, having reached the front of the stream of clients and having taken part in rather expensive ritual, received a response (in verse or prose) from the Pythia, who was seated on a tripod. There was an alternative method of divination, by means of lots, available at more frequent intervals. On the procedure for consulting the oracle at Delphi see H. W. Parke and D. E. W. Wormell, *The Delphic Oracle* (Oxford 1956) 1.17–45, H. W. Parke, *Greek Oracles* (London 1967) 72–89 and J. Fontenrose, *The Delphic Oracle: Its Responses and Operations* (Berkeley 1978) 196–228 (who argues that the Pythia spoke directly and intelligibly to the client and thus treats the consultation reported in Plutarch, *Moralia* 438a–b as exceptional: pp. 197, 208, 219, 226–7); on Alkmeonid influence at Delphi see H. W. Parke and D. E. W. Wormell, op. cit. 1.144–50 and W. G. Forrest, op. cit. and in *CAH*[2] 3.3.316–18. For a recent attempt to suggest that the Alkmeonidai used vase scenes connecting Herakles with Delphi to promote their political position before Peisistratos came to power, that Peisistratos took over and adopted the Herakles theme while tyrant, and that the Alkmeonidai introduced into art other Herakles stories, also sited in Delphi, for the first time after the fall of the tyrants, see D. J. R. Williams, in F. Lissarrague and F. Thelamon (eds), *Image et céramique grecque: Actes du Colloque de Rouen 25–26 novembre 1982* (Rouen 1983) 131–40, especially 136–40 (with much sceptical comment recorded from the subsequent discussion at 183–5).

6 The Peisistratid *summakhia* with the Thessalians, in other words, produced troops (who, however, fled early: 5.64.2), but the ties of *xenia* with the Spartans (reiterated by Herodotos at 5.90.1 [**95**] and 5.91.2; see note 8 on [**95**]) did not prevent a Spartan attack.

7 Herodotos gives the location in terms of what was in his time a deme. This aside in turn enables us to locate the deme Alopeke just outside the city wall to the south-east of the city centre (see, for example, *Chiron* 14 [1984] 19 and n. 64, and the map on p. 150). P. J. Bicknell (*Historia* 19 [1970] 130–1) suggests that, since the Alkmeonidai were prominent in Alopeke, some members of that family may have arranged a decent burial for Ankhimolios in their deme. It is, however, unlikely that any of Kleisthenes's relations were resident in Attike at the time of the first Spartan attack. Hence Ankhimolios might have been reburied after the overthrow of the tyrants.

8 Sparta had a king from each of two royal families; hence one had to be appointed general for a particular expedition. Kleomenes was the king from the Agiad house and reigned from before 519 to about 491 BC.

9 This was presumably the Mycenaean wall around the Akropolis; parts of it still survive. See R. J. Hopper, *The Acropolis* (London 1971) 25 (plan), 26 (photograph), 27–8.

10 So *Athenaion Politeia* 19.6 [**79**]. On the children of the Peisistratidai see Thucydides 6.55.1 [**69**].

11 For the Peisistratid interest in Sigeion compare Herodotos 5.94 [**95**].

12 Herodotos has thirty-six years as against Aristotle's thirty-five (*Politics* 1315b 31–4) because the historian considers Hippias's sole rule as four years (5.55 [**72**]) rather than a little over three (as Thucydides 6.59.4 [**78**]).

13 For the rest of this chapter see Chapter V, pp. 138–9 below [**80**].

Xenia

78 *Thucydides 6.59*

59 Such was the way in which the conspiracy of Harmodios and Aristogeiton had its origin in a lover's resentment and the reckless act of daring sprang from a moment of panic. (2) The Athenians experienced a harsher tyranny after this. Hippias, now more fearful, killed many of the citizens and at the same time began to look outside Athens for a place where he might obtain safe refuge in the event of a revolution. (3) At least he, although an Athenian, subsequently gave his daughter Arkhedike in marriage to a Lampsakene,[1] Aiantides son of Hippoklos the tyrant of Lampsakos, realising that they had great influence with king Dareios. Her tomb is in Lampsakos and bears this inscription.

Under this dust lies Arkhedike, her father Hippias
  Most illustrious among the Greeks of his time.
Though her father, husband, brothers and sons were tyrants
  Her mind was not raised to the sin of presumption.

(4) Hippias ruled as tyrant of Athens for three more years. He was stopped in the fourth[2] by the Spartans and, of Athenians in exile, the Alkmeonidai. He went under an agreement to Sigeion[3] and to Aiantides at Lampsakos, and thence to king Dareios. From there he set out for Marathon twenty years later when, as an old man, he campaigned with the Persians.[4]

Notes

1 This marriage alliance, from which Hippias later benefited (6.59.4 below), represented a reversal of foreign policy. Lampsakos, a city on the eastern shore near the northern end of the Hellespont, was a traditional enemy of the Chersonese (Herodotos 6.37–8), where the Peisistratid tyrants had sent members of the Philaid family (Herodotos 6.35, 6.39.1 [**98**]). As Thucydides says here, Hippias realised that the Lampsakenes had great influence with the Persian king (cf. M. E. White, in J. A. S. Evans [ed.], *Polis and Imperium: Studies in Honour of Edward Togo Salmon* [Toronto 1974] 81–95 at 88–9). Hippoklos may have been set up as tyrant by the Persians; certainly he joined Dareios on his expedition across the Danube and opposed Miltiades's plan to cut off Dareios's army (Herodotos 4.138.1).

2 511/10 BC.

3 At this time Sigeion, on the Asian mainland and near the entrance to the Hellespont, was under Peisistratid control: see Herodotos 5.94.1 [**95**].

4 Thucydides actually says 'in the twentieth year'. Since he is unlikely to be specifying a precise period of nineteen years between Hippias's move to

Dareios's court and the battle of Marathon in 490 BC or between Hippias's departure from Athens and the start of the Marathon campaign, he is probably speaking in round numbers, as we would say 'twenty years later, when he was an old man . . .'.

79 Athenaion Politeia *19*

19 The natural outcome of this episode[1] was that the tyranny became much harsher. For the vengeance Hippias exacted for his brother, executing many and banishing others, made him a universally distrusted, and hence vindictive, man. (2) About three years after the death of Hipparkhos, when the situation in the city was unfavourable, he began to fortify Mounikhia[2] with the intention of taking up residence there. While he was engaged on this task he was expelled by Kleomenes, king of the Lakedaimonians, because the Spartans had repeatedly received oracles telling them to overthrow the tyranny.[3] The cause of these oracles was as follows. (3) The exiles, who were headed by the Alkmeonidai, were unable to effect their return by their own strength and failed in all their attempts. In one of these abortive attempts, they fortified Leipsydrion in the country below Mount Parnes.[4] Some reinforcements joined them from the city, but they were besieged by the tyrants and forced to surrender. This gave rise to one of the drinking songs which was popular after the disaster:

Ah, Leipsydrion, betrayer of friends,
What warriors brave you destroyed!
Noble of birth, at that hour they showed
The qualities their forefathers bestowed.

(4) Having failed, then, in all other methods, they gained the contract to build the temple at Delphi and thereby acquired ample funds to enlist the help of the Spartans. Every time the Lakedaimonians consulted the oracle, the Pythia put pressure on them to free Athens,[5] to the point where she finally convinced the Spartan citizens to do it, despite the ties of hospitality which bound them to the Peisistratidai. No less a contribution to the Spartan decision was made by the alliance which the Peisistratidai had contracted with the Argives.[6] (5) First, then, the Spartans sent Ankhimolos[7] with an expeditionary force by sea. But he was defeated and killed, owing to the arrival of Kineas of Thessaly

Good Summ

with 1,000 cavalry to support the Peisistratidai. Their anger increased by this result, the Spartans sent their king, Kleomenes, by land with a larger force. He defeated the Thessalian cavalry as they barred his entry into Attike, shut up Hippias within the so-called Pelargic wall, and began to besiege him with the assistance of the Athenians.

(6) During the siege, it happened that the sons of the Peisistratidai were captured in an attempt to slip out. Upon their capture the Peisistratidai agreed to surrender in return for the safety of their children. They were allowed five days to remove their personal belongings and then they handed over the Akropolis to the Athenians. This took place in the arkhonship of Harpaktides,[8] the sons of Peisistratos having retained the tyranny for about seventeen years after their father's death. The whole length of the tyranny, including their father's rule, was forty-nine years.[9]

Notes

1 The murder of Hipparkhos is described in the previous chapter [**75**]. In this chapter the author briefly follows Herodotos's account [**77**] of the overthrow of the tyrants, but there are few verbal echoes. One is the use of προφέρειν for the pressure applied by the Pythia (Herodotos 5.63.1, *Athenaion Politeia* 19.4), perhaps by way of an oracular command or injunction. Another is the closeness of 'the sons of the Peisistratidai were captured in an attempt to slip out' (19.6) to 'the children of the Peisistratidai were captured as they were being secretly moved to safety outside the country' (Herodotos 5.65.1).

2 Mounikhia was a steep outcrop on the Peiraieus peninsula between the open beach at Phaleron (cf. Herodotos 5.63.3 [**77**]) and the main harbour on the west at Peiraieus. If Hippias controlled the sea, he could use the small harbour on the east of the peninsula for supplies while defending his family from land attack by the fortifications around his base.

3 The expulsion took place in 511/10 BC (cf. *Athenaion Politeia* 19.6 below). It is not clear why the author should alternate between 'Lakedaimonioi' and 'Lakones' here and in *Athenaion Politeia* 19.4. The one use of 'Spartiatai' (Spartan citizens in the strict sense) is in connection with their ties of hospitality with the Peisistratidai (see *Athenaion Politeia* 19.4 and note 6 below).

4 The papyrus says ὑπέρ, 'above' or 'beyond' Parnes, but the phrase 'below Parnes' occurs in a lexicon (*Etymologicon Magnum* 361.31) and that supports the correction of 'above' to 'below' by J. H. Wright (*HSCP* 3 [1892] 54 n. 2); this makes our author's location of Leipsydrion consistent with that of Herodotos (5.62.2 [**77**] with note 3).

5 See Herodotos 5.62.2–5.63.1 [**77**] with notes 4–5.

6 Here we have an indication of the importance in Greek inter-state relations of *xenia*, alluded to in 'ties of hospitality' above, and of *philia*, 'friendship' or 'alliance'. The latter relationship may be nearly as significant as that denoted by

the Roman counterpart, *amicitia*. The Spartans and the Argives were traditionally hostile to one another. Now Sparta abandons her *xenia* with the Peisistratidai when the latter form a *philia* with the Argives (cf. *Athenaion Politeia* 17.4 [**61**] and note 6 on Herodotos 5.63.2–3 [**77**]).

7 This spelling of the Spartan commander's name may be preferable to 'Ankhimolios' in Herodotos 5.63.2–4 [**77**].

8 511/10 BC.

9 Compare *Athenaion Politeia* 17.1 [**61**] with note 13 and see note 3 on [**55**].

V

KLEISTHENES

The struggle between Kleisthenes and Isagoras

It seems that after the overthrow of the tyrants the noble families expected the business of politics to continue in the same way as it had before Peisistratos succeeded in establishing himself as tyrant (Chapter III). The family which was so persistent in seeking to expel the tyrants, the Alkmeonidai, were at this time led by Kleisthenes, the son of the Megakles who had alternately collaborated with and opposed Peisistratos (Chapter III, pp. 91–9). Kleisthenes, having been arkhon in 525/4 BC (Chapter IV, pp. 111–12), was now a senior member of the Areopagos – even though he had been in exile for much of the intervening period. His great rival was Isagoras, from a family which Herodotos [**80**] says was famous but does not even name. The faction of Isagoras emerged as victorious and the symbol of their success may have been the election to the arkhonship of 508/7 BC of Isagoras himself or another member of his family with the same name. Kleisthenes, who came from a family which had been willing to bribe the priestess at Delphi (Chapter IV, pp. 130–7), had a brilliant idea: incorporation of the common people, who had previously been spurned by the Alkmeonidai and every other noble family, into his faction. His success in gaining the adhesion of the lower classes enabled him to pass his tribal reorganisation (and presumably the other changes he made). And this in turn enabled him to overcome his opponents. Isagoras's response to the Alkmeonid success was to call in the Spartan army, under the same king Kleomenes who had driven out the tyrant family from Athens. When the use of force failed, Isagoras had no choice but to leave the country.

80 *Herodotos 5.65.5–5.67.1, 5.69–5.70, 5.72.1–5.73.1*

(5) . . . I shall now relate all that is worth recounting of what the Athenians did and suffered after their liberation from the tyrants and before the Ionian revolt from Dareios and the arrival of

Aristagoras of Miletos in Athens to ask for their help.[1]

66 Athens had been great before[2] and grew greater after being liberated from the tyrants. There were two powerful men in Athens,[3] Kleisthenes the Alkmeonid, who is reported to have persuaded the Pythia,[4] and Isagoras son of Teisandros, who belonged to a famous family, though I cannot tell the history of it. His relatives, however, sacrifice to Karian Zeus. (2) These men were engaged in a struggle for power and Kleisthenes, who was losing,[5] formed an alliance with the common people.[6] Then he distributed the Athenians into ten tribes instead of four, dispensing with the names of the sons of Ion – Geleon, Aigikores, Argades and Hoples – and devising names taken from other heroes, all of native origin except Aias. He added the alien Aias because he was a neighbour and ally.[7] *67* This Kleisthenes acted in this matter, it seems to me, in imitation of his maternal grandfather, Kleisthenes the tyrant of Sikyon . . . .[8]

69 That is what the Sikyonian Kleisthenes had done. The Athenian Kleisthenes, who was the son of this Sikyonian's daughter and was named after him, imitated his namesake Kleisthenes, it seems to me, by despising the Ionians and refusing to let the Athenians have the same tribes as the Ionians. (2) For when he had completely gained for his own faction the common people in Athens, who had previously been spurned, he changed the names of the tribes and increased their number. He instituted ten Phularkhoi instead of four and distributed the demes among the ten tribes.[9] Having secured the adhesion of the common people he easily overcame his opponents.[10] *70* Isagoras in turn lost ground and contrived the following response. He summoned Kleomenes the Spartan, with whom he had formed ties of hospitality during the siege of the Peisistratidai; it was alleged that Kleomenes had had sexual intercourse with Isagoras's wife.[11] (2) First Kleomenes sent a messenger to Athens and tried to expel Kleisthenes and many other Athenians with him, describing them as 'accursed'. The messenger and proclamation were sent on the instruction of Isagoras, for the Alkmeonidai and the members of their faction were accused of the bloodshed which led to the label 'accursed', whereas he himself and his supporters had no connection with it . . . .[12]

72 When Kleomenes sent instructions and tried to expel Kleisthenes and the 'accursed', Kleisthenes himself left the country secretly.[13] But Kleomenes nevertheless arrived in Athens with a small force and drove out as 'accursed' 700 Athenian families[14] which were suggested to him by Isagoras. After this he tried to dissolve the Council and entrust the government to 300 partisans of Isagoras.[15] (2) When the Council opposed this and refused to co-operate,[16] Kleomenes, Isagoras and his partisans occupied the Akropolis. But the rest of the Athenians united and besieged them for two days. On the third, all of them who were Spartans left the country under a truce. (3) So the prophecy given to Kleomenes was fulfilled . . . .[17] (4) . . . The Athenians imprisoned the others and put them to death, including Timesitheos of Delphi, about whose deeds of strength and courage I could tell a great deal. *73* After the imprisonment and execution of these men the Athenians recalled Kleisthenes and the 700 families banished by Kleomenes and sent messengers to Sardis with the intention of making an alliance with the Persians, since they knew that Kleomenes and the Spartans were in a state of war with them.[18]

Notes

1 This sentence comes immediately after the passage 5.62.1–5.65.5 [**77**] on the expulsion of the Peisistratidai.

2 On the widespread connections of Athens under the Peisistratid tyranny see Herodotos 1.61.3–4 [**54**] with note 10, 5.94 [**95**] and *Athenaion Politeia* 17.3 [**61**] with note 16.

3 One could translate: 'Kleisthenes the Alkmeonid and Isagoras son of Teisandros were dynasts (*edunasteuon*)'.

4 Herodotos told the story a few pages earlier (see [**77**] with, especially, note 5). There, however, he attributed the bribery to the Alkmeonidai in general. It is only in this clause that he makes Kleisthenes the leader of the Alkmeonidai at Delphi.

5 *Athenaion Politeia* 21.1 [**81**] offers a detail which may mark the victory of Isagoras: he (or a younger relative of the same name: cf. D. J. McCargar, *Phoenix* 28 [1974] 275–81) was elected to the arkhonship of 508/7 BC. See further note 11 on [**81**].

6 Literally 'took the *demos* into his *hetaireia*'. *Hetaireia* was, at least in the late fifth and fourth centuries, a common term for a political association. This sentence indicates that Kleisthenes associated himself with the *demos* only as an afterthought.

7 Aias (stem *Aiant-*), known to English readers under the Latinised form 'Ajax', gave his name (*eponumia*, eponym) to the tribe Aiantis. He was associated with the Athenians in the *Iliad* (2.557–8) and was the hero of Salamis, the large island off the west coast of Attike in whose strait the famous sea-battle of 480 BC took place. For the story that Solon inserted verse 558 in the Catalogue of Ships in *Iliad* 2, see note 1 on [**100**].

8 Herodotos's insertion of 'in my opinion' or 'it seems to me' (here and in 5.69.1) may reveal that he was reluctant to state the real motivation of Kleisthenes, perhaps because it would offend the Alkmeonidai. There follows a digression on Kleisthenes of Sikyon (5.67.1–5.68.2), who changed the names of the Dorian tribes there, so that they should not be the same as the tribes of Argos.

9 Kleisthenes apparently moved his proposals as a private citizen in the Assembly. He did not have a special office, apart from being a long-standing member (since 524/3 BC; see [**64**]) of the Areopagos (so H. T. Wade-Gery, *CQ* 27 [1933] 17 = *Essays* 136; cf. Rhodes 241, 248 and M. Ostwald, in *CAH*^{2} 4.306). For more detailed commentary and explanation see the notes on [**82**] below. Phularkhoi means 'tribal leaders'; later it referred to cavalry commanders.

10 See note 4 on [**82**].

11 This is hardly an adequate explanation of the friendship. Perhaps it is a piece of Alkmeonid scandal (so Macan on this passage).

12 Note the factional connotations of the language in this sentence (I change the translations slightly to bring out these connotations): 'the Alkmeonidai and those who took their side in the *stasis*', 'Isagoras himself and his *philoi*'. Similarly earlier: 'These men were engaged in *stasis* concerning power' (5.66.2), 'he was far superior to his opponents in *stasis*' (5.69.2). Chapter 71 [**8**] tells the story of Kylon in order to explain the labelling of some Athenians as 'accursed'.

13 Naturally, Kleisthenes would not have accepted the label 'accursed', but he presumably realised the threat to himself; compare Peisistratos's withdrawal after his alliance with the Alkmeonidai broke down (Herodotos 1.61.2 [**54**]). Actual force arrived soon afterwards and drove out many of Kleisthenes's supporters.

14 These must be households or extended families, not clans. But the number 700 seems too high for expulsion by 'a small force' and for effective opposition to be mounted by the remaining Athenians against Kleomenes and Isagoras (5.72.2 below).

15 Again the language of factional struggle is prominent. The partisans (*stasiotai*, 5.72.1–2) of Isagoras were sufficiently numerous and competent to man a Council of Three Hundred and, when challenged, to seize the Akropolis. The participle that denotes the opposition of the existing Council (see next note), *antistatheisa*, is related to the noun for opponents in *stasis* (*antistasiotai*, 5.69.2).

16 This was probably the Council of the Areopagos, since if there was a Council of Four Hundred instituted by Solon, it is unlikely to have had the strength to organise resistance. The Kleisthenic Council of Five Hundred (see pp. 146–63 below) had probably not yet been instituted; even if it had, it would hardly have been powerful enough at this stage to resist Kleomenes after numerous families that supported Kleisthenes had been expelled. Compare *Athenaion Politeia* 20.3 [**81**] with note 6 and Hignett 93–5, 128 and 146.

17 Athene's warning to Kleomenes is recounted. Herodotos's narrative here leaves the impression that Isagoras was held in Athens, but he was to appear as an agent in a later attempt by Kleomenes to intervene in Athenian internal

affairs (5.74 [**95**]).

18 The Athenians (presumably by a decision of the Assembly) are thus the first Greeks to seek Persian intervention in internal Greek affairs. Artaphernes, governor of Sardis, refused an alliance except on terms of Athenian submission to Persia. It is a reasonable conclusion that Kleisthenes was behind this abortive embassy to Sardis. G. H. R. Horsley (*Museum Philologum Londiniense* 7 [1986] 99–107) links the embassy with an anecdote in Cicero, *On the Laws* 2.41 about Kleisthenes's deposit of money in the temple of Hera on Samos in trust for his daughters. He suggests that Kleisthenes was actually a member of the embassy to Sardis and suffered a radical political eclipse on his return. In any event, Kleisthenes vanishes from history at this point. Probably he simply died a natural death – something not spectacular enough to be included in Herodotos's narrative. He would have been at least 55 years old in 500 BC since he was arkhon (minimum age taken to be 30) in 525/4 BC (cf. Davies, *APF* 375). There is no need to suppose that he was a victim of his own institution of ostracism (see pp. 173–86), as Ailianos (*Historical Miscellanies* 13.24) alleged, or that he chose to reside outside Attike, like Solon (see *Athenaion Politeia* 11.1 [**47**], Plutarch, *Solon* 25.6 [**50**]) and other legislators (R. D. Cromey, *Historia* 28 [1979] 129–47). Unlike Solon, he was not idealised in subsequent Greek literature; indeed, he is mentioned comparatively rarely: see P. Lévêque and P. Vidal-Naquet, *Clisthène l'Athénien* [Annales Littéraires de l'Université de Besançon, 65] (Paris 1964) 117–22.

81 Athenaion Politeia *20.1–21.2*

20 After the overthrow of the tyranny a factional struggle broke out between Isagoras son of Teisandros, who was a supporter of the tyrants,[1] and Kleisthenes, who belonged to the family of the Alkmeonidai. Losing in the political clubs,[2] Kleisthenes attached the people to his following by handing over the state to the common people.[3] (2) Isagoras, falling behind in power, summoned back Kleomenes, who was bound to him by ties of hospitality, and persuaded him jointly 'to drive out the curse', since the Alkmeonidai were believed to be among the 'accursed'.[4] (3) Kleisthenes thereupon withdrew, [while Kleomenes arrived] with a few men and drove out as 'accursed' 700 Athenian households.[5] Having accomplished this, he tried to dissolve the Council[6] and set up Isagoras and 300 of his supporters as controllers of the city. But when the Council opposed this and the common people had been assembled, Kleomenes and Isagoras with their followers took refuge in the Akropolis. There the people settled down and besieged them for two days; but on the third day they permitted Kleomenes and all those with him to depart under a truce,[7] and they recalled Kleisthenes and the other exiles. (4) The people now gained control of affairs and Kleisthenes was their leader and champion of the people.[8] For it could scarcely be disputed that the major role in the expulsion of the tyrants was played by the Alkmeonidai, who were engaged in conflict with them for most of the time. (5) Even before, Kedon of the Alkmeonidai had made an attack on the tyrants.[9] Hence another drinking song, in his honour:

> Fill the cups yet again, boy, for Kedon;
> In this matter do not be remiss.
> If a toast must be given to any,
> Let the good and the brave not be missed.[10]

21 The factors mentioned above were the basis of the people's confidence in Kleisthenes. Now that he was leader of the common people, three years after the overthrow of the tyrants, in the arkhonship of Isagoras,[11] (2) he introduced his first change.

Notes

1 This clause is one of only four elements in *Athenaion Politeia* 20.1–3 that do not come from Herodotos. See H. T. Wade-Gery, *CQ* 27 (1933) 17–19 = *Essays* 136–9, who places alongside these sections the parallel portions from Herodotos 5.66.1–2, 70.1–2, 72.1–2, 73.1. Even if there were supporters of the tyrants in Athens at a later date (cf. *Athenaion Politeia* 22.4 [**91**] and note 4), Isagoras is unlikely to have been one because he tried to set up, with Kleomenes's help, a Council of Three Hundred (20.3 below). Indeed such an oligarchy would be more likely to gain Kleomenes's support than a tyranny, since Kleomenes led in the expulsion of the Peisistratidai (*Athenaion Politeia* 19.5 [**79**]). To eliminate the inconsistency within *Athenaion Politeia* 20.1–3 von Fritz and Kapp translate 'a former supporter of the tyrants'; this is possible, but the structure of the Greek implies that just as Kleisthenes was a member of the Alkmeonid family so Isagoras was a supporter of the tyrants at the time of the *stasis*. Wade-Gery suggests that this new element is an inference based on the narrative and connected with what is said of the Alkmeonidai in 20.4. However I do not think the author would introduce an inference which clearly conflicts with 20.3, as well as with Herodotos 5.70.1 [**80**] (Isagoras was a *xenos* of Kleomenes and assisted in the overthrow of the tyrants) and 5.92.1 (the Spartan record of opposition to tyranny). Rather it is an element of Alkmeonid propaganda, prepared for the impending ostracism vote (chapter 22 [**91**]); see *JHS* 90 (1970) 180, 182–3.

2 The word is *hetaireiai*; these associations were a normal medium of political activity (cf. note 6 on [**80**]). For a brief description of their role in classical Athens, see B. R. I. Sealey, *Historia* 9 (1960) 155–6 or W. R. Connor, *The New Politicians of Fifth-Century Athens* (Princeton 1971) 25–9. 'In the political

clubs' is not in Herodotos, but it is a natural expansion of Herodotos's statement (5.66.2 [**80**]; see note 6 on that passage) that 'Kleisthenes, who was losing, took the common people (*demos*) into his *hetaireia*.' In order to indicate the change of vocabulary – though the two words seem close to interchangeable in *Athenaion Politeia* 20–1 (cf. note 2 on [**18**] and note 2 on [**32**]) – I have translated *to plethos* as 'the common people' and *ho demos* as 'the people' in [**81**] and [**84**], though I have preferred 'the common people' for *ho demos*, in the interests of clarity, in Herodotos 5.66.2 and 5.69.2 [**80**].

3 This phrase replaces Herodotos's account of Kleisthenes's reforms together with those of his maternal grandfather, whom Herodotos suggests Kleisthenes was imitating (5.66.2–5.69.2 [**80**]); it also allows the author to postpone his account of Kleisthenes's reforms until the next chapter. E. David has recently argued that the phrase has no such function; rather, Herodotos describes a preliminary stage of Kleisthenes's reforms and the *Athenaion Politeia* in chapter 21 describes the reforms in their final form (*Classical Antiquity* 5 [1986] 1–13). But this view gives insufficient weight to the confinement of Herodotos's interest to Kleisthenes's political struggle against Isagoras (ibid. 3).

Politeia (here rendered 'the state') can mean 'citizenship, franchise' as in *Athenaion Politeia* 13.5 [**52**]; but *to plethos*, 'the common people', cannot refer only to those who had lost it (cf. 13.5, and Aristotle, *Politics* 1275b 34–9 [**88**], on which basis some translate 'giving back citizenship to those who had lost it'). For *politeia* in the sense of 'constitution, government, state', see *Athenaion Politeia* 2.2 [**17**], 5.1–2 [**18**], 8.4 [**42**], 9.1 [**46**], etc.

4 For the origin of this curse, see Herodotos 5.71 [**8**], Thucydides 1.126 [**9**] and other passages in Chapter I, pp. 17–26. The author of the *Athenaion Politeia* has already given an account of Kylon in chapter 1 [**10**] and, unlike Herodotos [**80**], does not offer an explanation of the curse in this passage.

5 The word for 'households' is *oikiai*, that is, families in the narrow sense. The word for families in the sense of all who claimed to be descended from a single ancestor is *gene*, 'clans'; the *genos* of the Alkmeonidai is mentioned in 20.1. The words 'while Kleomenes arrived' are inserted from Herodotos 5.72.1 [**80**].

6 So Herodotos 5.72.1–2 [**80**]. It is unlikely that the Council referred to is Kleisthenes's new Council of Five Hundred (see pp. 146–63), since its institution depended on the completion of the tribal reorganisation. Some scholars (e.g. Rhodes 246) have suggested that it is the Solonian Council of Four Hundred. Whether the latter existed or not the reference is most likely to be to the Council of the Areopagos, which is described as a 'Council' (*boule*) in *Athenaion Politeia* 3.6 [**1**], 8.2 [**42**], 23.1 and elsewhere. The Areopagos, and not the Councils of Four Hundred and Five Hundred, would have been sufficiently permanent and would have contained a sufficient accumulation of politically experienced men to organise resistance to a military force. A major thrust was the assembling of the common people – the verb 'had been assembled' is definitely passive – and this could have been achieved by the influence which ex-arkhon clan leaders in the Areopagos held over their retainers. See further note 16 on Herodotos 5.72.2 [**80**] and Hignett 93–5, 128 and 146.

7 Herodotos (5.72.2–5.73.1 [**80**]) says that all who were Lakedaimonians were

allowed to leave the country but the rest were imprisoned and executed. Yet this is contradicted in 5.74.1 [**95**], where the leader Isagoras is said to have escaped with Kleomenes. That Isagoras lived to make a second attempt on Athens is confirmed by an ancient commentator on Aristophanes, *Lysistrate* 273, who mentions a bronze tablet set up on the Akropolis that listed those condemned to death on the second occasion. (So H. T. Wade-Gery, *CQ* 27 [1933] 17–18 = *Essays* 136–7.) Hence the *Athenaion Politeia* is preferable to Herodotos [**80**] on this point, even if 'all' is an exaggeration.

8 Literally 'was their leader (*hegemon*) and leader of the people (*prostates tou demou*).' The redundancy indicates that 'leader of the people' was an epithet applied to any patron of the *demos*. Cf. *Athenaion Politeia* 2.2 [**17**] (Solon), 23.3 (Aristeides and Themistokles), 25.1 (Ephialtes), 36.1 (Theramenes) and the list of patrons of the *demos* in 28.1–4.

9 In isolation the Greek might be taken to say 'Even before the Alkmeonidai, however, Kedon had made an attack on the tyrants.' But after the previous sentence it is preferable to take the statement as including Kedon among the Alkmeonidai, even though nothing else is known of him and the name is rare in Athens (so Rhodes 248).

10 The original is an elegiac couplet (dactylic hexameter followed by a pentameter).

11 508/7 BC (see note 2 on [**84**]). This would still be the arkhonship of Isagoras, even though Isagoras had been forced to leave the country after his attempt to use force failed. The election of Isagoras (or a younger relative of the same name: see note 5 on [**80**]) to the eponymous arkhonship for 508/7 BC may have been the incident which showed that Kleisthenes was losing in the normal game of politics (Herodotos 5.66.2 [**80**]; *Athenaion Politeia* 20.1). Kleisthenes may have failed to have his protégé elected as arkhon (Kleisthenes himself had already held the arkhonship in 525/4 BC: see Meiggs and Lewis no. 6, Fragment *c* [**64**]).

* * *

How did Kleisthenes, holding no office but membership of the Areopagos, have his radical proposals put to the vote? Even if Isagoras as arkhon had a chairperson's power to prevent motions being voted on by the Assembly, he would probably have hesitated to take such drastic action in a revolutionary situation. Those who expected to gain from the passing of Kleisthenes's proposals may not have baulked at the use of violence if Isagoras had used his power to prevent the Assembly's voting on them. Compare R. J. Seager, *AJP* 84 (1963) 289 n. 9: 'The question is not a constitutional one; we presume that the followers of Cleisthenes were better equipped than their opponents with the basic weapons of practical democracy, e.g. bench-legs.'

The tribal reorganisation and the Council of Five Hundred

We do not know what Kleisthenes said to the common people in order to win them over to his faction. He can scarcely have spelled out all the details of the tribal reorganisation which in fact was instituted. He need, perhaps, have done no more than assure the common people that he would 'hand over the state' to them (passage [**81**]). But he may have indicated that he would break down the hold which other noble families had on their lower-class supporters by dividing up their blocs of support into several of his new 'tribes'. Perhaps he suggested that cult centres which had been used to strengthen ties of patronage would be isolated politically from the areas from which they drew adherents. (In the event, the people living immediately around a cult centre in the north-east of Attike were forced to associate for political purposes with villages far to the south.) He could have given examples of the 'deme' names which would be used for local communities in the new reorganisation, though the final list of 139 demes may have emerged later, after he or a commission set up under his bill had worked out the details. He probably mentioned that there would be an intermediate level between deme and tribe, called 'trittys' (no doubt understood as 'third', as there were three to a tribe), since this was crucial to the business of separating and associating communities artificially. A trittys was to consist of one or more (generally four to six) demes or local communities. Then Kleisthenes or his commission took a trittys from the city region (which included much farmland), a trittys from the coastal region and a trittys from the inland region, and formed a 'tribe'. (This process is illustrated with respect to three tribes on the map (p. 150), with accompanying explanation.)

The artificiality of this scheme is not mentioned by Herodotos, who does however refer to the demes and to the intention that ten new tribes were to replace for political purposes the four old tribes [**82**]. The role of the trittyes (plural of 'trittys') has to be deduced from the *Athenaion Politeia* [**84**]. This is also our source for the institution of the Council of Five Hundred, replacing Solon's Council of Four Hundred. Each deme sent a quota of representatives, ranging from one to twenty-two, to the Council each year.

82 *Herodotos 5.66.2–5.67.1, 5.69.1–2*

(2) . . . Kleisthenes distributed the Athenians into ten tribes instead of four, dispensing with the names of the sons of Ion – Geleon, Aigikores, Argades and Hoples – and devising names taken from other heroes, all of native origin except Aias. He added the alien Aias because he was a neighbour and ally.[1] *67* This Kleisthenes acted in this matter, it seems to me, in

imitation of his maternal grandfather, Kleisthenes the tyrant of Sikyon . . . .[2]

69 That is what the Sikyonian Kleisthenes had done. The Athenian Kleisthenes, who was the son of this Sikyonian's daughter and was named after him, imitated his namesake Kleisthenes, it seems to me, by despising the Ionians and refusing to let the Athenians have the same tribes as the Ionians. (2) For when he had completely gained for his own faction the common people in Athens, who had previously been spurned, he changed the names of the tribes and increased their number. He instituted ten Phularkhoi instead of four and distributed the demes among the ten tribes.[3] Having secured the adhesion of the common people he easily overcame his opponents.[4]

Notes

1 The method by which Kleisthenes replaced the four old tribes with ten artificial tribes (not in fact kinship groups; but our sources call both the old and the new 'tribes' *phulai*) is described briefly by Herodotos (5.66.2, 5.69.2) and in more detail by the *Athenaion Politeia* (21.2–6 [**84**]). The names of the ten Kleisthenic tribes were: Erekhtheis (I), Aigeis (II), Pandionis (III), Leontis (IV), Akamantis (V), Oineis (VI), Kekropis (VII), Hippothontis (VIII), Aiantis (IX) and Antiokhis (X) (Ps.-Demosthenes 60.27–31, Pausanias 1.5.2–4 and numerous inscriptions). On the choice of Aias as eponymous hero of tribe IX, see note 7 on [**80**].

2 Herodotos's insertion of 'in my opinion' or 'it seems to me' (here and in 5.69.1) may reveal that he was reluctant to state the real motivation of Kleisthenes, perhaps because it would offend the Alkmeonidai (cf. B. R. I. Sealey, *Historia* 9 [1960] 172–3). There follows (5.67.1–5.68.2) a digression on Kleisthenes of Sikyon. The only real parallel between the actions of the Athenian and those of the Sikyonian, on Herodotos's evidence, is the change in the *names* of the tribes. The Sikyonian is said by Herodotos to have changed the names of the Sikyonian tribes so that they were not the same as those of the Argives. The differences in the two policies far outweigh this parallel. Herodotos fails to substantiate the unlikely theory that Kleisthenes introduced major constitutional changes in imitation of his maternal grandfather's actions nearly a century before in another city. One may conclude that this theory is put forward not because Herodotos did not understand Greek politics, but because he did not wish to state Kleisthenes's real motivation. (For my view of Kleisthenes's motivation see note 2 on [**83**].)

3 This translation is based on an emendation (δέκαχα [Lolling] for δέκα), which gives the literal sense 'he distributed the demes in ten groups into the tribes'. The manuscript reading, 'ten' instead of 'in ten groups', has been defended, most recently by E. David, *Classical Antiquity* 5 (1986) 1–13 at 2, 4. But the clause then means literally 'he distributed the demes, ten in number, into the tribes'. This is an awkward way of saying, as D. Whitehead (*The*

Demes of Attica 508/7–ca.250 B.C.: A Political and Social Study [Princeton 1986] 18–19) and others have pointed out, that there were 100 demes and ten were assigned to each tribe. It is highly improbable, moreover, that there were only 100 demes in Kleisthenes's time. There is fifth-century evidence for more than 100 demes. Probably 139 demes go back to Kleisthenes. For lists of demes with their quotas of representatives on the Council of Five Hundred, see Bicknell, *Studies* 7–12, Traill, *Political Organization* 67–70 or D. Whitehead, op. cit. 369–73.

4 This chapter establishes that Kleisthenes formed his alliance with the *demos* for political purposes, and that the additional support of the *demos* enabled him to carry out his tribal reorganisation and overcome his opponents. Thus his constitutional changes had a partisan character.

83 *Aristotle,* Politics *1319b 19–27*

Other devices which are useful in the formation of the extreme type of democracy[1] are similar to those employed by Kleisthenes at Athens, when he wished to strengthen the democracy, and by the founders of popular government at Kyrene. New tribes and phratries should be created in addition to the old; private cults should be reduced in number and made public; every contrivance should be employed so that all mix with each other as much as possible and former loyalties are broken down.[2]

Notes

1 Aristotle means by the extreme type a democracy in which all classes participate. He prefers a democracy restricted to farmers.

2 After an important study of the framework which Kleisthenes imposed on the land of Attike, D. M. Lewis (*Historia* 12 [1963] 22–40) concludes that every increase in our knowledge shows that Kleisthenes worked towards the aim stated by Aristotle in this passage. All agree that Kleisthenes created new tribes – but not new phratries ('brotherhoods'; see *Athenaion Politeia* 21.6 [**84**] and Chapter VI, pp. 191–5) – and that the old tribes lost all importance. Lewis shows that some local cults were detached from the control of powerful aristocratic families and that the old loyalties were thus weakened. Kleisthenes does seem to have been concerned to mix people together, as is asserted here and twice in *Athenaion Politeia* 21.2–3 ([**84**] below). The question is, for whose good? My study of four new tribes concludes that Kleisthenes sought to benefit his own family, the Alkmeonidai; see *Chiron* 14 (1984) 1–41 and the notes on the map (p. 150). He presumably left unaffected his own family's cult centres while weakening the political control over retainers that was derived by other noble families from cult centres (ibid. 9–11, 41).

84 Athenaion Politeia *21*

21 The factors mentioned above[1] were the basis of the people's confidence in Kleisthenes. Now that he was leader of the common people, three years after the overthrow of the tyrants, in the arkhonship of Isagoras,[2] (2) he introduced his first change. This was to group the whole population into ten tribes instead of the old four, with the object of mixing them up so that more might have a share in the franchise.[3] Hence the proverbial saying 'Don't look at the tribes', originally directed against those who wished to scrutinise family backgrounds.[4] (3) Second, he set up a Council of Five Hundred to replace the Council of Four Hundred. It consisted of fifty members from each tribe, whereas there were 100 previously.[5] The reason why Kleisthenes did not organise the people into twelve tribes was that he wished to avoid a division in terms of the trittyes that already existed. For there were twelve trittyes from the four tribes;[6] to have used these would have frustrated a complete redistribution of the common people.[7] (4) He divided the country into thirty parts – ten from the areas about the city, ten from the coastal district, and ten from the interior – each composed of one or more demes. These parts he called trittyes, and he assigned three trittyes by lot to each tribe in such a way that each tribe should have a share in all three regions.[8] Furthermore, those who lived in each of the demes he made fellow demesmen, to prevent newly enfranchised citizens being exposed by the practice of calling people by their father's name. People were to be publicly known by the names of their demes; that is why the Athenians call themselves by the names of their demes. (5) He also instituted Demarchs with responsibilities identical with those of the former Naukraroi, since he replaced the naukraries by the demes.[9] He called some demes after their localities, others after their founders; for not all of them still corresponded with their original localities.[10] (6) However, he allowed everyone to retain his family connections, his phratry and his religious rites according to ancestral custom.[11] The eponymous heroes he established for the ten tribes were formally chosen by the Pythia from a pre-selection of 100 national heroes.[12] (*Notes follow on p. 152.*)

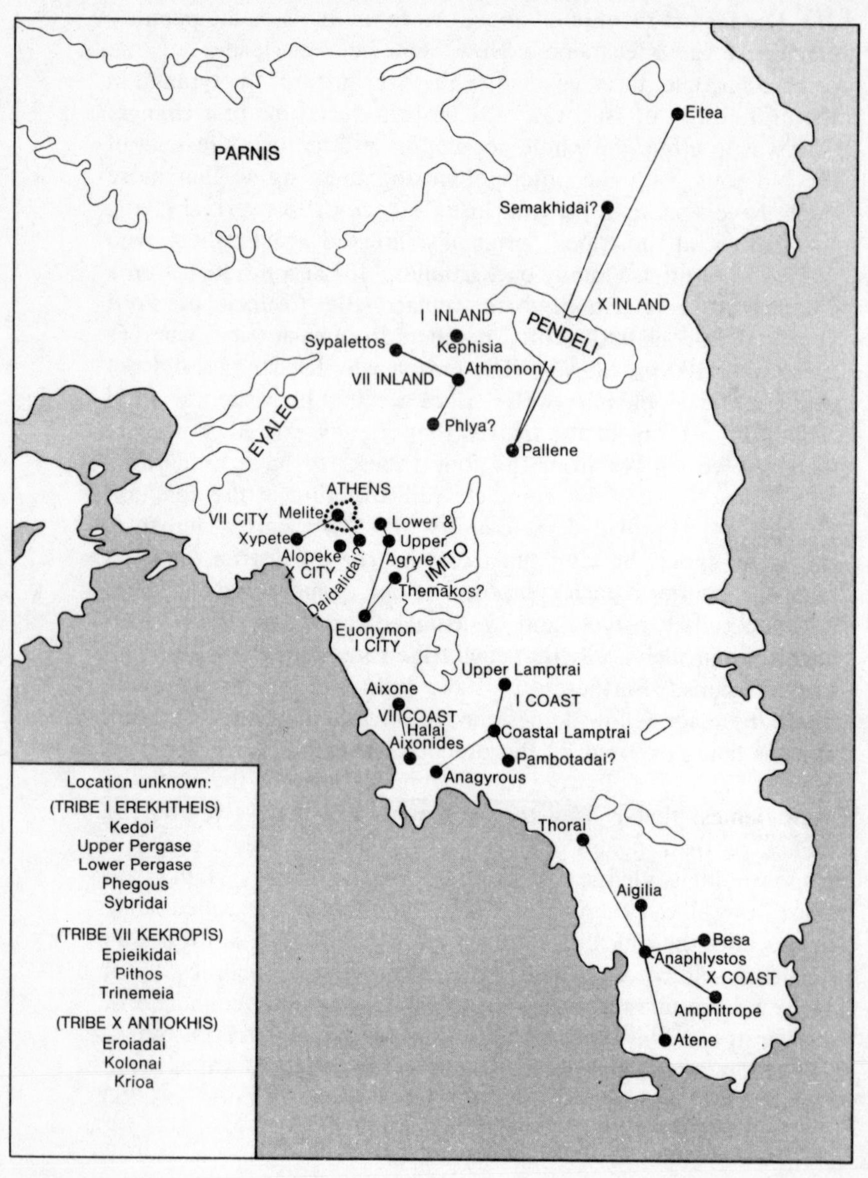
PARNIS
Eitea
Semakhidai?
X INLAND
I INLAND
PENDELI
Sypalettos
Kephisia
Athmonon
VII INLAND
Phlya?
Pallene
EYALEO
ATHENS
Melite
VII CITY
Xypete
Lower &
Upper
Agryle
Alopeke
X CITY
IMITO
Daidalidai?
Themakos?
Euonymon
I CITY
Upper Lamptrai
Aixone
I COAST
VII COAST
Halai
Aixonides
Coastal Lamptrai
Pambotadai?
Anagyrous
Thorai
Aigilia
Besa
Anaphlystos
X COAST
Amphitrope
Atene
Location unknown:
(TRIBE I EREKHTHEIS)
Kedoi
Upper Pergase
Lower Pergase
Phegous
Sybridai
(TRIBE VII KEKROPIS)
Epieikidai
Pithos
Trinemeia
(TRIBE X ANTIOKHIS)
Eroiadai
Kolonai
Krioa

The Reorganisation of Attike into 'Tribes' by Kleisthenes (*see map on facing page*)

At the end of the sixth century Kleisthenes had passed in the Assembly a distribution of Athenian citizens into ten artificial tribes. Erekhtheis (tribe I in the official order), Kekropis (VII) and Antiokhis (X) are illustrated opposite.

Each tribe was composed of three units called trittyes, one trittys from the city region, one from the coastal region, and one from the inland region. The city trittyes of the ten tribes occupied not only the built-up area of Athens but much of the plain on which it was situated, between Eyaleo on the west and Imito on the east. The inland trittyes were sited on the northern part of the same plain and north to Mount Parnis and the border with Boiotia, as well as east and south-east of Athens. The coastal trittyes were situated all around the coast, including the plain of Eleusis west of Eyaleo, but not the coast between Eyaleo and Imito, which was assigned to city trittyes. The trittyes of tribes I, VII, and X are indicated on the map by capitals (e.g. I CITY).

Each trittys comprised one or more demes. The city trittys of tribe X had only one deme, Alopeke. The coastal trittys of the same tribe had six demes in the southern part of Attike stretching towards Cape Sounion.

For the literary evidence describing the construction of these new tribes, see [**82**] and [**84**]. For inscriptional evidence bearing on the assignment of the demes of tribe X to their trittyes see [**86**] with notes. For later literary evidence crucial to the location of the demes along the coast from Aixone (in the coastal trittys of tribe VII) to Atene (in the coastal trittys of tribe X), see [**87**] with notes.

It can be seen from the map that the coastal trittyes of these three tribes, in which the Alkmeonidai – the family of Kleisthenes – can because of their earlier control of the Paralia ('the Coast'; see pp. 86–91) be supposed to have had political ascendancy, were fairly compact. The coastal trittys of tribe VII had just two demes with related names. The coastal trittys of tribe I can be seen as compact, though other demes from the box of unlocated demes may have to be added to this picture. It is fairly certain, however, that the unlocated demes in tribe X belonged to the inland trittys (see note 5 on [**86**]). So the coastal trittys was as indicated on the map. The city trittyes in which the Alkmeonidai can be located and in which they can be thought to have had some influence were also fairly compact (X CITY, with a single deme, was of course maximally compact). By contrast, the inland trittys of tribe X was spread far to the north of Mount Pendeli as well as to the south. It must have been very difficult for the opponents of the Alkmeonidai to organise support in advance of a political meeting.

Notes

1 That is, the major role in the overthrow of the tyrants played by the Alkmeonidai (Herodotos 5.62.2–5.63.1 [**77**]; *Athenaion Politeia* 19.2–4 [**79**], 20.4 [**81**]), probably led by Kleisthenes himself (cf. note 4 on [**80**]), together with Kleisthenes's wooing of the *demos* to his own faction (*Athenaion Politeia* 20.1 [**81**]).

2 508/7 BC. Dionysios of Halikarnassos provides the date by indicating that it was an Olympic year at the beginning of the sixty-eighth Olympiad (*Roman Antiquities* 1.74.6 with 5.1.1).

3 See pp. 165–7 below on the enfranchisement of aliens.

4 Later grammarians and lexicographers offer both a literal meaning 'to distinguish by tribe' (Pollux, Hesykhios) and a developed meaning 'to make too fine a distinction' or 'to examine too closely' (Phrynikhos, the Souda) for *phulokrinein*. But the earliest occurrence of the word in extant Greek literature already provides a transitional context in which both original and later meanings are present. Thucydides (6.18.2) has Alkibiades discourage the examination of racial background, responding in the literal sense of *phulokrinein* to the point by his opponent (6.11.7) that the people in Sicily seeking help are 'barbarians'; but Alkibiades is also urging the Athenians not to be inactive (stop quibbling and get on with the job). Our author is aware that the secondary meaning has developed and apparently indicates that the point of warning people not to examine tribal lists is that it will be a waste of time to make such an investigation now that the old tribes, which established citizenship by birth, have been replaced by tribes based on membership of a deme. Compare Rhodes 250–1 (including the initial comment on *Athenaion Politeia* 21.4, to the effect that the old tribes were based on actual or supposed kinship).

5 The author of the *Athenaion Politeia* believes (8.4 [**42**]) that Solon set up a Council of Four Hundred which had 100 representatives from each of the four old tribes. These two sentences (one sentence in Greek) provide the only explicit evidence that it was Kleisthenes who instituted the Council of Five Hundred. It drew fifty representatives from each of the ten new tribes. For an example of the representation of a tribe in the Council see *IG* II^2 1750 [**86**] with commentary.

6 Moore (p. 237) and Rhodes (p. 251) suggest that the author's logic is defective, since Kleisthenes could have created twelve completely new tribes (as with the ten tribes actually created); but the author apparently believes that use of the twelve trittyes already existing would have been irresistible had Kleisthenes opted for twelve tribes.

7 As this sentence indicates, the new tribes of Kleisthenes represented a complete redistribution of the population for political purposes. There were three 'trittyes' (singular 'trittys') in each of the new tribes, as there had been in each of the old. According to *Athenaion Politeia* 8.3 [**42**] the four old tribes (named after the sons of Ion: Herodotos 5.66.2 [**82**]) were divided into twelve trittyes and forty-eight naukraries. As explained in *Athenaion Politeia* 21.4 the ten Kleisthenic tribes had thirty trittyes. The thirty trittyes were established by dividing Attike into three areas – city, coast and inland – which had no connection with the three regional parties ('coast', 'plain' and 'beyond the

hills') described in Herodotos 1.59.3 **[51]** and *Athenaion Politeia* 13.4–5 **[52]**. Then each of these areas was divided into ten parts, called trittyes, so that there were thirty trittyes altogether. One trittys was selected from the city area, one from the coastal area and one from the interior; these three trittyes made up one new tribe. So each of the ten tribes had one trittys from each of the three areas. See the map on p. 150 for the structure of three of the ten tribes. The maps in Forrest 192–3 and Ehrenberg 95 show the coastal and inland trittyes of all tribes (however, it is misleading to draw boundaries for trittyes or demes; see *BSA* 79 [1984] 304–5). It can be seen that in the case of the tribe Aigeis (II, in the official order) its inland trittys and its coastal trittys were contiguous. But in most cases the tribe consisted of three quite separate areas.

Each trittys, as stated in *Athenaion Politeia* 21.4, was composed of one or more demes. Each deme (except in the city) comprised a village or two, from which the inhabitants went out to work the surrounding land. There were as many as eight or nine demes in some trittyes. The city trittys of the tribe Aiantis, on the other hand, contained only one deme. There was also one deme only in the city trittyes of Pandionis and Antiokhis and the inland trittyes of Oineis and Aiantis. For lists of demes arranged according to tribes (and trittyes, where known), see W. Judeich, *RE* 2 (Stuttgart 1896) 2227–30, A. W. Gomme, *The Population of Athens in the Fifth and Fourth Centuries B.C.* (Oxford 1933) 56–65, Bicknell, *Studies* 7–12 and, most authoritatively, Traill, *Political Organization* 37–54. For further explanation of the Kleisthenic reorganisation see the articles on 'demoi', 'phylai' and 'trittyes' by C. W. J. Eliot, A. W. Gomme and T. J. Cadoux in *OCD*^{2} (Oxford 1970) 329, 830–1 and 1095; or the accounts of Forrest 194–200 and Ehrenberg 93–5. For the view that the tribes of two cities in the north-east of the Peloponnese (Korinth and Phleious) were similarly organised on a regional basis see G. R. Stanton, *Classical Antiquity* 5 (1986) 139–53 (143–5 for the suggestion that Korinth had city, coastal and inland trittyes, and that Kleisthenes may have borrowed the idea from Korinth).

8 It seems that this statement about the use of lot must be rejected because (a) the trittyes varied considerably in size, but (b) the tribes were approximately equal.

(a) The quota of representatives which each deme sent to the Council of Five Hundred in the fourth century is known for most, but not all, demes. There is greater uncertainty about the assignment of demes to city, coastal and inland trittyes. Despite these areas of uncertainty, it is clear that the thirty trittyes varied considerably in the number of representatives which they sent to the Council. For example, more than half the fifty representatives of the tribe Antiokhis came from only one of the three trittyes, the coastal one. On the other hand, the inland trittys of the tribe Erekhtheis had considerably less than one-third of the fifty representatives and so did the city trittys of the tribe Aigeis.

(b) It is generally assumed that the ten tribes must have been approximately equal in population since a number of institutions in the state depended on approximate equality. See, for example, A. W. Gomme, *The Population of Athens in the Fifth and Fourth Centuries B.C.* (Oxford 1933) 49; Hignett

137–8; C. W. J. Eliot, *Coastal Demes of Attika: a Study of the Policy of Kleisthenes* [Phoenix Supplementary Volumes, 5] (Toronto 1962) 141; Rhodes 253. Certainly the army and the Council were organised around ten approximately equal tribes.

Such equal tribes could be obtained by the use of the lot, as asserted in *Athenaion Politeia* 21.4, only if the thirty trittyes were all equal in size, or if the city trittyes were all equal, the coastal trittyes all equal and the inland trittyes all equal. But we know that there was considerable variation in the quotas allotted to the trittyes for their representation in the Council of Five Hundred. Since no one could be councillor more than twice, the system of representation on the Council was in danger of breaking down if the tribes were not approximately equal in population.

On premises such as these C. W. J. Eliot argued (op. cit. 141–5) that the trittyes were grouped to form tribes not by accident but by design. Challenged by W. E. Thompson (*Historia* 13 [1964] 402–8), Eliot withdrew his arguments based on the occurrences of contiguity between coastal and inland trittyes in three tribes, but refined his arguments about the combinations of trittyes which might result from the use of the lot. Using the most reliable figures for trittys-representation then available (those established by J. S. Traill in his Ph.D. dissertation, which is summarised in *HSCP* 72 [1967] 403–5; these figures needed revision in the light of the re-study of all the lists of councillors undertaken by B. D. Meritt and J. S. Traill in *Agora* XV [Princeton 1974], a revision provided at Traill, *Political Organization* 71), Eliot calculated that 150 of the possible 1,000 combinations of city, coastal and inland trittyes would have differed from the norm by more than 20 per cent (*Phoenix* 22 [1968] 3–17). Sortition, for example by pulling trittys-names from three hats, has actually been performed by some scholars: M. H. Hansen, *Ancient World* 15 (1987) 43–4, and a post-graduate student at the University of New England, C. L. Tisdell. Both report quite satisfactory results from a couple of sortitions. However, my own view is that human manipulation was necessary in order to *guarantee* roughly equal tribes (given that Kleisthenes must have been aware of the adverse consequences of ending up with unequal tribes). The numbers of representatives of trittyes on the Council of Five Hundred, while possibly subject to gerrymandering by Kleisthenes or his commission, can be used as a very broad guide to the population of the trittyes. Kleisthenes cannot have allowed the possibility that a coastal trittys which could be claimed to justify twenty-seven representatives, an inland trittys with twenty-two representatives and a city trittys with nineteen representatives might comprise a tribe. Such a tribe would have to possess sufficient citizens to make a quota of sixty-eight councillors (as against the actual quota of fifty for each tribe) plausible. There would surely have been too many citizens in this tribe as compared with some other tribes. Since it seems likely that Kleisthenes created ten approximately equal tribes but unlikely that he would have risked his reforms and his reputation by tampering with the lot, the most probable conclusion is that the *Athenaion Politeia* is here mistaken in crediting Kleisthenes with the use of the lot. Whether the mistake arose because Kleisthenes foreshadowed use of the lot in proposing his legislation but found it impossible to use in practice (compare A. Andrewes, *CQ* n.s. 27 [1977] 245–6 with Rhodes 253), we do not know.

9 The position of naukraries and the responsibilities of their officers are mentioned briefly in *Athenaion Politeia* 8.3 [**42**]. See also Herodotos 5.71 [**8**] and note 3.

10 For the text translated (that of M. H. Chambers), which employs ἔτι from the London papyrus as well as ἐν from the Berlin papyrus, see P. N. Papagheorghiou, *Athena* 4 (1892) 553–4.

11 Here the author speaks of families in the wider sense, the *gene*. For the relationship of *oikiai* to *gene* and phratries see note 5 on *Athenaion Politeia* 20.3 [**81**] and Forrest 50–4. For the eclipse of phratries under the Kleisthenic reorganisation see Forrest 195–6 and 199–200.

12 The verb translated 'formally chosen' is the term for a response of the Delphic oracle to a consultant; the Pythia 'ordained' the eponyms (cf. note 1 on [**82**]) of the ten tribes. U. Kron, *Die zehn attischen Phylenheroen: Geschichte, Mythos, Kult und Darstellungen* [*AM* Beihefte, 5] (Berlin 1976) 29–31 denies that the Pythia made a selection from a longer list; she merely approved ten eponymous heroes chosen by Kleisthenes. The important point, however, is that he was intent on securing the support of Delphi for his tribal reorganisation. This approach is not mentioned by Herodotos in his account of Kleisthenes's changes (5.66.2, 5.69.1–2 [**80**], [**82**]). For the earlier connection of Kleisthenes's family with the Delphic oracle see Herodotos 5.62.2–5.63.1 [**77**] with notes 4–5 and *Athenaion Politeia* 19.2–4 [**79**].

* * *

What was Kleisthenes's motive in introducing this complex reorganisation of the body politic? It was not because he despised the Ionians in imitation of his maternal grandfather, as Herodotos alleges (see Hdt. 5.67.1, 5.69.1 [**80**], [**82**] with notes). The Athenians are unlikely to have approved changes on these grounds since they continued to celebrate the Ionian festival called Apatouria (Hdt. 1.147.2; on this festival, celebrated by phratries, see *IG* II^2 1237.28 [**96**] and note 8) and they claimed kinship with the Ionians (Hdt. 5.97.2, 9.106.3).

If Kleisthenes wished to substitute locality for birth as a basis for citizenship and membership in a tribe (in order, for example, to facilitate the enfranchisement of aliens or to break down the control of the Eupatridai in the phratry-network), he could have achieved this by much simpler changes in the tribes. The demes could have been emphasised at the expense of the phratries and they could have been grouped into ten or any number of regional tribes. But Kleisthenes grouped the demes into city, coastal and inland trittyes and the tribes were composed of trittyes from each region. The artificial superstructure of trittyes clearly has something to do with associating certain people or separating certain people or both. By this process of associating and/or separating people, Kleisthenes could have wished either to institute a permanent democracy in Athens or, while giving the *demos* some concessions, to further the political interests of his family and himself.

Among those who view Kleisthenes as an altruistic reformer, D. W. Bradeen (*TAPA* 86 [1955] 22–30) has the most carefully worked out explanation of the trittyes in the Kleisthenic changes. He argues that Kleisthenes introduced this superstructure in order that the *prutaneis*, the fifty members of one tribe who acted as the executive of the Council for one-tenth of the year, might be representative of the three regions of Attike; and more particularly, in order that the city area, where (Bradeen argues) the majority of the politically able Eupatridai lived, might be represented in every group of *prutaneis*. One of Bradeen's four presuppositions must be rejected entirely: it is not true that the demes in each trittys formed a compact geographical area. Moreover, it is doubtful whether another presupposition, that the inland and coastal trittyes of some tribes were contiguous, should be stressed more than the enclaves, the demes detached from the rest of their trittys.

Many of the details of the Kleisthenic reorganisation are uncertain. We cannot draw boundaries for the thirty trittyes (see note 7 above), we cannot assign all the demes to their trittyes with certainty and we do not know where all the families of political importance lived. However, in what we do know there seem to be too many coincidental benefits for the Alkmeonidai to reject the hypothesis that Kleisthenes was attempting to advance the political future of his own family, the Alkmeonidai. In the fifth century branches of the Alkmeonid family lived in three demes near the city (Alopeke, Agryle and Xypete) which belonged to the city trittyes of three different tribes (X, I and VII). Alluding to the connection between Alkibiades of Skambonidai and Kleisthenes (Isokrates 16 [*On the Team of Horses*].26–7; for the context see note 8 on [**102**]), W. G. Forrest says that a family politically allied with the Alkmeonidai occupied a fourth deme which was part of a fourth city trittys. 'Oddly enough these four urban *trittyes* were attached to just those four coastal *trittyes* which together covered the SW. coast, the old *Paralia* which Alkmeonids had once controlled . . .' (p. 199). The headquarters of the Alkmeonid faction was surely in the city deme of Alopeke, where are found not only many members of the family, such as Megakles son of Hippokrates (*Athenaion Politeia* 22.5 [**91**]), but also two families politically associated with them (D. M. Lewis, *Historia* 12 [1963] 23). It would be nice to say that Kleisthenes put the city trittys to which Alopeke belonged in the same tribe as the coastal trittys in which their country home was situated. But the identification of Aigilia as a country residence of the Alkmeonidai (C. W. J. Eliot, *Historia* 16 [1967] 279–86; cf. Forrest 178–9, 193 and 199–200) depends on the assumption that the Alkmeonidai were the most likely wealthy Athenian family to have named a son after the king of Lydia in the first half of the sixth century. We know too little about other families in this period to make such assumptions (see *Chiron* 14 [1984] 12–13). It does seem, however, that the Alkmeonidai may have controlled three of the new tribes (the three whose structure is seen in the map on p. 150) by virtue of their influence in both city and coastal trittyes of these tribes. The fourth tribe (Leontis) to which Forrest referred (see above) can be eliminated on the ground that all three of its trittyes were divided or scattered, making campaigning in advance of a political meeting difficult for whatever noble families were situated in them. But in the case of three tribes – Erekhtheis (I), Kekropis (VII) and Antiokhis (X) – there may well have been compact trittyes in both the city and coastal regions which the Alkmeonidai resident in those trittyes were able to influence. See, for the detailed evidence behind these conclusions, *Chiron* 14 (1984) 1–41.

Whereas before Kleisthenes's changes a noble family in Attike may have been influential in one of the four old tribes, under Kleisthenes's complex tribes this family's supporters would be scattered among several tribes. The same, of course, applied to the Alkmeonidai and we can identify the three new tribes (I, VII and X) to which they belonged. Where the Alkmeonidai may have gained while other families lost is in their control of the *city* trittyes of tribes. If one accepts the enfranchisement by Kleisthenes of many aliens resident in and around the city (pp. 165–7 below), then Alkmeonid control may have extended not merely to three but to most or all of the ten city trittyes. Now, the new tribes had three geographically separate components and if these components were to meet as a whole it would surely be in the city of Athens. The city members of a tribe could attend such meetings far more easily than members from outlying demes. In what institutions would this factor of attendance – not mentioned by the ancient sources – have enabled the Alkmeonidai to gain control?

One institution in which we may suspect but not prove that Kleisthenes gave his faction an advantage is the Council of Five Hundred. The quota of representatives which each deme sent to the Council was more or less fixed. However, we lack information about the population of the demes in Kleisthenes's time; the common attempt (e.g. Bicknell, *Studies* 1–51 at 23–8; Traill, *Political Organization* 64–70) to estimate the relative populations of the demes by the numbers of known members of the deme over five centuries must fail in the light of the fact that the numbers of known members of the larger entities, the tribes, are quite uneven when they should be roughly equal (see note 8 above). Hence we cannot determine whether or not there was gerrymandering in the establishment of the quotas for each deme or electorate (see further *Chiron* 14 [1984] 8–9 and the extended comment after note 5 on [**86**] below). What we can say, however, is that a member of the Council would have been detached from the influence of his old clan leader if that leader was now represented by a different tribal committee from his own. Instead this member would have been susceptible to the influence ı trittys and tribe. Alkmeonid control of a tribe could have an ffect on decisions made by the *prutaneis* and by the Council as

the Alkmeonidai gained directly was in the tribal assemblies which met in the city. Unfortunately we do not know much about the powers and duties of these assemblies of the tribe and can only guess at the precise administrative duties they performed. Moreover, although there were several boards of ten certainly or presumably composed of one representative from each tribe (the nine arkhons and secretary, the generals, various committees of the Council), it is uncertain which of these representatives were elected by the tribal assembly in the period following Kleisthenes's changes. (For a convenient list of administrative and financial boards from the whole period to c. 300 BC see N. F. Jones, *Public Organization in Ancient Greece: A Documentary Study* [Philadelphia 1987] 44–7.) The tribal assemblies may have been more important then than later. See further *Chiron* 14 (1984) 13–16.

One might have thought that there could be no gain for the Alkmeonidai in the Assembly, since men voted there as individuals, not by tribes, and there is no clue in this account by the *Athenaion Politeia* that Kleisthenes's reorganisation affected the Assembly. But there is literary evidence concerning a meeting of the Assembly in 406 BC which indicates that ballots were taken according to tribes (Xenophon, *Hellenika* 1.7.9–10). And there is inscriptional evidence closer to Kleisthenes's own time (see [**85**] below) which strongly suggests (though the issue remains controversial: see M. H. Hansen, *GRBS* 29 [1988] 51–8) that those attending the Assembly gathered around upright slabs which bore the names of individual trittyes. If the members of a trittys were loosely grouped around such a marker, they would be subject in meetings of the Assembly to the same kind of influence from the leading family or families in their trittys as they would experience if they represented their deme on the Council of Five Hundred.

Another way in which noble families other than the Alkmeonidai lost power through Kleisthenes's reorganisation can be detected. From an examination of the enclaves, demes which are attached to geographically distant trittyes, it can be shown that in at least two cases centres of important cults which must have consolidated the influence of the local aristocratic family were detached from their locality and associated with an area of different cults and traditions. The detachment of cult centres from their neighbourhood would serve to break down the political influence of local clan leaders. It was the traditional opponents of the Alkmeonidai, such as the Peisistratids and perhaps Isagoras's family, who were weakened by the attack on organisations which influenced a locality by religious ties. For a brief summary see Forrest 198–9; for a detailed study of the effects of Kleisthenes's reorganisation on local cults and other religious organisations see D. M. Lewis, *Historia* 12 (1963) 30–40, who argues that while Kleisthenes manipulated the structure of the tribes to the disadvantage of traditional opponents he attempted to unify Attike by mixing new citizens with old and making men from different areas work and fight together.

This last view of Kleisthenes's motives seems rather optimistic. The removal from his rivals of political influence exercised through cult celebrations can be combined with the insertion of a city element in every tribe (and the assumption that those enfranchised by Kleisthenes lived in and around the city) and with the association in three tribes of coastal and city trittyes in which the Alkmeonidai can be thought to have possessed some influence, to reach the conclusion that Kleisthenes was looking to the political future of his own family in instituting these changes.

85 *Trittys markers*

Trittys of Lakiadai
[Tr]ittys of [Ker]ameis
Trittys of [Sk]a[m]bo[nidai]
Tritt[ys of] Sphet[tos][1]

Note

1 These four inscriptions seem to have been set up on the meeting place of the Assembly, the Pnyx, though two of them were found a few hundred metres away at the southern edge of the Agora. The first two have been published in *Inscriptiones Graecae* I² (884 and 883), the second two in *Supplementum Epigraphicum Graecum* (X.370 and XXI.109); the four will be republished as nos 1120, 1118, 1119 and 1117 in the second fascicule of *IG* I³. The first inscription is the most interesting, since when discovered in 1846 it was still embedded in an irregular block of local limestone (and it can be seen in that condition today in the National Epigraphical Museum in Athens). Although not found *in situ*, this combination of marble inscription and lump of limestone was too bulky to have been moved far from its original site. The lump of limestone was surely used to stand the marble slab upright in the earth fill at the front of the original auditorium on the Pnyx (a hill just south-west of the Akropolis). In the subsequent rebuilding of the auditorium (in the second and third stages the slope of the hill was artificially reversed) the combination of inscription and limestone block was no doubt used as fill. See G. R. Stanton and P. J. Bicknell, *GRBS* 28 (1987) 51–92, especially 52–6.

The fact that there is archaeological evidence for ten divisions of the latest (probably mid-fourth century BC) auditorium, known as Pnyx III – ten divisions corresponding to the ten tribes (ibid. 56–65) – encourages one to look for archaeological indications of tribal or trittys divisions on the original Pnyx. And there is a series of cuttings in the rock floor of the original Pnyx which could hold inscriptions like these four trittys markers. The fourth marker above, before it was cut down for reuse in some other construction, probably sat in just such a slot, since Sphettos was an inland trittys and the terrace of earth fill at the front was apparently reserved for city trittyes. But the other three markers are for city trittyes. The limestone block holding the inscription 'Trittys of Lakiadai' was certainly ready to be stood upright in the earth fill at the front of the auditorium and the stone bearing the inscription 'Trittys of Skambonidai' (also a city trittys) is substantial enough to have stood in earth fill without any further weighting underneath (ibid. 65–9).

86 IG *II^2 1750 (334/3 BC)*[1]

The *prutaneis* from [A]ntiokhis in the [a]rkhonship of Ktesi[kles][2] who have been [aw]arded a crown for their excellence and jus[ti]ce by the Counc[il and] the Assembly:

From Anaphlystos:
Hierokles/Hieron[3]

Eratostratos/Nausikydes
Kyknos/Philokhoros
Demetrios/Pythippos
[A]pollodoros/Olympikhos
Epikrates/Alexiades
Theagenes/Akesandros
[Ph]ilaigides/Leokedes
Pausanias/Thrasyllos
Demetrios/Kallippos
From Amphitrope:
Diokles/Philarkhides
Aiskhylos/Aiskhylos
From Besa:
Kephisostratos/Arkhi[a]s
Aristeus/Theogenes
From Atene:
Aristodamas/Kallias
Gnathios/Euphiletos
Euphiletos/Gnathios

From Aigilia:
Kratinos/Kratylos

Kratios/Kratylos
Aristodemos/Epikrates
Phainippos/Sostratos
Euxippos/Thersippos
Arkhedem[o]s/Pheidiades
From Thorai:
Kleandrides/Kleandros
Kharikles/Athenodoros
Philokles/Bison
Kharikles
From Pallene:
Arkhebios/Arkhenautes
Hegesileos/Deisitheos
[Kh]airestratos/Gniphon
Kleopeithes/Theopompos
Timotheos/Smikrias
Kephisios/Kephisodemos
Theodotos
Secretary of the
Co[u]ncil
and the Assembly:
Pronapes/Proxenos
of Prospalta

From Alopeke:
Philoxenos/Xenophon
Diogenes/Diogeiton[4]
Autophontides/Deinias
Khairestratos/Euxitheos
Antimakho[s]/[. . . . n]
Antiphon/Solon
Theodoros/Antiphanes
Nikon/Arkhino[s]
Aphthonetos/Pha[ne]s
Kleon/[Di?]agoras
(vacant space)
From Krioa:
Theophilos/Khaireas
From Kolonai:
Epikharinos/Euthykrate[s]
Eukri[to]s/Eukritos
From Eitea:
Hieros/Melanopos
From Eroiada[i]:
Anthippos/Antikh[ar-]
From Semakhidai:
Komaios/Komon[5]

The Council
the tribesmen
(crown)
Kyknos
son of Philokhoros
of Anaphlystos

The Council
the tribesmen
(crown)
Eratostrato[s]
son of Nausikydes
of Anaphlystos

Notes

1 This inscription lists the fifty representatives from the tribe Antiokhis who were members of the Council of Five Hundred and it records the honours voted to them for their service as *prutaneis*, that is, as the executive of the Council for one-tenth of the year. During this period the *prutaneis* ate together at public expense in a circular building near the council chamber and they had the duty of convening the Council and the Assembly and of preparing the agenda for both bodies (*Athenaion Politeia* 43.2–4). Wreathes are engraved around the honours from the Council and the fellow members of the tribe recorded in the two circles at the bottom of the inscription; the two *prutaneis* so honoured are also the second and third names in the whole register. Despite the rejoinder of J. S. Traill (*Demos and Trittys* 110 n. 7), I have preferred to translate the older edition of the inscription by J. Kirchner in *Inscriptiones Graecae* II^2 since my readings of the stone are closer to his than to Traill's in *Agora* XV 44 (see *BSA* 79 [1984] 289–91, especially 289 n. 2).

2 This dates the inscription to 334/3 BC.

3 The names of the councillors (e.g. Hierokles) are followed by their patronymics, that is, the names of their fathers in the possessive case (e.g. *Hieronos*, 'son of Hieron'). In order to give a more accurate impression of the layout of the inscription, on which conclusions have been based (see note 5), I have given the name and the patronymic together on the same line – as on the original inscription. Thus 'Hierokles/Hieron' means 'Hierokles son of Hieron'.

4 This name is written in the adequate space between the lines which record Philoxenos and Autophontides.

5 The list of *prutaneis*, grouped under deme-names, enables us to calculate the number of representatives which each deme in Antiokhis (tribe X) had in the Council of Five Hundred. According to this inscription the thirteen demes belonging to the tribe Antiokhis were represented as follows in 334/3 BC:

[Column I]		[Column II]		[Column III]	
Anaphlystos:	10	Aigilia:	6	Alopeke:	10
Amphitrope:	2	Thorai:	4	Krioa:	1
Besa:	2	Pallene:	7	Kolonai:	2
Atene:	3			Eitea:	1
				Eroiadai:	1
				Semakhidai:	1
				Total:	50

However, representation of the demes could vary slightly: we know from a largely illegible list of the whole Council of Five Hundred for the preceding year, 335/4 BC (*IG* II^2 1700), that Pallene had only six representatives in that year, while Eitea had two. Since representation varied and may not have been strictly proportionate to the population of a deme, the figures must be used with care. But the comparatively large number of representatives for a rural deme like Anaphlystos implies that the deme may have comprised two centres of population or a very large village. It has often been suspected that the demes are arranged on this inscription according to their geographical trittyes: see, for example, R. Löper, *AM* 17 (1892) 426–7, C. W. J. Eliot, *Coastal Demes of*

Attika: A Study of the Policy of Kleisthenes [Phoenix Supplementary Volumes, 5] (Toronto 1962) 126–7, or P. Siewert, *Die Trittyen Attikas und die Heeresreform des Kleisthenes* [Vestigia, 33] (München 1982) 18–19. I sought to strengthen this suggestion by an analysis of the list of the whole Council for the preceding year (*IG* II^2 1700); it may be that on this latter stone vacant spaces are left between the rosters for the three trittyes of Antiokhis (*BSA* 79 [1984] 289–306 at 289–91). If this is correct, it is easier to discern an arrangement of demes by trittyes on the present inscription:

[Column I]	[Column II]	[Column III]
4 deme-names and 17 councillors from the coastal trittys, headed by Anaphlystos (which gave its name to the coastal trittys)	2 deme-names and 10 councillors from the coastal trittys followed by	Sole city deme-name and 10 councillors
		followed by vacant line, then
	Pallene (also the name of the inland trittys) and 7 councillors from the inland trittys	remaining 5 deme-names and 6 councillors from the inland trittys

Such an arrangement would mean, for example, that Atene can be identified as a deme belonging to the coastal trittys of the tribe because of its position in the list between Anaphlystos and Aigilia, known as coastal demes from Strabon 9.1.21 [**87**]. This conclusion in turn strengthens the emendation of the non-existent 'Azene' in that passage to 'Atene' rather than to 'Azenia'. For the locations of the demes of this tribe, see the map on p. 150.

Some scholars, building on observations by W. E. Thompson (*Historia* 15 [1966] 1–10), have argued that in the fourth century the topographical trittyes of Kleisthenes were changed for administrative convenience in order to obtain more equal numbers of councillors in a 'trittys of *prutaneis*'. See, most recently, Siewert, op. cit. and J. S. Traill, *Demos and Trittys*. But it is very dangerous to argue from inscriptions such as the present one which are divided into three columns that, for example, the two coastal demes at the top of column II were obliged for administrative purposes to associate with the inland deme of Pallene (as Traill suggests, ibid. 109–10 and map). See, for arguments against the proposed 'modified geographical trittyes' of Siewert and others, *Chiron* 14 (1984) 1–41, especially 3–7 and 29–32, and *BSA* 79 (1984) 303–4.

* * *

Was there fair representation of the population of each deme on the Council of Five Hundred? The author of the *Athenaion Politeia* tells us (62.1) that the councillors were selected by the demes, not by the tribes as a whole. This would prevent the citizens of city demes at a tribal assembly, which they could attend more easily than the citizens of rural demes, gaining disproportionate representation on the Council. But were the quotas of representatives which Kleisthenes assigned to each deme just? There is not enough evidence at present to answer this question. Estimates of the population of each deme in the fifth century are based on the assumption that the demes were in fact given proportionate representation and that the quotas varied little before 307/6 BC (when there was a change from Kleisthenes's ten tribes to twelve). Another guide to population is to see how many Athenians are known from each deme. But citizens of outlying demes may be under-represented in our knowledge because they were less likely to come into the city to hold political office or to conduct business in such a way that their names would be preserved (on inscriptions or in literary references). There are, in any case, large variations among the smaller demes in terms of known members. From those demes which sent two representatives to the Council of Five Hundred, as few as twenty-five or as many as 100 citizens are known to us (see A. W. Gomme, *The Population of Athens in the Fifth and Fourth Centuries B.C.* [Oxford 1933] 55–65 or Traill, *Political Organization* 65–70). For a contrary view, that the accuracy of the system of representation in proportion to population can be determined, and that 'all classes and elements of the population were represented in the council pretty much in proportion to their strength', see J. A. O. Larsen, *Representative Government in Greek and Roman History* [Sather Classical Lectures, 28] (Berkeley 1955) 5–11. For cautions about the use of fourth-century deme-quotas and the use of numbers of known demesmen over five centuries to calculate the population of demes in the late sixth or fifth centuries, see W. E. Thompson, *Historia* 13 (1964) 409–12.

87 *Strabon 9.1.21 (398C)*

After Peiraieus the deme of Phaleron is next along the coast. Then come Halimous, Aixone, Halai Aixonides and Anagyrous; then Thorai, Lamptrai, Aigilia, Anaphlystos and Atene. These are the demes as far as Cape Sounion. Amid the demes listed is a long promontory, Zoster, the first after Aixone; then another, Astypalaia, after Thorai . . . . In the vicinity of Anaphlystos is the shrine of Pan and the temple of Aphrodite Kolias . . . .[1]

Note

1 This is an example of the literary evidence which can be used to locate the demes of ancient Attike, the basic units from which Kleisthenes constructed his trittyes and thus his tribes. Writing about 500 years after the institution of Kleisthenes's changes, Strabon describes Attike from the sea. In this passage he lists the demes along the western coast of Attike from Peiraieus, the harbour of Athens, to Cape Sounion, the southern extremity of Attike. If one can identify the location of, say, Halimous by other means (such as the finding place of a

decree of the deme Halimous: see J. J. E. Hondius, *BSA* 24 [1919–21] 156–7 and J. Day, *AJA* 36 [1932] 1–2), then on Strabon's evidence Aixone is south of this location and not too distant. Also on Strabon's evidence, Aixone comes before the long promontory called Zoster and Anaphlystos is near the temple of Aphrodite Kolias (if that can be identified). The passage, however, contains some problems: in the text translated (that of A. Meineke [Leipzig 1852–3], but with the emendation Ἀτηνεῖς [R. Löper and V. von Schöffer] for Ἀζηνεῖς in place of Meineke's Ἀζηνιεῖς) five of the names are emendations by modern editors and scholars wish to transpose the names Thorai and Lamptrai.

In the nineteenth century much work was carried out on the identification of demes and their distribution among the tribes of Kleisthenes. See, for example, W. M. Leake, *The Topography of Athens and the Demi*[2] 2 (London 1841); L. Ross, *Die Demen von Attika und ihre Vertheilung unter die Phylen* (Halle 1846); C. Hanriot, *Recherches sur la topographie des dèmes de l'Attique* (Napoléon-Vendée 1853); A. Milchhöfer, *Untersuchungen über die Demenordnung des Kleisthenes* [Abhand. königl. Akad. Wissenschaft. zu Berlin] (Berlin 1892); also his work in *SBAW* [1887, 4] 41–56 and in E. Curtius and J. A. Kaupert (eds), *Karten von Attika* [Berlin 1881–1900]; R. Löper, *AM* 17 (1892) 319–433. Good examples of more recent work are E. Kirsten in A. Philippson, *Die griechischen Landschaften* 1.3 (Frankfurt am Main 1952) and in *Atti del terzo congresso internazionale di epigrafia greca e latina* (Roma 1959) 155–71 with map on plate 26; D. M. Lewis, *BSA* 50 (1955) 12–17; C. W. J. Eliot (see below); W. E. Thompson, *Historia* 15 (1966) 1–10 and *Hesperia* 39 (1970) 64–7; E. Vanderpool, *Hesperia* 39 (1970) 47–53. Many of Vanderpool's conclusions are incorporated in Traill's *Political Organization* 37–54. The revised version of this conspectus in *Demos and Trittys* 125–40 (cf. 124–5 n. 8 and 148–9) is now the standard source for deme locations.

A detailed examination of ten coastal demes in southern Attike (which come from three coastal trittyes) is undertaken by C. W. J. Eliot, *Coastal Demes of Attika: A Study of the Policy of Kleisthenes* [Phoenix Supplementary Volumes, 5] (Toronto 1962). Eliot uses four kinds of evidence to locate the demes and establish their boundaries:

(i) Ancient references. Each reference has to be weighed independently. For an example of the use of an ancient authority, see the commentary above on Strabon 9.1.21, a passage which is discussed by Eliot on pages 6, 25–6, 47–51, 65, 74 n. 22, 125–6.

(ii) Names. The name of a deme may refer to some topographical feature. A few of the names have survived in some form (e.g. modern Anavysso from the deme-name Anaphlystos). Inferences that modern names indicate the location of ancient deme centres must, however, be made with caution, since both names and settlements can move. Moreover an ancient name may be revived through antiquarian interest.

(iii) Inscriptions. The sites (often, however, vaguely recorded) where decrees passed by a deme were found are likely to indicate the location of that deme. The finding places of isolated gravestones recording members of a deme are not reliable guides since a family retained its deme-membership, no matter where it lived. Inscriptions recording mining leases in the Laureion area provide topographical evidence relevant to three of the demes studied by Eliot.

(iv) Remains. The village which was the administrative centre of a deme can be located by the remains of an inhabited settlement securely dated to the classical period. Some demes seem to have had more than one village concentration. One is often dependent on the reports of travellers of the seventeenth, eighteenth and nineteenth centuries for descriptions of remains no longer visible and on twentieth-century archaeologists for records of objects removed in their surveys and excavations.

Using evidence from at least two categories for each deme, Eliot feels that he has identified nine of the ten demes studied with certainty. Indeed, seven of his identifications are accepted in the latest summary by J. S. Traill (*Demos and Trittys* 125–40), who provides a conspectus of locations for all 139 Attic demes. For my views on the locations of the demes of the three coastal trittyes studied by Eliot, see the map on p. 150.

The enfranchisement of aliens

In the Classical world politicians were suspicious of any of their number who sought to grant citizenship to large numbers of non-citizens. They foresaw that such newly enfranchised citizens would be added to the body of clients attached to the politician who had the enfranchisement enacted. In Rome, for example, the narrow clique that controlled the Senate sent M. Fulvius Flaccus, one of the consuls of 125 BC, off to a command in Gaul when he proposed citizenship for Rome's allies in Italy. So we can expect that rival factions would have opposed the successful attempt by Kleisthenes to enfranchise aliens in Athens. If, as seems likely, these aliens were people who had previously possessed citizenship, then the family of Kleisthenes, the Alkmeonidai, was adding to its faction people who would see the Alkmeonidai as the guarantors of their restored privileges.

88 *Aristotle,* Politics *1275b 34–9*

There is more room for debate, perhaps, in the case of those who acquired citizenship rights after a revolutionary change of constitution. Take, for example, the action of Kleisthenes at Athens after the expulsion of the tyrants. He enrolled in the tribes many resident aliens of foreign and slave origin.[1] The question with respect to these men is not 'who is a citizen?' but 'is he a citizen rightly or wrongly?' And there may be the further question. . . .[2]

Notes

1 This translation, taking *xenoi* and *douloi* as adjectives qualifying *metoikoi*,

'resident aliens', rather than nouns ('guest-friends, foreigners' and 'slaves'), is based on suggestions by J. Bernays, *Die heraklitischen Briefe: Ein Beitrag zur philosophischen und religionsgeschichtlichen Litteratur* (Berlin 1869) 155–6, W. L. Newman (ed.), *The Politics of Aristotle* (Oxford 1887–1902) 1.231 n. 1, 3.146 and G. Luzi, *ASNP*[3] 10 (1980) 71–8.

2 Aristotle is discussing the definition of citizenship. He defends a functional definition: a citizen is one who shares in the administration of justice and the holding of office (*Politics* 1275a 22–3). The passage above is direct and indisputable evidence for the enfranchisement of aliens by Kleisthenes. In *Historia* 9 (1960) 503–5 J. H. Oliver argues that something has fallen out of the text after 'constitution' and translates the vital sentence: 'For he enrolled many foreigners and slaves in a classification as metics.' This novel interpretation was adversely noticed by D. M. Lewis (*Historia* 12 [1963] 37 n. 135) and effectively refuted by D. Kagan (*Historia* 12 [1963] 41–6). Apart from the linguistic arguments there is the major objection that Oliver's interpretation makes nonsense of the context. If Aristotle is not assuming that Kleisthenes made citizens of resident aliens, there is no point in his raising the question of justice, 'is he a citizen rightly or wrongly?'

89 Athenaion Politeia *21.2, 21.4*[1]

(2) Kleisthenes's first change was to group the whole population into ten tribes instead of the old four, with the object of mixing them up so that more might have a share in the franchise.[2] . . . (4) . . . Furthermore, those who lived in each of the demes he made fellow demesmen, to prevent newly enfranchised citizens being exposed by the practice of calling people by their father's name. Men were to be publicly known by the names of their demes; that is why the Athenians call themselves by the names of their demes.[3]

Notes

1 The whole chapter is translated on p. 149 above [**84**].

2 This clause could be rendered 'so that more might have a share in the government' (*politeia* can mean 'constitution, government, state' as well as 'citizenship, franchise'; see note 3 on *Athenaion Politeia* 20.1 [**81**], where my reasons are given for translating that passage 'by handing over the state [*politeia*] to the common people'). The translation of *politeia* by 'franchise' in the present passage is justified by the passage from Aristotle's *Politics* quoted above [**88**]. For a contrary view see Rhodes 250.

The enfranchisement of aliens was politically advantageous for Kleisthenes's family. Not only would the newly enfranchised feel that they owed their citizenship to him, but they would also feel bound to maintain the power of the Alkmeonidai so that there was no risk of their being disenfranchised. Moreover, the people whose enfranchisement Kleisthenes saw through the Assembly may have included those who, according to *Athenaion Politeia* 13.5

[**52**], could not establish pure descent and lost their citizenship in a revision of rolls after the overthrow of the tyrants. Such a group would be a particularly valuable bloc of support for the Alkmeonidai, since their previous possession of citizenship would have made them politically conscious to some extent. Whether these people were given back their citizenship or not, the Alkmeonidai must have gained from the concentration of resident aliens in the city and port of Athens. For most resident aliens would have been skilled workers or merchants attracted to Athens by the development of secondary industry and trade since Solon's time and especially under the tyrants (cf. K.-W. Welwei, *Gymnasium* 74 [1967] 423–37; P. J. Bicknell, *PP* 24 [1969] 34–5; J. K. Davies, *CJ* 73 [1977–8] 115–17; Rhodes 188, 255–6; G. R. Stanton, *Chiron* 14 [1984] 39–40). The enfranchisement of aliens resident in city demes gave the Alkmeonidai a bloc of supporters in each of the new tribes and these supporters were able to attend assemblies held in the city with relative ease.

3 There is a definite reference here to the 'newly enfranchised citizens'. On the difficulties of translating *neopolitai* by 'citizens of the new community' and *patrothen* in such a way that it does not refer to the patronymic (see below), see D. Kagan, *Historia* 12 (1963) 43–5. An immigrant might be exposed as such because, while he personally had an Athenian name, his father did not. To counteract such prejudice Kleisthenes encouraged – rather than ordered (cf. Rhodes 254–5) – Athenians to say, for example, 'Aristeides of Alopeke' (i.e. of the deme of Alopeke) instead of 'Aristeides son of Lysimakhos'. The inscriptions attached to early Akropolis dedications and the ostraka of the 480s indicate that the Athenians accepted the use of their demotics (names of their demes) reluctantly and did not completely abandon the use of their patronymics (names of their fathers). The use of demotics, whether or not patronymics were also used, was more popular with people from outlying demes. The members of old aristocratic families are generally referred to by their patronymics. See A. E. Raubitschek, *DAA* 472–6; *Actes du deuxième congrès international d'épigraphie grecque et latine* (Paris 1953) 67–9; Vanderpool 220–2.

The first election of ten generals

The change from the four old tribes to ten artificial tribes led to a change in the army organisation: from 501/0 BC there was one general from each of the ten new tribes. It is not certain that Kleisthenes was responsible for this change; it is not attributed to him in the only direct evidence (passage [**90**]) and conceivably someone else developed his ideas and applied them to the army. But it is possible to discern a means by which Kleisthenes and his family benefited from the election of the generals by the new tribes meeting in their tribal assemblies (as seems to be the case, to judge by the point which is emphasised in the brief report). For the new tribes, composed of trittyes from three different regions, must have met in the city region, and hence their meetings were more easily attended by citizens resident in or around the city and its port. And it was precisely in the city components of the various tribes that the

Alkmeonidai had a base of support – particularly from the families which felt that the Alkmeonidai were the guarantors of their citizenship.

90 Athenaion Politeia *22.1–3*

22 By these measures[1] the constitution became far more democratic than that of Solon. For the laws of Solon had been virtually abrogated through disuse under the tyranny,[2] and they were replaced by fresh laws enacted by Kleisthenes with a view to winning the favour of the common people. Among them was the law concerning ostracism.

(2) Four years after the establishment of this system, in the arkhonship of Hermokreon,[3] they first imposed on the Council of Five Hundred the oath which they still swear at the present time.[4] Second,[5] they began to elect the generals tribe by tribe, one from each tribe, though the Polemarkhos remained the overall commander of the army.[6] (3) Eleven years later, in the arkhonship of Phainippos, they won the battle of Marathon.

Notes

1 The reference is to the constitutional changes of Kleisthenes described in chapter 21 [**84**].

2 This can hardly stand in the face of Herodotos 1.59.6 [**54**], Thucydides 6.54.6 [**69**] and *Athenaion Politeia* 16.8 [**61**].

3 The eponymous arkhon for 504/3 BC, four years after the arkhonship of Isagoras (*Athenaion Politeia* 21.1 [**84**] with note 2), was Akestorides (Dionysios of Halikarnassos, *Roman Antiquities* 5.37.1), not Hermokreon. However, if one uses the dating given in 22.3 Hermokreon was arkhon eleven years before the arkhon year (490/89 BC) in which the battle of Marathon was fought, that is, in 501/0 BC. It is not necessary to change the text to 'seven years after . . .'; the text can be understood as evidence that the complex changes of chapter 21 [**84**] took some three years to establish. *Katastasis* can be rendered 'establishment' as readily as 'institution'. Moreover, this explanation, combining calculation back from Marathon and inclusive reckoning ('in the twelfth year after this' interpreted as 'eleven years later'), enables us to accept a statement in a late lexicographer called Pollux:

> '. . . in the arkhonship of Alkmeon [the tribes] became ten' (8.110).

The reforms of Kleisthenes were passed in the arkhonship of Isagoras (508/7) and, after the abortive attempt of Kleomenes to block them, began to be implemented. The ten tribes came into force in the arkhonship of Alkmeon (505/4) and either then or four years later (the date of the oath: see note 5 below) the first Council of Five Hundred sat. An advantage of this reconstruction is that we can locate the arkhonship of Alkmeon (in 505/4 rather than in 507/6, where it is placed by T. J. Cadoux, *JHS* 68 [1948] 70–123 at 114,

116 n. 249 and A. E. Samuel, *Greek and Roman Chronology: Calendars and Years in Classical Antiquity* (Handbuch der Altertumswissenschaft, 1.7) [München 1972] 204–5), without altering the text of *Athenaion Politeia*.

4 For the content of the oath, to which some additions had been made since Kleisthenes's time, see H. T. Wade-Gery, *BSA* 33 (1932–3) 113–22 (Greek text) and P. J. Rhodes, *The Athenian Boule* (Oxford 1972) 194–9.

5 The phraseology here ('first . . . second') is identical with that in 21.2–3 [**84**] where the tribal reorganisation and institution of the Council of Five Hundred are closely linked. Hence there need not be a period of time between the imposition of the oath on the Council and the first election of ten generals. Both can belong to 501/0 BC. For discussion of the dates of Kleisthenes's tribal organisation, the oath imposed on the Council and the first election of ten generals, see T. J. Cadoux, *JHS* 68 (1948) 113–16, Hignett 331–7, B. R. I. Sealey, *Historia* 9 (1960) 175–7, G. V. Sumner, *CQ* n.s. 11 (1961) 35–7, C. W. Fornara, *CQ* n.s. 13 (1963) 104, G. V. Sumner, *BICS* 11 (1964) 84–5, D. J. McCargar, *RhM* 119 (1976) 315–23 and Rhodes 262–4.

6 On the generals, their election and powers, see K. J. Beloch, *Die attische Politik seit Perikles* (Leipzig 1884) 265–330; A. Hauvette-Besnault, *Les stratèges athéniens* (Paris 1885); W. Schwahn, *RE* Suppl. 6 (Stuttgart 1935) 1071–81; Hignett 169–73, 244–51, 347–56; M. H. Jameson, *TAPA* 86 (1955) 63–87; A. H. M. Jones, *Athenian Democracy* (Oxford 1957) 124–8; B. R. I. Sealey, *PACA* 1 (1958) 65–78, 82–7; K. J. Dover, *JHS* 80 (1960) 61–77; E. S. Staveley, *Anc. Soc. Inst.* 275–88; N. G. L. Hammond, *CQ* n.s. 19 (1969) 111–44 = *Studies in Greek History* (Oxford 1973) 346–94; E. Badian, *Antichthon* 5 (1971) 1–34; C. W. Fornara, *The Athenian Board of Generals from 501 to 404* [Historia Einzelschriften, 16] (Wiesbaden 1971); Bicknell, *Studies* 101–12; E. S. Staveley, *Greek and Roman Voting and Elections* (London 1972) 40–7; P. J. Bicknell, *Historia* 23 (1974) 156–7; M. Piérart, *BCH* 98 (1974) 125–46; G. R. Stanton, *Chiron* 14 (1984) 1–41 at 11, 13–16 and 40. For a brief statement, see D. M. MacDowell, *OCD*² (Oxford 1970) 1017–18.

* * *

The meaning of this brief notice has been disputed. For our author it cannot mean that generals (*strategoi*) were elected for the first time, unless we assume both that the statements about generals under the 'constitution of Drakon' (*Athenaion Politeia* 4.2 [**15**]) are part of a later forgery and that the reference to Peisistratos's generalship a few lines later (22.3 [**91**]) is not to a formal office. It cannot refer to a change in the power of the generals *vis-à-vis* the Polemarkhos, in view of the second part of the sentence, which is substantiated by Herodotos's account of the battle of Marathon (6.111.1: Kallimakhos the Polemarkhos commanded the right wing). The natural meaning of the passage is that there was a change in the method of electing the generals. Indeed, if the earlier generals had commanded tribal regiments, a change in the appointment of generals was essential after Kleisthenes's tribal reorganisation. G. Busolt and H. Swoboda (*Griechische*

Staatskunde [München 1926] 881) and, with some reservations, Hignett (pp. 169–73) argue that the essence of the reform was a change not in the body from which the generals were chosen, but in the body by which they were chosen. Previously, in their view, each tribe may have elected its own general; now the people as a whole elected the generals. This view receives some support from the vague 'they' in *Athenaion Politeia* 22.2. However, such a change would give too much prominence to the generals at this stage, when the Polemarkhos was still the overall commander of the army. It is difficult to perceive in *Athenaion Politeia* 22.2 a reference to a change in the body by which the generals were elected (see also C. W. Fornara, op. cit. 3–5). Rather, the emphasis of the passage is on the election of one general from each of the ten new tribes. If the change was introduced to suit the ten new tribes, it is natural to assume that each tribe elected its own general in its tribal assembly (cf. C. W. Fornara, op. cit. 9–10). This view is strengthened by noticing the point which is emphasised here: 'one from each tribe' is added to 'according to tribes' or 'tribe by tribe'.

The change to ten generals elected from the ten new tribes may have been delayed by the lengthy process of establishing the new tribes and by Athens' involvement in war after the recall of Kleisthenes (see Herodotos 5.74–91 [**95**]; cf. G. V. Sumner, *CQ* n.s. 11 [1961] 37). During this period of war the Athenians no doubt retained their old system of military leadership, which may have been to choose generals for a particular campaign or may have been to elect four generals regularly, each commanding a regiment from one of the four old tribes (examples of references to generals earlier in the sixth century: Andokides 1.106, *Athenaion Politeia* 22.3 [**91**]). In any case, there is no time-gap which prevents our attributing the change to Kleisthenes. Strictly, all one can say is that the ten generals could not have been instituted before the ten tribes were established by Kleisthenes. The changes of 501/0 BC are, however, a logical extension of the changes which can definitely be attributed to Kleisthenes. We are, in part, in a situation where it is necessary to decide simultaneously on what Kleisthenes did and what his motives were. The attribution to Kleisthenes of the *strategia* change of 501/0 BC is accepted in the discussion below because it reveals more of Kleisthenes's probable motives.

If the ten generals were elected by the tribes in their tribal assemblies, it is possible to explain a well-known phenomenon of politics in fifth-century Athens and to argue that Kleisthenes's complex tribal reorganisation was, at least in part, intended to further the political interests of his family. Several scholars have pointed out that almost all the prominent politicians between Kleisthenes's constitutional changes and the outbreak of the Peloponnesian War came from city demes – not necessarily demes which were urban in character, but demes assigned by Kleisthenes to the city trittyes of the ten tribes. These politicians include most of the Alkmeonidai, Miltiades, Hipparkhos son of Kharmos, Xanthippos, Aristeides, Kimon, Kallias, Thoukydides son of Melesias, Sophokles and Perikles. The notable exception is Themistokles of Phrearrhioi, a coastal deme. (For more details see A. W. Gomme, *The Population of Athens in the Fifth and Fourth Centuries B.C.* [Oxford 1933] 37–9.) Now, not all of these men can be shown to have been generals at some stage in their career; nevertheless the prominence of most of them is closely bound up with holding the office of general. If we look at the demes of the generals whose deme is known, again a surprising proportion in the period down to the Peloponnesian War came from city demes. The earliest decade for which we have reasonable statistics is that immediately preceding the war, 441/0–432/1 BC. For that decade eighteen generals are known to have come from city demes, but only twelve from coastal and inland demes combined. Using the lists in G. F. Hill, R. Meiggs and A. Andrewes, *Sources for Greek History*[2] (Oxford 1951) 401–2, B. R. I. Sealey classified the generals from 441/0 to 412/11 BC in terms of demes within the city trittyes, demes within easy reach of the city and demes far outside the city, and showed that during the Peloponnesian War the ascendancy of the city families was broken (*PACA* 1 [1958] 61–87 at 72–7). Sealey's classification of demes can be applied to a list of generals drawn up later by C. W. Fornara, *The Athenian Board of Generals from 501 to 404* [Historia Einzelschriften, 16] (Wiesbaden 1971) 48–66. One would hope to gain a degree of objectivity by employing a list drawn up for other purposes (in this case, to look for instances where a tribe was represented by more than one general). But there are some dangers in this procedure, for Fornara wanted to assign as many generals to their demes as possible; however, one of his doubtful identifications of deme (the assignment of Phormion son of Asopios to Paiania) is accepted also by Sealey, op. cit. 66. Also, the figures are distorted by the prominence of certain men who are shown by our literary sources to have held several generalships, while less prominent generals are not known. But within these limitations it can be calculated that 60 per cent of the generalships during the decade 441/0–432/1 BC for which a deme can be identified were held by men from city demes, whereas during the first two decades of the Peloponnesian War (431/0–412/11 BC) only 32 per cent of the known generalships were held by men whose demes belonged to city trittyes. During the war, then, men who did not belong to the city aristocracy seized the initiative in politics. Of course, the families of prominent new men like Nikias and Demosthenes may have migrated to the city earlier than 431/0 BC (cf. Thucydides 2.14.1 [**5**]). Such migration made possible the fact that most prominent politicians of the fourth century belonged to rural demes, although the layout of the second stage of the Pnyx (note 1 on [**85**]) seems to have aided politicians from inland trittyes in the period 400/399–346/5 BC (G. R. Stanton and P. J. Bicknell, *GRBS* 28 [1987] 51–92 at 80–6, 89–92). The statistical evidence is not, of course, as plentiful as one would wish: 441/0 BC, for which we have the evidence of Androtion (*FGrH* 324 F 38), appears to be the only year in the fifth century for which we can assign all ten generals to their demes; the decade 431/0–422/1 BC is the only one in the century for which we can assign as many as forty-four of the 100 generals to demes. Nevertheless, it seems clear that a majority of the generals before the Peloponnesian War belonged to city demes.

The explanation for the predominance of city families among the prominent politicians of the period 500–431 BC appears to be that the generals were elected by their tribes in tribal assemblies which met in the city. Since the new tribes created by Kleisthenes were artificial and had their membership dispersed, the city was the obvious place for them to meet. Citizens resident in the city or close to it could attend these meetings more readily than citizens from outlying demes. The latter might well have given greater priority to assemblies of the whole citizen body (of which there were at least forty per year) than to tribal assemblies. Thus citizens resident in and around the city are likely to have constituted a majority in the tribal assemblies and thereby to have succeeded in getting candidates from city families elected as generals.

Who would have gained from this situation? Two groups of beneficiaries can be named. One is composed of the newly enfranchised citizens, most of whom were attracted to Attike by business opportunities and hence lived in or near the city. Now these men owed their citizenship to Kleisthenes and its continuation to his thorough reorganisation of the body politic. Those who had been citizens before the overthrow of the tyranny (cf. *Athenaion Politeia* 13.5 [**52**]) would have been politically aware. So they could make the most of their voting strength in the new tribal assemblies. The other group to benefit was politically associated with the newly-enfranchised: the Alkmeonidai themselves. The estates of the Alkmeonidai seem to have been situated just south (south-west to south-east) of the city. Alkmeonidai are found in three demes, Alopeke, Agryle and Xypete, which belong to three separate tribes (D. M. Lewis, *Historia* 12 [1963] 23; Forrest 199–200; cf. B. R. I. Sealey, *Historia* 9 [1960] 163 and n. 41; C. W. J. Eliot, *Historia* 16 [1967] 279–86; G. R. Stanton, *Chiron* 14 [1984] 12–13; see map on p. 150). While the Alkmeonidai and their political allies were able to influence three of the new tribes directly, their supporters in and near the city were spread through all ten tribes. There was the possibility that their candidates for general would be elected in all ten tribal assemblies.

The introduction of ostracism

Whereas the ancient sources do not attribute the first election of generals to Kleisthenes, they do assign to him the law concerning ostracism. Ostracism was a peculiar device whereby a person was exiled from Athens for ten years (few politicians were able to make a comeback after losing the decade in which they were most likely to be running affairs), though they were able to live on the income from their property, which remained intact. Precisely because it is such a peculiar institution, modern scholars believe that it must have been introduced for immediate application; however, the *Athenaion Politeia* (passage [**91**]) indicates that this sword lay rusting in its sheath (to use Beloch's metaphor) for thirteen to twenty years after it was introduced by Kleisthenes. It is possible to explain the delay in its first use by the flight of Isagoras after the law was passed but before it was applied. The passages ([**92**]–[**93**]) describing the procedure for ostracism, combined with the wide scatter vote attested by the surviving ostraka (examples in [**94**]), make it clear that a man could be ostracised on far less than 50 per cent of the quorum of 6,000 votes.

91 Athenaion Politeia *22.1, 22.3–8*[1]

(1) The laws of Solon . . . were replaced by fresh laws enacted by Kleisthenes with a view to winning the favour of the common people. Among them was the law concerning ostracism.

(3) . . . in the arkhonship of Phainippos they won the battle of Marathon; and two years after this victory, when the common people were self-assured, they employed the law concerning ostracism for the first time.[2] This law had been enacted because of the suspicion felt concerning those in power, for Peisistratos had used his position as a popular leader and general to establish himself as a tyrant. (4) The first person to be ostracised was one of Peisistratos's relatives – Hipparkhos son of Kharmos, of the deme of Kollytos.[3] It was largely on his account that Kleisthenes had enacted the law, since he wished to banish him. For the Athenians, with the usual leniency of the democracy, had allowed the supporters of the tyrants to remain in the city, provided that they had not actively participated in the crimes committed during the civil disturbances. The chief and leader of these people was Hipparkhos.[4] (5) In the year immediately following, the arkhonship of Telesinos, they selected, for the first time since the tyranny, by lot and tribe by tribe, the nine arkhons

out of 100 candidates previously elected by the demes;[5] all previous elections of arkhons had been by vote.[6] Megakles son of Hippokrates, of the deme of Alopeke, was ostracised in the same year. (6) Thus for three years they continued to ostracise the supporters of the tyrants,[7] on whose account the law had been passed. But then in the fourth year they began to remove as well others who appeared to be too influential. The first of those not associated with the tyranny to be ostracised was Xanthippos son of Ariphron.

(7) Two years later, in the arkhonship of Nikodemos,[8] the mines at Maroneia[9] were discovered, and the state gained a profit of 100 talents from their exploitation. There was a proposal to distribute the money among the people, but Themistokles intervened. He did not say just how he proposed to use the money, but he urged them to lend 1 talent each to the 100 wealthiest citizens of Athens. Then, if the way in which it was used was satisfactory, the expenditure should be met by the state; but if not, the money should be recovered from the borrowers. Granted the money on these conditions, Themistokles had 100 triremes built, each of the 100 citizens building one; and with these ships they fought the battle of Salamis against the barbarians.[10]

At this time Aristeides son of Lysimakhos was ostracised. (8) But three years later, in the arkhonship of Hypsikhides,[11] they recalled, in view of Xerxes's expedition,[12] all those who had been ostracised. And they laid down the principle that in future those who were under sentence of ostracism must reside on the other side of a line drawn between Geraistos and Skyllaion,[13] or else lose their citizenship absolutely.

Notes

1 *Athenaion Politeia* 22.1–3 as far as 'Marathon' is translated in passage **[90]** above.

2 That is, in 488/7 BC. Twice in this chapter the author of the *Athenaion Politeia* attributes the law on ostracism to Kleisthenes (22.1 and 22.4; other ancient sources do so too). Depending on the date of Kleisthenes's laws, this leaves a gap of thirteen to twenty years between the institution of ostracism and its first use. But is not ostracism precisely the kind of instrument which must have been introduced for immediate use? The author of the *Athenaion Politeia* apparently felt this difficulty and in 22.4 he seeks to explain the long gap between the introduction and the first use of ostracism. But his explanation should be rejected: if Hipparkhos was allowed to remain in Attike after the expulsion of the tyrants he is unlikely to have been an important rival of

Kleisthenes. A better explanation is that Kleisthenes proposed ostracism in the expectation that Isagoras would be ostracised; Isagoras then called in Kleomenes; but when this last resort (force) failed, Isagoras withdrew and there was no point in Kleisthenes's risking an ostracism vote. The law was not used after this until 488/7 BC because no proposals to hold an *ostrakophoria* (vote of ostracism) were passed until then (one had to be very sure of one's position before calling for an *ostrakophoria*) or because *ostrakophoriai* were held but a quorum was not reached. For these views on the introduction of ostracism see *JHS* 90 (1970) 180–2; cf. Thomsen 133–4 and M. Ostwald, in *CAH*^{2} 4.334–46, especially 344–5. Some scholars think that Androtion (*FGrH* 324 F 6) dated the law to the year of its first successful use, but probably Androtion held the same view as the author of the *Athenaion Politeia* (*JHS* 90 [1970] 180; cf. K. J. Dover, *CR* n.s. 13 [1963] 256–7, J. J. Keaney, *Historia* 19 [1970] 1–11, K. R. Walters, *RhM* 127 [1984] 223–6).

3 B. M. Lavelle, *CP* 83 (1988) 131–5, argues that this clause should be translated 'The first of Peisistratos's relatives to be ostracised was Hipparkhos . . .', precisely parallel to 'the first of those not associated with the tyranny to be ostracised was Xanthippos . . .' in 22.6. While he correctly points out that *philoi* (see note 3 on [**31**]) embraces relatives (*sungeneis*) as well as 'friends' in a political context, the phrase 'friends (supporters) of the tyrants' is probably a piece of Alkmeonid propaganda (see note 4 below). Much of Lavelle's case turns on the brief marriage of Megakles's daughter to Peisistratos (Herodotos 1.61.1–2 [**54**]). The case would be a good deal stronger if the word which embraced Hipparkhos and Megakles (and the unknown victim of 485 BC; see the note on [**94** (ii)]) was not *sungeneis*, which refers primarily to relatives by descent, but *kedestai*, 'relatives by marriage'. The latter word is consistently used by the speaker of Lysias 19 (*On the Property of Aristophanes*) to describe the connection formed by his father with the family of Aristophanes (e.g. 19.9, 12, 13), while *sungeneis* is not used at all in the speech.

4 Hipparkhos was alleged to have been *hegemon* and *prostates* of the 'supporters of the tyrants', just as Kleisthenes had become *hegemon* and *prostates* of the *demos* (*Athenaion Politeia* 20.4 [**81**] with note 8). For my view that 'supporter of the tyrants' was a piece of adverse propaganda designed to aid in getting a person ostracised see *JHS* 90 (1970) 180, 182–3 and (briefly) note 1 on *Athenaion Politeia* 20.1 [**81**].

5 487/6 BC. For the view that this change in the selection of arkhons made no recognisable difference in the quality of men who held the eponymous arkhonship and that any radical changes were made by Kleisthenes and not by the reform of 487/6 BC, see E. Badian, *Antichthon* 5 (1971) 1–34. It may be that under this procedure an election was held among relatively few candidates ('500' [perhaps once abbreviated as $\bar{\phi}$] of the papyri has been corrected to '100' [$\bar{\rho}$]) and that chance (in the form of the 'bean') was used to allocate portfolios to the nine successful candidates; cf. Badian, op. cit. 17–19, 21–6 and Rhodes 260, 272–4.

6 If the author is consistent with what he says in *Athenaion Politeia* 8.1 [**42**], this must mean 'all previous elections since the tyranny'. But see note 11 on *Athenaion Politeia* 8.1.

7 487–485 BC (since ostracism votes [*ostrakophoriai*] were held in the spring, we do not need to indicate the full arkhon years, such as 488/7). It is possible that all three were either Alkmeonidai or connected with the Alkmeonidai. Megakles was the nephew of Kleisthenes and the fourth man to be ostracised, Xanthippos, was Megakles's brother-in-law. (See further the note on [**94** (ii)] below.) The label 'supporter of the tyrants' does not fit members of the Alkmeonidai family, which was responsible for the expulsion of the tyrants, any better than it fits Isagoras: see note 1 on *Athenaion Politeia* 20.1 [**81**], note 4 above on *Athenaion Politeia* 22.4 and *JHS* 90 (1970) 183 and n. 27.

8 483/2 BC.

9 In the south-east of Attike. For the area and its mines see E. Ardaillon, *Les mines du Laurion dans l'antiquité* [Bibliothèque des Écoles françaises d'Athènes et de Rome, 77] (Paris 1897) 138–40, 213–14 and map; J. Labarbe, *La loi navale de Thémistocle* [Bibliothèque de la Faculté de Philosophie et Lettres de l'Université de Liège, 143] (Paris 1957) 25–37 with map on 27; R. J. Hopper, *BSA* 63 (1968) 298–300, 313 with notes, 316–17, reprinting Ardaillon's map as plate 65; K. E. Konophagos, Τό ἀρχαῖο Λαύριο καί ἡ ἑλληνική τεχνική παραγωγῆς τοῦ ἀργύρου (Athens 1980) 93, 164 with maps at 18–19 and in box; H. Kalcyk, *Untersuchungen zum attischen Silberbergbau: Gebietsstruktur, Geschichte und Technik* [Europäische Hochschulschriften, 160] (Frankfurt am Main 1982) 56, 64 and 75 (maps), 77–9. Maroneia lies near modern Aghios Konstandinos (formerly Kamareza), north of Cape Sounion and west-north-west of Lavrion.

10 That is, against the Persians in Xerxes's expedition (480 BC). The shipbuilding programme is mentioned by other writers. But the idea that the plan was kept secret, as claimed alone by our author, is not credible, as nothing could be gained from such secrecy (Rhodes 277–81). The version of Herodotos (7.144.1–2) is to be preferred: Themistokles proposed that ships should be built with the surplus, offering the war with Aigina (see note 6 on [**95**]), rather than the more remote prospect of a Persian invasion, as the persuasive argument. This would still allow the detail in the *Athenaion Politeia* that a number of rich citizens were each responsible for the construction of one ship (so Burn, *Persia and the Greeks* 292; G. S. Maridakis, in *Studi in onore di Biondo Biondi* [Milan 1965] 2.207–18).

11 481/0 BC ('three' is probably a mistake for 'two'). 'They', as in *Athenaion Politeia* 22.2 [**90**], must refer to 'the Athenians'.

12 For a few passages of the *Athenaion Politeia*, including 22.4–8, we have a papyrus in Berlin as well as the main (London) papyrus. The Berlin papyrus reads 'expedition', the London 'army' ('in the face of Xerxes' army') here; either word is appropriate.

13 That is, between the south-eastern tip of Euboia and the eastern tip of Argolis. Generally, Athenians ostracised after 481/0 BC resided beyond this line (but our information is limited). See also Philokhoros, *FGrH* 328 F 30 [**92**] and note 7. The text translated here (that of M. H. Chambers) incorporates an emendation of ἐντός 'on this side of' in the London (and perhaps also the Berlin) papyrus to ἐκτός, 'on the other side of' – a change suggested by W. Wyse (*CR* 5 [1891] 105–23 at 112) soon after publication of the London papyrus. T. J. Figueira (*GRBS* 28 [1987] 281–305, especially 284

and n. 11) accepts the alternative suggestion (by G. Kaibel, *Stil und Text der ΠΟΛΙΤΕΙΑ ΑΘΗΝΑΙΩΝ des Aristoteles* [Berlin 1893] 177) that a 'not' be inserted before the verb. But Figueira seems to assume that the emendation 'beyond' must go with ὁρίζειν, which I have translated 'laid down the principle', rather than with 'reside'. This alternative emendation has the same effect: ostracised people were to keep away from Attike. Other scholars prefer to retain the unemended text, so that the rule keeps the ostracised closer to Athens and away from Persian territory.

Wyse added the suggestion (op. cit. 274) that Aristeides's residence on Aigina – close to Attike – provided the motive for this rule. See also K. J. Beloch, *Griechische Geschichte* 2.2 (Strassburg 1916) 143 and n. 1 and F. Jacoby, *CQ* 41 (1947) 8 for the view that this provision of 481/0 BC was intended to keep the ostracised away from the vicinity of Athens. Figueira (op. cit. 281–305) has developed the suggestion, arguing that the change in the ostracism law was designed to inhibit active interference in factional politics by the ostracised, from a site within easy reach of Athens by sea, in the way that Aristeides had managed from Aigina; but some of his other conclusions, such as the attribution of the change to Themistokles, lack a firm basis.

92 *Philokhoros,* FGrH *328 F 30*[1]

The procedure for ostracism. Philokhoros has the following explanation of ostracism in his third book: 'Ostra[cism was as follows]: The people used to take a preliminary vote before the eighth prytany[2] as to whether to hold an ostracism vote. When they decided to do so, the Agora was fenced in with barricades and ten approaches were left through which they entered, tribe by tribe,[3] and deposited their ostraka[4] with the inscriptions concealed. The nine arkhons and the Council supervised the voting. When the votes were counted, the one who received the greatest number – provided that was not less than 6,000[5] – had to settle his private business affairs in the courts and leave the city within ten days for a period of ten years (later the period became five years).[6] He enjoyed the income from his property but was not to come on this side[7] of Geraistos, the promontory of Euboia . . . .'[8] Hyperbolos was the only disreputable person to be ostracised because of depraved behaviour and not because of suspicion that he might attempt a tyranny. After his exile the custom was abandoned. It had been originated by the legislation of Kleisthenes, after he had overthrown the tyrants, in order to drive out their supporters with them.

Notes

1 References of this kind are to F. Jacoby, *Die Fragmente der griechischen*

Historiker (Berlin 1923–30; Leiden 1940–58). Philokhoros is historian no. 328 in Jacoby's compilation. He wrote a history of Attike (known as an *Atthis*) which covered the period to his death in the 60s of the third century BC. The following quotation from the third book of his *Atthis* is reconstructed from four excerpts in late, mainly lexicographical, writings. The source of the excerpts may be Didymos, a scholar of the first century BC.

2 According to *Athenaion Politeia* 43.5 a vote was taken in the sixth prytany (that is, the sixth month of the Council's year) as to whether to hold an *ostrakophoria* (ostracism vote). This passage, from the section of the *Athenaion Politeia* dealing with the constitution of Athens in the author's own time, shows that the law on ostracism was still on the books ninety years after its last use. The unusual wording in the excerpts from Philokhoros ('before the eighth prytany') is perhaps the result of abridging a statement that the preliminary vote was taken in the sixth prytany (during the winter) and, if that decision was affirmative, the *ostrakophoria* was held in the eighth prytany (in the spring).

3 Philokhoros implies that each tribe of Athenian citizens entered by a separate approach (presumably so that the voters could be identified as eligible to vote by tribal and deme officials).

4 The ostraka were pieces of broken pottery on which people inscribed the name of the man whom they wished to be banished (examples are given in [**94**]).

5 The number 6,000 is common to two variant traditions. That preserved in the excerpts from Philokhoros assumed a single count of votes and a minimum number of 6,000 against the man to be ostracised. The other tradition, preserved by Plutarch (*Aristeides* 7.6 [**93**] below), makes 6,000 votes a quorum; unless there were 6,000 votes cast, there was no sorting by the names of the 'candidates' and no second count of the votes against each 'candidate'. There is no reason to doubt the clear account of a double counting in Plutarch; moreover, 6,000 is a quorum required in the Assembly for other matters. Philokhoros may have given the same version and in that case the mistake may be due to inaccurate excerpting or misleading abridgement by the lexicographer.

6 The period of ten years is confirmed by Plutarch, *Aristeides* 7.6 [**93**] and other sources. F. Jacoby, *FGrH* 3B Suppl. 1.317 assumes that the mistake about five years is not Philokhoros's and that another author was quoted for five years, his view later being distorted into a change in the period of exile.

7 The excerpts vary here and one point (the promontory) does not easily provide a boundary. In *Athenaion Politeia* 22.8 also there is a textual difficulty (see note 13 on [**91**]).

8 It appears that Philokhoros is quoted only for the procedure and not for the history of ostracism. Consequently we cannot prove that he regarded Kleisthenes as the founder of ostracism. But it is probable that he followed the consensus of the Atthidographers in ascribing the law to Kleisthenes. If the historical part is also based on Philokhoros, there was presumably at this point in the text a list of men ostracised before Hyperbolos. Such a list is provided by the scholion (for such notes by ancient commentators see note 1 on [**12**]) on Aristophanes, *Hippeis* 855, a passage which also has an abbreviated version of the procedural part and a statement about Hyperbolos.

* * *

A late Byzantine document which has been republished by J. J. Keaney and A. E. Raubitschek (*AJP* 93 [1972] 87–91) suggests an earlier stage of ostracism procedure in which the Council (of Five Hundred, presumably) was the body that voted. For an English translation see C. W. Fornara (ed.), *Archaic Times to the Peloponnesian War* [Translated Documents of Greece and Rome, 1] (Baltimore 1977) 41. While the evidence has been accepted by some scholars (e.g. D. J. McCargar, *CP* 71 [1976] 248–52, C. Pecorella Longo, *Historia* 29 [1980] 257–81), the expression is so poor and the reliability of the document in other parts so variable that we cannot place any trust in it (cf. R. Develin, *Antichthon* 19 [1985] 7–15).

93 *Plutarch,* Aristeides *7.2, 7.5–8*

(2) The people assembled in the city from all parts of the country and ostracised Aristeides,[1] representing their envy of his reputation as fear that he would become a tyrant. For ostracism was not a punishment for crime, but was called for the sake of a dignified appearance a curtailment of excessive influence. It was a humane way of relieving envy; the enmity it provokes could find an outlet in exiling for ten years and not in some irreparable harm . . . .[2]

(5) The procedure for ostracism was, to be brief, as follows. Each man took an ostrakon,[3] wrote on it the name of a citizen whom he wished to exile and carried it to a place in the Agora which was fenced in with barricades. (6) The arkhons first counted the total number of ostraka. For if there were less than 6,000 voters, the ostracism was invalid. Then they sorted the ostraka by individual names and the one whose name had been written by the greatest number of voters was exiled for ten years, though he enjoyed the income from his property.[4]

(7) When the ostraka were being inscribed on that occasion, an illiterate country fellow is said to have brought his ostrakon to Aristeides, as if he were just one of the bystanders, and to have asked him to write 'Aristeides' on it. Aristeides was surprised and enquired whether Aristeides had done him any harm. 'None at all', he replied, 'I do not even know the man, but I'm annoyed at hearing him everywhere called "the Just".' (8) When Aristeides heard this he made no reply, but wrote his name on the ostrakon and gave it back.[5]

Notes

1 483/2 BC, according to *Athenaion Politeia* 22.7 [**91**] above.

2 Plutarch makes the same assertions about ostracism when relating the ostracism of Themistokles (*Themistokles* 22.4–5). A similar judgment appears in Diodoros's account of the ostracism of Themistokles (11.55.3, probably based on Ephoros). In *Aristeides* 7.3–4 Plutarch says that worthless non-aristocrats were later subjected to ostracism and the practice was discontinued after the exile of Hyperbolos. He describes the manner in which the two leading candidates for ostracism on that occasion, Alkibiades and Nikias, combined their factions in order to secure the ostracism of Hyperbolos.

3 A piece of broken pottery.

4 It seems clear from this that a quorum of 6,000 votes was essential but that on the second count a man with considerably less than 3,000 votes against him could be exiled. The ostraka found by archaeologists have shown that the 'scatter vote' (that is, votes not cast against the leading candidates) was quite extensive. 'Enjoying the income from his property', a phrase which also appears in the excerpts from Philokhoros [**92**], seems to have been part of the ostracism law.

5 An ostrakon has been found by excavators in the Agora which illustrates this story nicely, though it would be too much of a coincidence to think that we have the actual ostrakon. The name 'Aristeides' has been inscribed faintly but correctly around the top of the potsherd. Then an attempt has been made to write his patronymic, but the attempt was abandoned half-way through the name, after one or two mistakes. Underneath that the writer has tried to inscribe the demotic of Aristeides, but lost his way towards the end of the word. Finally, someone else has taken the task in hand, crossed out the confused second and third lines, and written underneath them in an authoritative style the patronymic, so that a scrutineer could recognise the vote as 'Aristeides son of Lysimakhos'. See Vanderpool 229–30 and figs 41–2.

94 *Ostraka (examples)*

These inscribed pieces of pottery are, of course, contemporary with the *ostrakophoriai* in which they were cast as votes. They are placed here, after the literary evidence, for the sake of clarity.

There are about 10,600 ostraka which have been recovered in excavations. Approximately 9,300 of these have been found in the Kerameikos, the ancient cemetery area in Athens, and most of the rest come from the Agora. The overwhelming majority of the Kerameikos ostraka were found in 1965–8 and have not yet been published. The comments below are based mainly on the published ostraka, about 1,700 in number. First the inscription is given and then the comment. Square brackets enclose letters *not* on the potsherd; the examples below have more written on them than the average ostrakon. From the extensive literature on ostracism, I recommend the following as sensible discussions of ostracism which use the ostraka as historical evidence: A. E.

Raubitschek, *Actes du deuxième congrès international d'épigraphie grecque et latine* (Paris 1953) 59–74 (a slightly shortened version in *CJ* 48 [1952–3] 113–22); A. R. Hands, *JHS* 79 (1959) 69–79; Meiggs and Lewis 40–7; Vanderpool (two lectures delivered in 1969 with accompanying illustrations and notes); Thomsen.

(i) Kallixenos son of Aristonymos

Kallixenos of Xiphete

[Kalli]xenos son of [Arist]onymos [of] Xyp[ete]

[Of the Alk]meon[idai Kal]lixen[os son of Ar]isto[nymos]

[Kall]ixenos [the tr]aitor

On the first ostrakon Kallixenos is identified by his patronymic, on the second by his demotic (the name of his deme; see note 3 on [**89**]), which is misspelt ('iph' for 'yp'), and on the third by both patronymic and demotic. The description of Kallixenos on the fourth ostrakon as an Alkmeonid may have pejorative as well as descriptive motives. The fifth ostrakon apparently accuses Kallixenos of pro-Persian sympathies, a charge to which the Alkmeonidai in general were open (cf. Herodotos 6.121.1 [**102**], 6.123.1). Kallixenos must be a descendant of the marriage between Megakles the Alkmeonid and Agariste daughter of the tyrant of Sikyon (Herodotos 6.126–31), since his father's name is the same as that of Agariste's grandfather (6.126.1 [**102**]). He was unknown to us from the literary sources, yet he was the subject of a strong campaign in the 480s. Among the ostraka recovered to date, his name appears frequently. For a discussion of Kallixenos see G. A. Stamires and E. Vanderpool, *Hesperia* 19 (1950) 376–90 or (more briefly) Vanderpool 231–5. Full bibliography is given by Thomsen 75–6 n. 111. The particular examples here are published in E. Vanderpool, *Hesperia* 15 (1946) 272–3 nos 8–9 and plate 26 (first and third examples); Stamires and Vanderpool, op. cit. 388–90 nos 26, 30 and 32 with figures 19, 22 and 24 (second, fourth and fifth examples).

(ii) Hippokrates of Alopeke

[Hip]pokrates son of [A]lkmeonides

Hippokrat[es son of] Alkmeoni[des]

Publication: T. L. Shear, *Hesperia* 7 (1938) 361; E. Vanderpool, *Hesperia* 15 (1946) 274–5 no. 13 and plate 26; Vanderpool 245 fig. 3. This man also was unknown until his name was found on ostraka dated, like most of the published ostraka, before 480 BC. He too is an Alkmeonid, probably a younger cousin of Kleisthenes. There seems, indeed, to have been a campaign against the Alkmeonidai in the 480s.

Hipparkhos son of Kharmos, the first man to be ostracised (in the spring of 487 BC), may have been connected with the Alkmeonidai (see Hignett 180–2); the second (486), Megakles son of Hippokrates, was the nephew of Kleisthenes; and the fourth (484), Xanthippos, father of the famous Perikles, was married to the sister of Megakles (a niece of Kleisthenes). See *Athenaion Politeia* 22.4–6 [**91**] and [iii] below.

Another man who was probably an Alkmeonid and against whom many votes were cast in the 480s or 470s is Kallias son of Kratios of Alopeke. He comes from a deme in which the Alkmeonidai were important (on the connection of the Alkmeonidai with the deme see the extended notes above on [**84**] and [**90**]). According to the new orthodoxy (cf. G. M. E. Williams, *ZPE* 31 [1978] 112–13; O. Murray, *Early Greece* [Glasgow 1980] 264), he was not only a 'candidate' for ostracism but was actually ostracised in 485 (the unnamed 'friend of the tyrants' ostracised in that year: see *Athenaion Politeia* 22.6 [**91**]). But the fact that three names have been confidently placed in this vacant slot should suggest that there is something wrong with the methodology. First Alkibiades the elder (see table below, p. 183) was thought to be the victim of 485 (G. De Sanctis, *RFIC* 20 [1892] 152–3; J. Carcopino, *L'ostracisme athénien*, 2nd edn [Paris 1935] 145–8; W. B. Dinsmoor, *Observations on the Hephaisteion* [Hesperia Supplements, 5] [Princeton 1941] 161 n. 346; J. Hatzfeld, *Alcibiade: Étude sur l'histoire d'Athènes à la fin du Ve siècle* [Paris 1951] 13–15; against this view see Vanderpool 236–8). Then, when E. Vanderpool showed that Alkibiades's ostracism could not belong in the 480s, he suggested 460 BC for Alkibiades's ostracism and Hippokrates son of Anaxileos (see table below, p. 183) as the victim of 485 (*Hesperia* 21 [1952] 1–8; cf. A. R. Burn, *Persia and the Greeks* 287–8). Since the discovery of the great Kerameikos deposit, Kallias son of Kratios of the deme of Alopeke has been placed in that slot (G. Daux, *BCH* 92 [1968] 732; Vanderpool 235–7; H. B. Mattingly, *The University of Leeds Review* 14 (1971) 277–97 at 282; Bicknell, *Studies* 64–71). It is better to declare the victim of 485 still unknown, though we should indeed look for an Alkmeonid in view of the vulnerability to ostracism of that family and its connections in the 480s.

The comparatively large number of votes cast against two previously unknown Alkmeonidai, Kallixenos son of Aristonymos (a name derived from the Sikyonian family from which Kleisthenes was descended on his mother's side: see note on (i) above) and Hippokrates son of Alkmeonides, are shown in the following table of known ostraka against a selection of Athenian citizens. The figures for ostraka discovered in excavations prior to the great Kerameikos find are based on Meiggs and Lewis 45–7, with the addition of the ostraka reported by E. Vanderpool, *Hesperia* 37 (1968) 117–20 and 43 (1974) 189–93 at 192. The figures for the finds of 1965–8 are likely to grow as joins of fragments are made, but they still have to be based on the reports of the excavator, F. Willemsen, in *AM* 80 (1965) 102 and *AD* 23 (1968) B'1 28–9 (with a correction for Kallias son of Kratios made by reference to A. H. S. Megaw *AR* 13 [1966–7] 4 and G. Daux, *BCH* 92 [1968] 732; cf. also Vanderpool 235) and of R. Thomsen, one of only two or three scholars unconnected with the excavation who has been permitted to study the great Kerameikos find of ostraka (cf. H. B. Mattingly, op. cit. 280–9; A. J. Podlecki, *The Life of Themistocles: A Critical Survey of the Literary and Archaeological Evidence* [Montreal 1975] 193). See especially for the figures the notes to Thomsen 81–5, 101–6.

Alkibiades son of Kleinias of Skambonidai (the elder; ostracised 475–450 BC)	9
Aristeides son of Lysimakhos of Alopeke (ostracised 482 BC)	114
Hipparkhos son of Kharmos [of Kollytos] (ostracised 487 BC)	12
Hippokrates son of Alkmeonides of Alopeke	127
Hippokrates son of Anaxileos	46
Hippokrates (uncertain which)	21
Kallias son of Kratios of Alopeke	792
Kallixenos son of Aristonymos of Xypete	265
Kimon son of Miltiades [of Lakiadai] (ostracised 461 BC)	563
Leagros son of Glaukon of Kerameis	83
Megakles son of Hippokrates of Alopeke (ostracised 486 BC)	4,662
Menon son of Menekleides of Gargettos	749
Perikles son of Xanthippos [of Kholargos]	3
Themistokles son of Neokles of Phrearrhioi (ostracised 475–470 BC)	2,264
Xanthippos son of Ariphron [of Kholargos] (ostracised 484 BC)	23

(iii) Xanth[ippos] son of [Arri]phron, [this] ostrak[on] declares,
Does the m[o]st wrong of all the accursed le[a]ders.

Most ostraka against Xanthippos have only his name or his name and patronymic. The voter who cast this ostrakon (first published by A. E. Raubitschek, *AJA* 51 [1947] 257–62) wrote a two-line poem (an elegiac couplet) in two concentric circles on a kylix base. The exact interpretation of the poem is in doubt; for the one given, and references to this and alternative interpretations, see Meiggs and Lewis 42 or Vanderpool 223 (with photograph in fig. 20). To their references can be added R. Merkelbach, *ZPE* 4 (1969) 201–2 and T. J. Figueira, *Historia* 35 (1986) 257–79. The latter suggests that the couplet falls in a tradition of partisan poetry (pp. 258–60) and records a particular culpable action by Xanthippos, namely failure by the *prutaneis* of the Naukraroi (of which he is assumed to have been the most eminent) to produce sufficient battle-worthy ships to support a coup in Aigina in 489 or 488 BC (pp. 274–5). However, there are difficulties with his endeavour (pp. 267–74) to link this ostrakon with the *prutaneis* of the Naukraroi mentioned in connection with Kylon's attempt to become tyrant (Chapter I, pp. 17–19) and to argue that these officers survived into the 480s: see note 3 on [**8**]. Rather, Xanthippos was one of a series of men linked with the Alkmeonidai to suffer ostracism: see note 7 on *Athenaion Politeia* 22.6 [**91**]. The voter who composed this poem may be referring in 'accursed leaders' to the curse employed against the Alkmeonidai (Herodotos 5.70.2–5.72.1 [**8**] and note 1).

(iv) Megakles son of Hippokrates

Themisthokles of Phrearrhioi

Kimon son of Miltiades

These three were 'candidates' at the same *ostrakophoria* (vote of ostracism). Ostracism-day entrepreneurs made a vote against Megakles and a vote against Themistokles out of the same vase. There are at least three cases from the great Kerameikos find where ostraka bearing the name of Megakles join with ostraka bearing the name of Themistokles. In addition, there is one case where an ostrakon of Themistokles joins an ostrakon of Kimon, who was not finally ostracised until 461 BC. (For illustrations of joining ostraka with different names on them see F. Willemsen, *AD* 23 [1968] B'1 plate 19a and c, G. Daux, *BCH* 92 (1968) 731 figs 5 and 7, A. J. Podlecki, *The Life of Themistocles: A Critical Survey of the Literary and Archaeological Evidence* [Montreal 1975] plate 8 [facing 177] or Sealey 165.) We have here the handiwork of persons who used their skill in literacy and sold ostraka already inscribed to lazy or illiterate voters. Most significant of all is a pot from which votes against Megakles, Themistokles and Kimon were all carved (the pieces do not join): see Thomsen 95 with n. 262.

It is natural to think that Megakles cannot have been a 'candidate' for ostracism after 486 BC, the year in which he was ostracised (*Athenaion*

Politeia 22.5 [**91**]). Hence scholars (e.g. Thomsen 95 with n. 262) have concluded that the votes against Kimon and Themistokles which come from the same pot must have been cast in that or the preceding year. It is somewhat surprising that Themistokles, who is described by Herodotos (7.143.1) as having 'recently' come to the fore in 481 BC and who was not ostracised until the late 470s, was a 'candidate' so early. But it is even more remarkable that Kimon was sufficiently prominent only three years after his father's death (at which time, according to Plutarch [*Kimon* 4.4], he was 'a mere lad') to make it worthwhile for a scribe to prepare ostracism votes with his name on them. We also have to believe that Kimon was the subject of ostracism campaigns over a period of twenty-five years – possible (D. M. Lewis, *ZPE* 14 [1974] 2), but unparalleled. The difficulties can be overcome by presuming that some at least of the ostraka from the great Kerameikos find belong in the 470s, not the 480s. Lewis (ibid. 1–4) and P. J. Bicknell (*AC* 44 [1975] 172–5) have resurrected a piece of literary evidence (Lysias 14.39) to the effect that Megakles was ostracised twice. These votes, then, may indicate that Megakles, Themistokles and Kimon were all candidates at some *ostrakophoria* held after the invasion of Xerxes in 480 BC.

Information about rival 'candidates' at a particular *ostrakophoria* will rarely come, as in this case, from potsherds from the same vase (which are unlikely to have been used at two or more *ostrakophoriai*). There is more hope of gaining such information from groups of ostraka which have been deposited and sealed off from other ostraka by an accumulation of debris. However, some of the groups of ostraka described by A. R. Hands, *JHS* 79 (1959) 76–8 and by Meiggs and Lewis 43–5 are not securely closed. If we are to eliminate some ostraka as intrusive (for example, ostraka belonging to the latter half of the fifth century in a group attributed to the 480s), can we be certain about a handful of votes cast against a person active in the 480s or 470s, but not certainly a 'candidate' in the particular year to which the group is attributed? Unfortunately the large quantity of ostraka recovered in 1965–8 in the Kerameikos cannot be placed in closed groups. The site is a low one near the Eridanos stream and was so waterlogged that despite continuous pumping the excavators were obliged to reach down into the mud and extract ostraka without being able to study their archaeological context. This is not made clear in the otherwise invaluable news reports: A. H. S. Megaw, *AR* 13 (1966–7) 4; M. Ervin, *AJA* 71 (1967) 295; G. Daux, *BCH* 92 (1968) 732–3; F. Willemsen, *AD* 23 (1968) B'1 28–32.

(v) Themisthokles son of Neokles

Themisthokles son of Neokles: let him go

There are more ostraka with Themistokles's name than with the name of any other 'candidate' for ostracism with the single exception of Megakles. In 1937 a group of 190 were found together in a well on the north slope of the Akropolis. They were prepared by relatively few people (fourteen hands have been identified). Apparently one of the anti-Themistokles factions collected a mass of broken pots, mainly attractive kylix bases, from a potter's shop and prepared votes to hand out on ostracism day. They seem to have had a quantity of inscribed potsherds left over and dumped them in a well. About 40 per cent of this group is on display in the Stoa of Attalos Museum in the Agora: see Vanderpool plates 30 and 31 and, for a full account, O. Broneer, *Hesperia* 7 (1938) 228–43. There are in the group four ostraka of the second, 'out with Themistokles', variety (O. Broneer, op. cit. 233–4 and fig. 63). Themistokles's name is spelled with 'th' instead of 't' in the third syllable in the great majority of cases. Cf. Vanderpool 227.

(vi) Hyperbolos son of Antiphanes

This is one of the few painted ostraka surviving. Most ostraka have the name scratched on them. But when an ostracism-day entrepreneur or a political faction wished to prepare a large number of votes, it was easier to paint the name on the ostraka. At the same time the paint tends to fade and hence to escape modern detection. Painted ostraka such as the above were surely prepared by the coalition of opposing factions which engineered Hyperbolos's ostracism about 417 BC (see note 2 on Plutarch, *Aristeides* 7 [**93**]). Painted ostraka were also prepared against Phaiax, one of Hyperbolos's rival 'candidates' at this last ostracism. On painted ostraka see Vanderpool 226–7, 233–4 and 240; on votes cast in this last ostracism see Vanderpool 242–3.

Attike after the recall of Kleisthenes

Although the Athenians successfully opposed the original attempt to block the constitutional changes of Kleisthenes (pp. 138–45), they were attacked from three directions after the reforms came into force. The Spartans marched from the south-east of the Peloponnese and attacked Athens from the west, the Boiotians attacked from the north-west, and the Chalkidians came across the strait of Euripos from the island of Euboia and attacked from the north-east. The Athenians, however, succeeded in repelling these invasions, though they subsequently toyed with the idea of forming an alliance with Persia and inviting Persian intervention in Greek affairs. Our major source for these events, Herodotos (passage [**95**]), makes some interesting observations in favour of the limited form of democracy which Athens had after the constitutional changes of Kleisthenes (chapter 78).

95 *Herodotos 5.74, 5.77.1–2, 5.78–5.79.1, 5.90.1–5.91.1, 5.94*

74 Kleomenes considered that he had been shamefully insulted by the Athenians in word and deed. He gathered an army from the whole Peloponnese without making known the purpose for which he gathered it,[1] wishing to take vengeance on the common people of Athens and desiring to set up as tyrant Isagoras, who had escaped from the Akropolis with him. (2) So Kleomenes invaded Eleusis with a large expeditionary force, the Boiotians acting in concert captured Oinoe and Hysiai, villages on the border of Attike, and the Chalkidians attacked Attike on the other side[2] and ravaged the country. Although attacked on both sides the Athenians decided to remember the Boiotians and Chalkidians later and took up a position against the Peloponnesians at Eleusis . . . .[3]

77 So when this expeditionary force broke up ingloriously, the Athenians in their desire to take vengeance undertook an expedition first against the Chalkidians. The Boiotians went to the help of the Chalkidians at the Euripos channel. Seeing the reinforcements the Athenians decided to attack the Boiotians before the Chalkidians. (2) The Athenians engaged the Boiotians in battle and won a great victory, killing a large number and taking 700 of them captive. On the same day, the Athenians crossed to Euboia and engaged the Chalkidians in battle, winning again and leaving 4,000 Athenian settlers on the land of the 'horse-keepers', as the wealthy Chalkidians used to be called . . . .[4]

78 So the Athenians had become stronger. It is clear that equality[5] is an excellent thing not in one respect only, but in all respects. For when the Athenians were governed by tyrants they were in no sense militarily superior to those who lived around them, but when they were liberated from the tyrants they became by far the best. Clearly when they were suppressed they fought badly on purpose, as men working for a master, but when they were freed each was eager to achieve something for himself. *79* In view of the Athenian successes, the Thebans desired to take vengeance on the Athenians and sent messengers to the god . . . .[6]

90 While the Athenians were preparing to take vengeance [on Aigina], they encountered trouble from Sparta. For when the

Spartans learned what the Alkmeonidai had devised against the Pythia and what the Pythia had devised against themselves and the Peisistratidai,[7] they considered it a double disaster that they had expelled from their home people who had ties of hospitality with them[8] and that no benefit had materialised from the Athenians for their having done this. (2) They were further incited by prophecies which said that they would suffer many injuries at the hands of the Athenians. Previously they had been ignorant of these prophecies, but they knew them well after Kleomenes brought them to Sparta. Kleomenes obtained the prophecies on the Akropolis of Athens, where they had previously been in the possession of the Peisistratidai.[9] They left the prophecies behind in the temple when they were driven out and Kleomenes picked them up. *91* When the Spartans received the prophecies and perceived that the Athenians were growing stronger and were by no means ready to obey the Spartans, they thought that if the people of Attike were free they might become a match for themselves, whereas if they were suppressed by a tyranny they would be weak and ready to be obedient.[10] Learning all this, they recalled Hippias son of Peisistratos from Sigeion at the Hellespont . . . .[11]

94 When the Spartan plans were stopped, Hippias was expelled from Sparta. Amyntas the Makedonian offered to give him Anthemous and the Thessalians to give him Iolkos.[12] But he chose neither of these places and retired again to Sigeion. Peisistratos had captured Sigeion by the spear from the Mytilenaians and after gaining possession of it set up as tyrant his illegitimate son Hegesistratos, born of an Argive woman.[13] He did not keep without a battle what he received from Peisistratos, (2) for there was war for a long time between the Mytilenaians and the Athenians, using as bases the cities of Akhilleion and Sigeion.[14] The former demanded the return of the territory, while the Athenians rejected this claim and tried to prove by argument that the Aiolians should have no greater share in the land of Ilion than they themselves and all the other Greeks who had helped Menelaos exact vengeance for the abduction of Helen . . . .[15]

Notes

1 This appears to be the first occasion on which a Spartan king led an army from the whole Peloponnese. Note that he acts as a military despot, but that the

allied contingents are free to withdraw. On the obligation of Spartan citizens to obey their king see Herodotos 6.56.

2 Presumably near Oropos. Thus the Spartans were attacking from the west, the Boiotians from the north-west and the Chalkidians from the north or north-east.

3 L. A. Tritle, *Historia* 37 (1988) 457–60 accepts the detail from a scholiast on Aristophanes, *Lysistrate* 273 that Kleomenes on his retreat from Athens (Herodotos 5.72.2 [**80**]), together with his Athenian partisans (who, according to Herodotos 5.73.1 [**80**], were put to death) occupied Eleusis. However, he then has to imagine that his garrison of Athenian partisans soon lost Eleusis to the central Athenian government. It is easier to believe, with this present passage, that the Peloponnesians seized Eleusis when they invaded. Chapter 75 says that the Korinthians decided that they were not acting correctly and left the Peloponnesian army, that the other Spartan king disagreed with Kleomenes over the expedition, and that the rest of the allied forces then withdrew from Attike. Chapter 76 lists the four Dorian invasions of Attike: (i) when Megara was founded; (ii) and (iii) against the Peisistratidai; and (iv) this one at Eleusis.

4 Herodotos goes on to describe Athenian memorials of their victories over Boiotia and Chalkis. We have fragments of an inscription dating from this time, together with fragments of a mid-fifth-century replacement which transposes the two hexameter verses (Meiggs and Lewis 15 = *CEG* 179 = *IG* I^3 501). The inscription can be restored from Herodotos, who quotes the later version at 5.77.4, as follows:

> Athenian sons quenched by their valour in war
>   Insolent pride in distressing fetters of iron,
> Subdued companies of Boiotians and Chalkidians,
>   And from ransom gave this chariot as tithe to Athene.

For discussion see, in addition to the commentaries by Meiggs and Lewis and by Hansen (in *CEG*), Friedländer and Hoffleit 135–7; Raubitschek, *DAA* 191–4, 201–5, 458; D. L. Page, *Further Greek Epigrams* (Cambridge 1981) 191–3; J. W. Day, in *The Greek Historians: Literature and History: Papers Presented to A.E. Raubitschek* (Stanford 1985) 33–4. The preoccupation of the Athenians with the Spartans, Boiotians, Chalkidians and Aiginetans (5.74–89) during the years after the recall of Kleisthenes makes it very unlikely that the military reform involving the introduction of ten Strategoi belongs to these years. See D. W. Knight, *Some Studies in Athenian Politics in the Fifth Century B.C.* [Historia Einzelschriften, 13] (Wiesbaden 1970) 24.

5 *Isegoria*, a situation in which all have an equal right to speak on affairs. This chapter reveals Herodotos's high opinion of the limited democracy resulting from the Kleisthenic reforms. In similar vein Herodotos describes the second and third invasions of Attike listed in chapter 76 as 'for the good of the common people (*to plethos*) of Athens'. On the concept of *isegoria* and its introduction at Athens, see G. T. Griffith, *Anc. Soc. Inst.* 115–38, A. G. Woodhead, *Historia* 16 (1967) 129–40, J. D. Lewis, *Historia* 20 (1971) 129–40 and Y. Nakategawa, *Historia* 37 (1988) 257–75.

6 Herodotos describes the efforts to interpret the oracular response (79–80),

Theban success in getting Aigina to destroy Phaleron and many other villages along the coast of Attike (81), varying versions of the origin of the enmity between Athens and Aigina (82–8) and Athens's preparations to punish Aigina (89). For a recent discussion of Herodotos's description of the confrontation between Athens and Aigina see T. J. Figueira, *AJP* 106 (1985) 49–74 (the same author discusses the early fifth-century conflict [Herodotos 6.49–94], which he dates to the period after the battle of Marathon, in *QUCC* n.s. 28 [1988] 49–89).

7 See Herodotos 5.62.2–5.65.5 [**77**].

8 Now the Spartans pay attention to the obligations of *xenia*; cf. Herodotos 5.63.2–3 [**77**] and note 6. The idea appears again in Herodotos 5.91.2 (omitted in this present excerpt), in a speech attributed to the Spartans.

9 Great understanding of oracles is attributed to Hippias in Herodotos 5.93.2; cf. 7.6.3.

10 The idea that a state which was not independent was incapable of energetic action is found also in the Hippocratic corpus (*Airs, Waters, Places* 23). However, Herodotos's argument (5.78 above) that Athens under the tyrants was militarily inferior to any city around them (e.g. Chalkis, Eretria, Aigina, Megara, Thebes) probably overstates the case (cf. E. S. Shuckburgh's comment on 5.78 in his edition of Book 5 [Cambridge 1890]). The Peisistratid family had ties with Eretria (which would have made neighbouring Chalkis hesitate to attack Athens earlier) and with Thebes (*Athenaion Politeia* 15.2 [**55**]).

11 There follows an account of a meeting of Sparta's allies at Sparta, at which the Korinthian delegate attacks the proposal to institute a tyranny at Athens on the basis of Korinth's experience (5.92).

12 For Peisistratos's links with the Thermaic gulf (adjacent to Makedonia) see *Athenaion Politeia* 15.2 [**55**]; for his and his sons' links with the Thessalians see Herodotos 5.63.3 [**77**], *Athenaion Politeia* 17.3 [**61**] and 19.5 [**79**].

13 For Hegesistratos and the other sons of Peisistratos see note 16 on *Athenaion Politeia* 17.3 [**61**].

14 Hippias had fled to Sigeion, on the Asian mainland just south of the entrance to the Hellespont, when overthrown in 511/10 BC (Herodotos 5.65.3 [**77**], Thucydides 6.59.4 [**78**]) and was recalled from there by the Spartans c. 505 BC (Herodotos 5.91.1 above). Although Herodotos describes Akhilleion as a *polis*, he probably refers to the 'small settlement' (so Strabon 13.1.39 [600C]) in the Troad ('the land of Ilion' in Herodotos) where the monument of Akhilleus (Achilles) stood (so Macan on this passage), rather than Akhilleion south of (and so on the other side of) Mytilene. Herodotos's account in this chapter may be less precise (e.g. 'there was war for a long time', 5.94.2) than modern readers would like, but there is no reason to doubt its accuracy (for a recent defence see P. Giannini, *QUCC* n.s. 16 [1984] 7–30, especially 13 and 25).

15 After telling a story about the poet Alkaios, Herodotos describes the hostility between Hippias and the Persians on the one side and the Athenians on the other. It was in this situation that Aristagoras of Miletos arrived in Athens to seek support for the Ionians in their revolt against Persia. Aristagoras's arrival was mentioned by Herodotos in 5.55 [**72**] and the intervening chapters have been taken up with notes on the history of Athens.

VI
THE NOBLE FAMILIES

Clans and phratries

In early Athens every citizen belonged to one of the old four tribes (that is, the pre-Kleisthenic tribes) and to one of the constituent trittyes ('thirds') of that tribe. He also belonged to another unit, known as a phratry (*phratria*, 'brotherhood'). It is possible, though not certain, that each phratry had a *genos* ('clan') as its nucleus (see note 3 on [**109**]). At least, not all members of a phratry were also *gennetai* (members of a *genos*). The word *phrater* is related to other Indo-European words for 'brother', yet the Greeks adopted different words for a literal brother. So we can picture clans forming themselves and their non-noble dependants into wider associations, to which the word 'brotherhood' was applied (inappropriately, in a strict sense). We do not possess any early descriptions of the activities of phratries and clans, but we do have a later inscription [**96**] which records several attempts in the first half of the fourth century BC to refine procedures for admission to membership of a particular phratry. By that time membership of a phratry was not an essential ingredient of Athenian citizenship; after the reforms of Kleisthenes (Chapter V) people established their citizenship by calling witnesses that they were members of a deme. But it seems that membership of a phratry, with its religious and social functions, was still normal and, as this inscription implies, desired by people. At an earlier stage, according to a fragmentary statement by Philokhoros [**97**], there was an attempt to make it easier for men who had been approved by more exclusive bodies, such as the *genos*, to be accepted also as members of a phratry.

96 Inscriptiones Graecae *II[2] 1237, lines 1–68 (396/5 BC)*[1]

Of Zeus of the Phratries[2]

The priest Theodoros son of Euphantides had the pillar inscribed and erected.

The following are to be given to the (5) priest as perquisites: from the Lesser Sacrifice a thigh, a side, an ear,[3] and 3 obols in money; from the Youth Sacrifice a thigh, a side, an ear, a flattened loaf weighing a *khoinix*, half a *khous* of wine, and a drakhme in money.

(10) The following resolutions were passed by the members of the phratry[4] in the arkhonship of Phormion in Athens and when Pantakles of the deme of Oion was phratriarch.[5]

Hierokles proposed: With regard to all those whose cases have not yet been adjudicated according to the law of the Demotionidai, (15) the members of the phratry are to adjudicate their cases immediately, pledging themselves by Zeus of the Phratries and taking their ballot from the altar.[6] Let the priest (20) and the phratriarch erase from the register kept in (the records) of the Demotionidai, and from the copy, the name of anyone who, it is resolved, has been introduced (as a member) although he is not a member of the phratry.[7] Let the man who introduced the rejected person be liable to a fine of 100 drakhmai, which are to be devoted to Zeus of the Phratries. The priest and the phratriarch are to collect (25) this fine or else be liable for it themselves. In future the adjudication is to take place in the year following that in which the Youth Sacrifice is made, on Youth Day of the Apatouria festival. The ballots are to be taken from the altar.

If (30) any of those rejected wish to appeal to the Demotionidai, they are to be allowed to do so. The house of the Dekeleieis is to elect as commissioners in their cases five men over the age of 30 and let (35) the phratriarch and the priest make them swear that they will conduct their commission by the highest standards of justice and not allow anyone who is not a member to participate in the phratry. Let any appellant who is rejected by the Demotionidai be liable to a fine of 1,000 drakhmai, (40) which are to be devoted to Zeus of the Phratries. Let the priest of the house of the Dekeleieis collect this fine or else be liable for it himself. Any member of the phratry who so wishes is to be allowed to collect it for the common fund. These arrangements (45) are to be in force from the arkhonship of Phormion. The phratriarch is to put to the vote the question concerning those whose cases (of admission) must be adjudicated year by year. If he does not put it to the vote, let him be liable to a fine of 500 drakhmai, which are to be devoted to Zeus of the Phratri[es]. The priest [a]nd anyo[ne else who w]ishes is to collec[t th]is fine [for the common fund].

In future the [Lesser Sacrifices and the Yout]h Sacrifices are to be brought to t[he altar] at Dekeleia. [Let anyone who does not sa]crifice them on the altar be li[able to a fine of 50] drakhmai, which are to be devoted t[o Zeus of the Phratries.] Let the pri[est co]llect [this fine or else be] liable for it himself, [unless there be some plague or war.(?)] If any of these events interferes, the Lesser Sacrifices and the Youth Sacrifices are to be brought to wherever the priest gives notice. Such notice is to be given four days before the Dorpia,[8] on a whitened board no less than a handspan across, at a place that the Dekeleieis frequent in the city.[9]

The priest is to have this decree and the perquisites inscribed on a marble pillar in front of the altar at Dekeleia at his own expense.

Notes

1 Since this inscription preserves (lines 65–8) the instruction that it be set up in the sanctuary at Dekeleia, its finding place at Tatoï in the far north of Attike can be taken to indicate part of the territory of the ancient deme of Dekeleia. The inscription records decisions taken by one of the Athenian phratries, probably called Dekeleieis (see note 7 below), on three occasions: 396/5 BC (the decree of Hierokles, lines 13–68), at the same meeting or shortly after (the amendments of Nikodemos, lines 68–113), and (to judge from the script) about half a century later (a fragmentary record, lines 114–26, at the bottom of the back side of the stone). Only the first decree, dated shortly after the end of the Peloponnesian War (for the last decade of which Dekeleia was occupied by the Peloponnesians), is translated here. As with other inscriptions (e.g. [**13**], [**64**], [**86**]) in this book, words or letters corresponding to the parts of the translation placed in square brackets are not preserved on the stone and have been restored by modern editors.

2 The name of the god, in his role as protector of phratries (literally 'Zeus Phratrios') is put in the possessive case at the head of the inscription in larger letters, so that the god to whom the altar belongs can be immediately identified. The fines exacted in cases of false claims to membership of the phratry (lines 23–4, 39–40) and for other delinquencies (lines 49–50, 55–6) are to be given to Zeus of the Phratries.

3 These parts of the sacrificial victim, along with the monetary payment (3 obols is half a drakhme), are assigned to the priest as a kind of fringe benefit.

4 'Members of the phratry' translates *phrateres*, the 'brothers'. A phratry was a social grouping smaller than a 'tribe' but containing many families (though usually only one noble clan). For attempts to define *genos* ('clan') and phratry see H. T. Wade-Gery, *CQ* 25 (1931) 1–2 = *Essays* 86–8, Forrest 50–4, Sealey

22–3 or Rhodes 68–71; for an introduction to the problems see Fine, *Ancient Greeks* 183–8. It seems that women also could be associated with phratries (M. Golden, *CQ* n.s. 35 [1985] 9–13; for a contrary view, see S. G. Cole, *ZPE* 55 [1984] 233–44, especially 235–8).

5 *Phratriarkhos* must be the chief official of the phratry. There were two demes named Oion and Pantakles's deme is no doubt the one near Dekeleia, called Oion Dekeleikon. We do not of course know the years when particular men were officials of this phratry, but from other evidence we can date the arkhonship – a statewide office – of Phormion to 396/5 BC.

6 For another example of the solemn procedure of members of a phratry taking their ballot from the altar of Zeus of the Phratries see [Demosthenes] 43 (*Against Makartatos*).14; and for the Areopagos voting in this way on a religious issue c. 343 BC see Demosthenes 18 (*On the Crown*).134.

7 There has been dispute as to whether the members of the phratry were called Demotionidai or Dekeleieis (the same as the members of the deme in which the sanctuary was based). It can be seen from this inscription that the Demotionidai possess law (14–15), keep archives including a membership register (20–1), hear appeals through a commission elected by the Dekeleieis (30–3, 38–9), while 'the house of the Dekeleieis' provides that commission and has a priest (41–2). U. von Wilamowitz-Möllendorff (*Aristoteles und Athen* [Berlin 1893] 259–79 at 261) asserts that the name of the phratry is Demotionidai, while 'the house of the Dekeleieis' was a privileged subdivision of the phratry. H. T. Wade-Gery (*CQ* 25 [1931] 129–43 = *Essays* 116–34) maintains that Dekeleieis is the name of the phratry and the Demotionidai were some kind of aristocratic corporation with a privileged position. A. Andrewes (*JHS* 81 [1961] 1–15) believes that the Demotionidai were a *genos* ('clan') with a privileged position inside the phratry. W. E. Thompson (*SO* 42 [1967] 51–68 at 52–6) regards Wade-Gery's view as convincing and Andrewes's suggestion as probable.

8 The first day of the Apatouria festival, marked by sumptuous reunion dinners in the evening (J. D. Mikalson, *The Sacred and Civil Calendar of the Athenian Year* [Princeton 1975] 79; H. W. Parke, *Festivals of the Athenians* [London 1977] 88–92 at 91). The Youth Day, 'Koureotis' (line 28), was the third day of the festival.

9 It seems that although meetings of this phratry normally took place in the Agora at Dekeleia (lines 85–6, not translated here, refer to 'all members of the phratry present in the Agora') the Dekeleieis would normally congregate in the city itself. A meeting place in the early fourth century is revealed to us by the orator Lysias (23.2–3): the barber's shop 'beside the *hermai*', apparently a stretch of the Panathenaic Way at the north-west corner of the Agora which was lined with monuments on both sides (J. Threpsiades and E. Vanderpool, *AD* 18 (1963) A' 99–114, especially 109; for an earlier view see A. von Domaszewski, *Die Hermen der Agora zu Athen* [*SHAW* 1914, 10], especially 7–9).

97 *Philokhoros*, FGrH *328 F 35*[1]

(a) . . . concerning *orgeones* Philokhoros also has written: 'The members of the phratry are to accept automatically *orgeones* as well as *homogalaktes*, whom we call *gennetai*.'

(b) Philokhoros in the fourth book of his *Atthis* says that what are now called *gennetai* were formally called *homogalaktes*.[2]

Notes

1 On Philokhoros see note 1 on [**92**]. This fragment (35) comes from the fourth book of the *Atthis* and has been reconstructed in two versions (called a and b by Jacoby) from lexicographers who wrote as late as the tenth century (Harpokration, Photios, the Souda).

2 The members of the clan (*genos*) were typically called *gennetai*, but here the unusual word *homogalaktes* is explained: it literally means those who sucked the same milk, that is, a kind of 'milk-brotherhood'. *Orgeones*, on the other hand, were not linked with each other or with the clansmen by blood; they shared among themselves a common cult.

This fragment has been much discussed. I follow here, in the main, A. Andrewes's interpretation in *JHS* 81 (1961) 1–15. The fragment (in version a) seems to preserve a law directing the members of the phratry (literally 'brotherhood') to accept automatically the upper-class families known as *orgeones* as well as the *gennetai*, the members of clans. While these two groups, one belonging to an aristocracy of birth and the other perhaps not, were exempt from scrutiny by the phratry, the great mass of commoners presumably had their qualifications for membership scrutinised.

Andrewes (ibid. 3–9) cites other evidence which suggests that a clan (e.g. the Demotionidai [**96**]) could have decisive influence within its phratry (in their case, Dekeleieis), even as late as the fourth century BC. In the archaic period a clan's dependants were no doubt organised in phratries, which the clan dominated (ibid. 15).

The Philaidai

One of the wealthiest families in sixth-century Athens was that which produced men named Miltiades (including the general at the battle of Marathon) and Kimon. They engaged in the expensive but ostentatious sport of racing four-horse chariots at the festivals held at Olympia and elsewhere. They offered hospitality to foreign leaders with a view to a comparable or greater return. They were able to found settlements in distant places which were looked on as hereditary possessions of the family as well as Athenian bases. And they were the family most at loggerheads with the tyrants in Athens, despite their ability to work in concert with the tyrant family from time to time. Many scholars have held that Miltiades, Kimon and their descendants were related to the Philaidai by marriage and were not Philaidai themselves; but some aspects of the family's history are easier to understand if they were in fact Philaidai.

98 *Herodotos 6.34.1–6.36.1, 6.38.1–6.39.2*

34 Until this time[1] Miltiades son of Kimon and grandson of Stesagoras was tyrant of these cities. This power had been acquired earlier by Miltiades son of Kypselos in the following way.[2]

This Chersonese was in the hands of the Dolonkoi, who are Thracians. Being hard pressed in war by the Apsinthioi, these Dolonkoi sent their princes to Delphi to enquire about the war. (2) The Pythia replied that they should take home as founding hero for their state whoever first offered them hospitality after they left the temple. The Dolonkoi, travelling along the Sacred Way, went through Phokis and Boiotia. When no one invited them in, they turned and made for Athens.

35 In Athens at this particular time Peisistratos held all the power, but Miltiades son of Kypselos was a powerful man.[3] His family engaged in four-horse chariot racing. Originally he was descended from Aiakos and Aigina, but further down the line he was Athenian, being descended from Philaios son of Aias, who was the first member of this family to be Athenian. (2) This Miltiades was sitting outside his front door when he saw the Dolonkoi coming past[4] and noticed that their clothing was not local and they were carrying spears. He called to them and when they came over he offered them a respite from their travels and hospitality.[5] They accepted his offer and were given hospitality by him. They revealed the whole oracular response to him and asked him to obey the god. (3) When he heard their story Miltiades was immediately persuaded; for he disliked the rule of Peisistratos and wished to be out of the way.[6] He set out immediately for Delphi to enquire of the oracle whether he should do what the Dolonkoi asked of him. *36* The Pythia confirmed the request. So Miltiades son of Kypselos, who before this had won a prize at Olympia with a four-horse chariot, took with him every Athenian who wanted to be part of the expedition, sailed with the Dolonkoi and took possession of the country. And those who brought him made him tyrant . . . .[7]

38 This man, then, escaped through the intervention of Kroisos, but he later died childless. He bequeathed his rule and his resources to Stesagoras son of Kimon (Kimon was his half-brother on his mother's side). Since the death of Miltiades the people of the Chersonese have sacrificed to him as is customary to a founding hero and have instituted in his honour both chariot and athletic contests, in which no one from Lampsakos is allowed to compete. (2) It happened during a war with Lampsakos that Stesagoras also died childless. He was struck on the head with an axe in the Prytaneion, by a man who said he was a deserter but who was in fact an enemy of his, and a rather incensed one. *39* After Stesagoras's death in this manner Miltiades, the son of Kimon and brother of the dead Stesagoras, was sent with a trireme to take charge of affairs in the Chersonese by the Peisistratidai, who had treated him well at Athens, as though they were not responsible for his father's death. How that happened I shall tell you in another place.[8] (2) On arrival in the Chersonese Miltiades kept to his house, giving the impression that he was honouring his dead brother Stesagoras. When the people of the Chersonese learned of this, the influential men in all the cities gathered together from everywhere and came in a single band to join in his mourning. But he put them in chains. So Miltiades seized hold of the Chersonese. He maintained 500 mercenaries and married Hegesipyle, daughter of the Thracian king Oloros.

Notes

1 493 BC, when the Phoenician fleet conquered the cities of the Thracian Chersonese (the Gallipoli peninsula), in the north-eastern Aegean. On the structure of the narrative see F. Prontera, *PP* 27 (1972) 111–23, especially 115, 119, 123.

2 The family stemma which emerges from this and other passages (notably [**99**]–[**100**] below) is as shown on the following page. See in general J. Töpffer, *Attische Genealogie* (Berlin 1889) 269–86 and Davies, *APF* 294–6, 298–304. For the view that the family of Miltiades as well as the family of Agamestor were Philaidai, see Burn, *Lyric Age* 311.

3 For the verb used (*dunasteuein*) see note 3 on Herodotos 5.66.1 [**80**].

4 This confirms that the home of the Philaidai was in Lakiadai, to the west of the city on the Sacred Way; the Dolonkoi had come through Eleutherai and Eleusis (D. M. Lewis, *Historia* 12 [1963] 25). There does not seem to be any special connection of the Philaidai with Brauron, which was included by Kleisthenes in the deme called Philaidai (see note 3 on [**100**]). Miltiades son of Kimon (arkhon 524/3 BC) did not capture Lemnos principally because of the abduction of Athenian women from the festival of Artemis at Brauron (Herodotos 6.138.1); rather he cited the oracle from Delphi which prescribed punishment for the Lemnians for the subsequent murder of these Athenian mistresses and their children (Herodotos 6.140.1; cf. 6.139.2).

5 The Philaidai belonged to the wealthiest aristocratic stratum of society: they

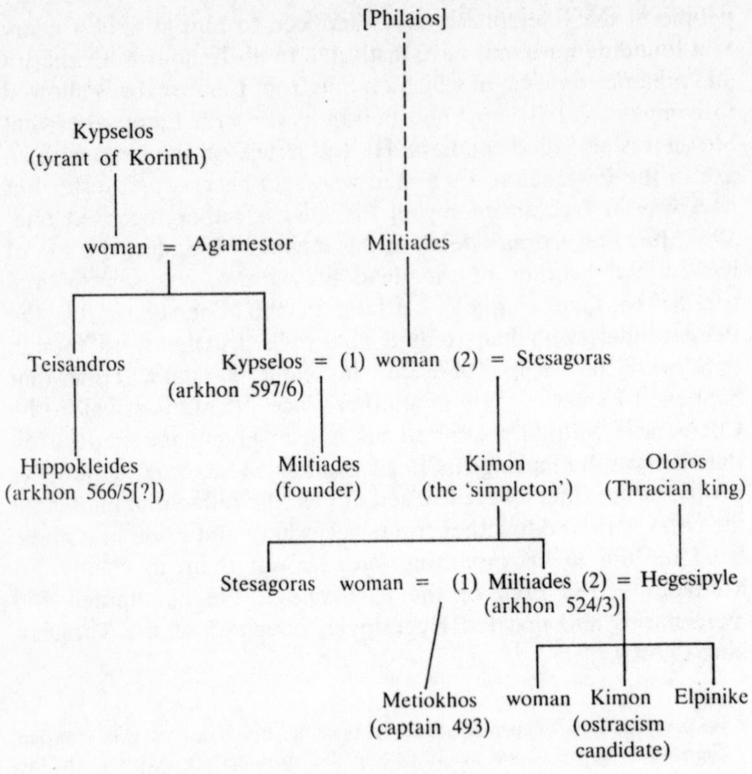

raced four-horse chariots at festivals and provided lodging and hospitality to strangers with a view to a return.

6 As Davies (*APF* 299–300) points out, it was the family of Miltiades and Kimon, not the Alkmeonidai, that were the most obvious opponents of the tyrants in the 540s and later.

7 The return for the benefits bestowed on the Dolonkoi by Miltiades was a tyranny in the Thracian Chersonese. In the section omitted Herodotos relates that Miltiades had initial success in warding off the Apsinthioi (cf. 6.34.1 above), but was captured by the Greeks of Lampsakos and only freed through the intervention of Kroisos of Lydia (on whom see notes 1–2 on [**29**]).

8 The passage to which Herodotos refers is 6.103.1–104.1 below [**99**], in which he recounts the murder of Kimon son of Stesagoras by the Peisistratidai near the Prytaneion in Athens.

99 *Herodotos 6.103.1–6.104.1*

(*103*) . . . They[1] were led by ten generals, one of whom was Miltiades. This man's father, Kimon son of Stesagoras, had been banished from Athens by Peisistratos son of Hippokrates.[2] (2) During his exile he won a victory at Olympia with a four-horse chariot, and in winning this victory he gained the same honour as Miltiades, his half-brother on his mother's side. At the next Olympic festival he won with the same mares, but allowed Peisistratos to be proclaimed victor. (3) Having ceded the victory to Peisistratos, he was brought home with a guarantee of safety. He won yet a third Olympic victory with the same mares,[3] but after the death of Peisistratos he died at the hands of Peisistratos's sons, who set men in ambush for him at night near the Prytaneion. Kimon is buried outside the city, on the other side of the road which is called 'through Koile'. Opposite him are buried those mares which won the three victories at Olympia. (4) . . . The elder of Kimon's sons, Stesagoras, was at that particular time living with his uncle Miltiades in the Chersonese, while the younger son was living at Athens with Kimon himself; he was named Miltiades after Miltiades the founding hero of the Chersonese.[4] *104* It was, then, this Miltiades who was now a general of the Athenians, having come from the Chersonese and twice escaped death.

Notes

1 The Athenians at Marathon in 490 BC.

2 That is, when Peisistratos was tyrant (Chapter IV, pp. 103–10).

3 Probably the three victories belong to the Olympic Games of 536, 532 and 528 BC.

4 Compare Herodotos 6.34.1–6.36.1 [**98**]. N. G. L. Hammond (*CQ* n.s. 6 [1956] 113–29) thought it odd that the older Miltiades should be described in two different ways in this sentence and postulated a third Miltiades. But his theory has been answered by D. Bradeen (*Hesperia* 31 [1963] 193–7, 206–8), when he published further fragments of the arkhon list [**64**] that shows that Miltiades was eponymous arkhon shortly after Hippias himself. Fragment *a* of the same inscription (Meiggs and Lewis no. 6) shows the father of the founding hero holding the arkhonship, perhaps in 597/6 BC (see note 5 on [**19**]):

[. . .]N[-----]
[Ky]pselo[s]
[Te]lekle[---]
[Phil]omb[rotos?]
------

100 *Plutarch,* Solon *10.3*

(3) But the Athenians themselves think that this story is nonsense.[1] They say that Solon proved to the judges that Philaios and Eurysakes, the sons of Aias, adopted Athenian citizenship

and in exchange handed over the island to them. One of them settled at Brauron in Attike, the other in Melite;[2] the Athenians have a deme Philaidai, from which Peisistratos came,[3] named after Philaios.

Notes

1 The long struggle between the Megarians and the Athenians for control of the island of Salamis culminated in the appointment of Spartans as arbitrators ('judges' in this passage). Plutarch has just cited the popular story that Solon convinced the judges by invoking the authority of Homer and inserting a verse linking Aias (Ajax), the hero from Salamis, with the Athenians in the Catalogue of Ships (*Iliad* 2.558; on this story see L. Piccirilli (ed.), *Gli arbitrati interstatali greci* 1 [Pisa 1973] 46–56 and note 7 on [**80**]). Then Plutarch gives the Athenian version of Solon's case.

2 Melite is a deme extending west and south-west of the Agora in Athens. Although we have a few inscriptions which were set up in the Eurysakeion, the shrine named after Aias's son Eurysakes, they all seem to have been moved from the site of the Eurysakeion. H. A. Thompson and R. E. Wycherley suggest a location south-west of the temple of Hephaistos: *The Athenian Agora* 14 (Princeton 1972) 40–1, 228.

3 Perhaps to avoid a revival of Peisistratid influence after the overthrow of their tyranny, Kleisthenes did not call the deme (the local political unit: see Herodotos 5.69.2 [**82**], *Athenaion Politeia* 21.4 [**84**] and Strabon 9.1.21 [**87**]) which included Brauron by that name, but gave it the name Philaidai. This may have been a political disadvantage not only for the Peisistratidai (cf. note 3 on [**56**]) but also for the Philaidai, to which Miltiades and Kimon belonged. They can be associated only with the city deme Lakiadai (see note 4 on Herodotos 6.35.2 [**98**]). Kleisthenes may have used the name Philaidai for a deme where there were patently no Philaidai, thus encouraging confusion about a rival family. See D. M. Lewis, *Historia* 12 (1963) 25–7.

The Alkmeonidai

This family appears among the first individuals who can be identified in Athenian history, in the person of that Megakles who, with his family, was held responsible for the massacre of the supporters of the would-be tyrant Kylon (Chapter I, pp. 19–24). His son Alkmeon is generally held to have been the Athenian leader in the so-called First Sacred War (passage [**103**]). A later Megakles was the head of the Alkmeonidai when they opposed factions led by Lykourgos (see below pp. 208–9, [**108**]–[**111**]) and Peisistratos. By various coalitions with these factions they were able first to thwart Peisistratos's initial attempt to become tyrant, then to put him back into power and finally by dissolving a marriage alliance to drive him out a second time (Chapter III, pp. 91–102). When Peisistratos returned some years later with an invincible army, they went into exile again, but were collaborating with

Peisistratos in time for the young Kleisthenes to be arkhon in the years immediately after Peisistratos's death (Chapter IV, pp. 111–12). Twenty years later Kleisthenes brought in a radical reform of the basis of Athenian politics and the evidence suggests (Chapter V) that special benefits were intended to flow to the Alkmeonidai.

Herodotos is a major source for the various activities of the Alkmeonidai. He openly says that they used bribery to persuade the Pythia to work against the Peisistratidai (Chapter IV, pp. 130–3), but he defends them stoutly against the charge of treason after the battle of Marathon (passage [**102**]). That defence may well be justified, but there are other points where he can be shown to have taken an excessively pro-Alkmeonid line. In this very passage he obscures the collaboration of the Alkmeonidai with the tyrants, alleging that they were in exile for the whole period of the tyranny. And in introducing Kleisthenes's reforms he gives such an unreasonable motive (imitation of his maternal grandfather) that we may conclude that he preferred not to reveal Kleisthenes's main motive (passage [**82**] and note 2).

101 *Pindar,* Pythian Odes *7*[1]

The mighty city of Athens is the noblest prelude on which to found a monument of song in honour of the family of the Alkmeonidai, powerful in many places, for their chariot victory. In what native land, in what house will you dwell if you are to declare it more illustrious of report in Greece? For there haunts every city, Apollon, the tale of those citizens of Erekhtheus who built your home, marvellous to behold, in resplendent Python.[2]

Five victories at the Isthmos prompt me, one conspicuous victory at the Olympian festival of Zeus, two at Kirrha, Megakles, victories of your family and your forebears. Your new success[3] gives me some joy. But this I grieve at, that envy is the recompense for noble deeds. Yet prosperity, they say, which thus continues in bloom for a man brings with it now this, now that.[4]

Notes

1 Although E. L. Bundy, *Studia Pindarica* [University of California Publications in Classical Philology, 18.1–2] (Berkeley 1962) 28, took the conclusion of this ode (verses 19–22) as foil with a general truth concerning vicissitudes, there seems to be a particular reference, in envy (*phthonos*) as a response to aristocratic achievement, to Megakles's ostracism from Athens in the spring of 486 BC (see *Athenaion Politeia* 22.5 [**91**] with note 7). On this view Megakles

won the four-horse chariot race at Delphi while in exile and subsequently commissioned this short ode from Pindar. The poet sings of the earlier victories of the Alkmeonid family (verses 13–17) as well as this recent success (verse 18).

2 After identifying the family and the city being honoured, the poet mentions one of the family's traditions, in this case the Alkmeonid rebuilding of the temple of Apollon at Delphi (here called 'Python'; compare Apollon's epithet 'Pythian' in Meiggs and Lewis no. 11 [**65**] and the title of the priestess 'Pythia' in Herodotos 5.63.1 [**77**]). 'Kirrha' below also refers to Delphi (compare Plutarch, *Solon* 11.1 [**103**] with note 4), where the Pythian Games were held. For the magnificent completion of the façade of the temple at Delphi see Herodotos 5.62.2–3 [**77**] with notes 4–5. For Erekhtheus compare Apollodoros 3.15.1 [**110**] with note 2.

3 The victory at Delphi in 486 BC (see note 1 above). The Olympic victory was won by Alkmeon, the great-grandfather of Megakles (Herodotos 6.125.5 [**102**]; for a partial stemma of the family see p. 205).

4 Envy refers to the jealousy of humans – hence the ostracism of an Alkmeonid – as well as the envy of the gods which blights a human's success. Some ancient commentators on verse 18 of this ode, however, thought that the adverse circumstance encountered by Megakles was the death of his father Hippokrates about this time.

102 *Herodotos 6.121.1, 6.123.1–6.125.1, 6.125.5–6.126.1, 6.131.1–2*

121 It is a wonder to me and I do not accept the story that the Alkmeonidai by agreement signalled with a shield to the Persians with the intention that Athens should be under the control of the Persians and of Hippias. For they were clearly haters of tyranny. . . .[1] (*123*) . . . For the Alkmeonidai were in exile from the tyrants for the whole period[2] and it was by their contrivance that the Peisistratidai were expelled from the tyranny. (2) This family was the liberator of Athens, in my judgment, much more than Harmodios and Aristogeiton. For they, by killing Hipparkhos, made the remaining Peisistratidai more savage and did not end their tyranny.[3] But the Alkmeonidai were clearly the liberators if it was really they who persuaded the Pythia to proclaim to the Spartans that they should free Athens, as I have related above.[4] *124* One might say that they betrayed their country because of a grudge against the common people of Athens. But no family had a higher reputation or were more honoured than they among the Athenians. (2) So reason does not establish that this family signalled with a shield for such a purpose. That a shield was used as a signal, it is not possible to deny. For it happened. But as to who signalled, I am unable to say more than this.[5]

125 Now the Alkmeonidai had been distinguished from earliest times in Athens,[6] but after Alkmeon and then Megakles they became exceedingly distinguished. . . .[7] (5) . . . This was how the family became very wealthy and Alkmeon was able to keep horses, with which he won the four-horse chariot race at Olympia.[8] *126* Then, in the next generation, Kleisthenes the tyrant of Sikyon so exalted the family that it became much more renowned in Greece than before. For Kleisthenes son of Aristonymos, son of Myron, son of Andrees, had a daughter named Agariste. He wished to marry her to the man he found to be the best of the Greeks . . . .[9]

131 . . . From the marriage of Megakles and Agariste was born Kleisthenes, who instituted the Athenian tribes and the democracy. He was named after his maternal grandfather, the Sikyonian. (2) Hippokrates also was a son of Megakles, and he was the father of another Megakles and another Agariste, who was named after Agariste the daughter of Kleisthenes. She married Xanthippos son of Ariphron and, when pregnant, saw a vision in her sleep to the effect that she would give birth to a lion. A few days later she gave birth to Perikles by Xanthippos.[10]

Notes

1 There follows a comparison of the Alkmeonidai with Kallias, who is said to have been the only one to offer to buy the possessions of Peisistratos when they were put up for auction. Much of the comparison is omitted by the better manuscripts of Herodotos. Herodotos has referred to the shield signal and the accusation against the Alkmeonidai in 6.115. For the view that the Alkmeonidai were indeed the strongest candidates for treason in 490 BC, see D. Gillis, *GRBS* 10 (1969) 133–45 = *Collaboration with the Persians* [Historia Einzelschriften, 34] (Wiesbaden 1979) 45–58.

2 This claim that the Alkmeonidai were in exile from the final establishment of Peisistratos's tyranny until the expulsion of his sons (c. 546–510 BC) is refuted by the fragment of an arkhon list [**64**] in Chapter IV, pp. 111–12. Unless Herodotos pushed back the date of a single exile which began under Hippias (P. J. Bicknell, *Historia* 19 [1970] 129–31), we must conclude that the Alkmeonidai went into exile twice during the tyranny: when Peisistratos originally established himself as tyrant (Herodotos 1.64.3 [**60**]) and again between Kleisthenes's arkhonship in 525/4 BC and their unsuccessful fortification of Leipsydrion (Herodotos 5.62.2 [**77**]). In either case Herodotos apparently succumbed to Alkmeonid propaganda.

3 Herodotos ([**72**], [**77**]) and Thucydides ([**73**]–[**74**], [**78**]) both reject the common errors (preserved, for example, in the drinking songs in Chapter IV, pp. 119–20 [**71**]) that Harmodios and Aristogeiton freed Athens from the tyranny and that Hipparkhos was the successor to Peisistratos as tyrant. Thus Herodotos describes Hipparkhos in 5.55 [**72**] as 'the brother of *the tyrant*

Hippias'. For the worsening of the tyranny after the death of Hipparkhos see Thucydides 6.59.2 [**78**] and *Athenaion Politeia* 19.1–2 [**79**].

4 Herodotos 5.62.2–5.63.1 [**77**].

5 Herodotos dismisses the motive attributed to the Alkmeonidai with conviction and does not mention any strong evidence that they signalled to the Persians. However, his claim, based on their fight against the Peisistratidai, that the Alkmeonidai were great haters of tyranny (6.121.1, 6.123.1) is weakened by (i) Megakles's coalition with Peisistratos, which enabled his second tyranny (1.60.1–1.61.1 [**54**]); (ii) Alkmeonid collaboration with the Peisistratidai (note 2 above and [**64**]); (iii) their marriage connection with Kleisthenes tyrant of Sikyon (6.128–6.130); (iv) their relations with Kroisos of Lydia (6.125; cf. note 7 below).

6 This deliberate statement by Herodotos tells against the view of H. T. Wade-Gery, *CQ* 25 (1931) 82–3 = *Essays* 106–8 and Rhodes 70, 84, 243 that the Alkmeonidai were not a *genos*. A similar statement is made by Herodotos in 5.62.3 [**77**]. J. K. Davies (*APF* 369, 445) believes that the Alkmeonidai were not only a *genos* but also Eupatridai.

7 In 6.125.2–5 Herodotos tells of Alkmeon's connection with Kroisos of Lydia, as a result of which the Alkmeonid clan became very wealthy.

8 The fourth-century orator Isokrates (16 [*On the Team of Horses*].25) makes this the first victory by an Athenian; he is speaking of the famous Alkibiades (see note 1 on [**74**]):

> On his mother's side he came from the Alkmeonidai, who left behind a very great monument of their wealth. For Alkmeon was the first of our citizens to win a victory with a team of horses at Olympia.

9 There follows (6.126.1–6.130.2) an account of the contest conducted by Kleisthenes for the hand of his daughter, Agariste. The finalists were both Athenians, but Hippokleides ruined his chances by immodest dancing. So Kleisthenes gave his daughter to the Alkmeonid Megakles.

10 The genealogical information given in Herodotos 6.125–6.131 can be represented diagrammatically as shown on the opposite page. For notes on these figures see J. Töpffer, *Attische Genealogie* (Berlin 1889) 242–4; Davies, *APF* 370–80 and 599; J. Kleine, *Untersuchungen zur Chronologie der attischen Kunst von Peisistratos bis Themistokles* [Istanbuler Mitteilungen: Beihefte, 8] (Tübingen 1973) 145–9, 152 (stemma).

103 *Plutarch,* Solon *11*

11 Solon was already famous and influential as a result of these events.[1] But he became more admired and acclaimed among the Greeks when he urged them to support the temple at Delphi and not condone the insult of the Kirrhaians to the oracle, but defend Delphi on behalf of the god. For it was at his persuasion that the Amphiktyonic Council[2] went to war, as many writers testify, including Aristotle in his list of victors in the Pythian Games,

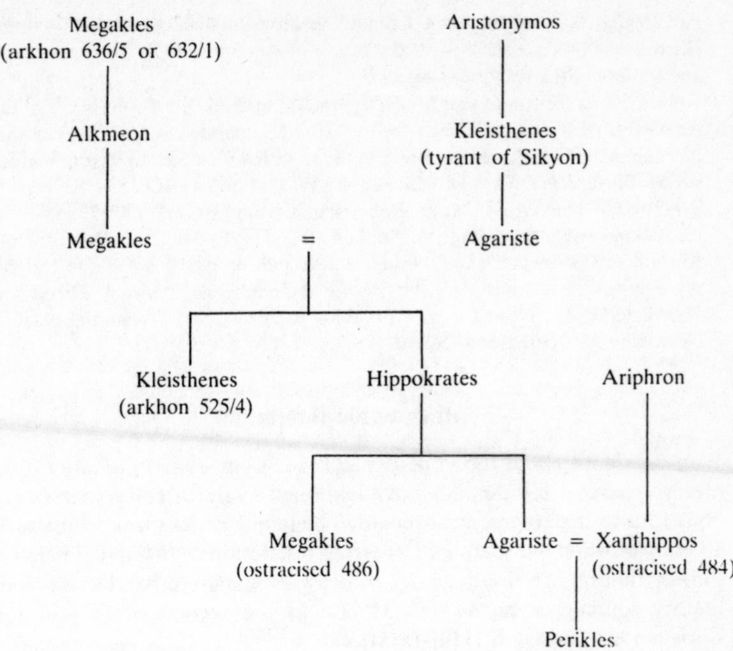

where he attributes the advice to Solon. (2) He was not, however, appointed general for this war, as Euanthes of Samos is reported by Hermippos as saying.[3] For Aiskhines the orator makes no such statement, and in the records at Delphi Alkmaion, not Solon, is named as Athenian general.[4]

Notes

1 Probably Plutarch refers only to Solon's part in the long struggle between Megara and Athens for control of the island of Salamis (*Solon* 8–10). Plutarch has not yet begun to describe Solon's reforms.

2 'The Amphiktyones' (as the Greek says literally) refers to the Council of the most important Amphiktyonic League, the one which maintained the temple and cult of Demeter at Anthela near Thermopylai and of Apollon at Delphi; it also (in association with the city of Delphi) organised the Pythian Games. The League consisted of twelve tribal states and (as indicated by this passage) could engage in foreign policy, including war.

3 Aristotle, *Fragment* 615 Rose is derived from this passage, as is Hermippos, *FHG* III 39. The Pythian Games were held at Delphi (note 2 on [**101**] above). (Apollon had the epithet 'Pythian'; see Meiggs and Lewis no. 11 [**65**] and Thucydides 6.54.6 [**69**].) There must have been records (*hypomnemata*) at Delphi which Plutarch, as a priest of Apollon, was able to consult. Aiskhines, in his speech against Ktesiphon (3.107–111), says that Solon proposed the

motion that the Amphiktyonic League passed, to march against the accursed [Kirrhaians] in accordance with the oracle of Apollon, but he does not name any leaders in this victorious attack.

4 Alkmeon was the son of that Megakles who, as arkhon, led the massacre of the supporters of Kylon (Chapter I, pp. 17–26). This passage is our evidence that he commanded the Athenian forces in the so-called First Sacred War (on which see M. Sordi, *RFIC* n.s. 31 [1953] 320–46, W. G. Forrest, *BCH* 80 [1956] 33–52 [49–51 on Alkmeon] and N. D. Robertson, *CQ* n.s. 28 [1978] 38–73 [66–8, 73 on Alkmeon]). According to Strabon (9.3.4 [418–19C]) Kirrha, on the Korinthian Gulf near Delphi, wished to levy tolls on pilgrims going to Delphi. As a result of the war declared by the Amphiktyonic League, Kirrha was annihilated c. 590 BC and it was forbidden to anyone to cultivate the plain of Krisa between Kirrha and Delphi.

Other noble families

While we learn about the Philaidai and the Alkmeonidai primarily from literary sources, for families not mentioned in the literary sources we must turn to the epigraphical record. The family of Khairion is just such a family of whom we learn entirely from inscriptions ([**104**]–[**106**] below). Information on the Boutadai, by contrast, is mainly to be gleaned from literary sources, some written as late as the second century of the Christian era (passages [**110**]–[**111**]).

104 Inscriptiones Graecae *I²* *467 = I³ 590*

[This altar was de]dicated to Athene by Khairion [son of] Kleidikos(?), while [t]reasurer.[1]

Note

1 This inscription, engraved from right to left about the middle of the sixth century BC on what may have been the crowning member of an altar, was found in 1889 near the South Wall of the Athenian Akropolis. A. E. Raubitschek (*DAA* 364–5 no. 330) believes this dedication had an official character. But the dedication of an altar to Apollon by Peisistratos the younger (Meiggs and Lewis no. 11 [**65**] with note) seems rather to be an act of private munificence drawing attention to his public office.

105 Inscriptiones Graecae *XII.9.296*

Khairion of Athens, an Eupatrid, lies here.[1]

Note

1 This inscription, found at Eretria on the island of Euboia, belongs to the time when the Peisistratidai were in power in Athens (Chapter IV, pp. 110–18). Peisistratos had the support of the government of Eretria in his final, successful

attempt to become tyrant (see *Athenaion Politeia* 15.2 [**55**]). It is conceivable that Peisistratos or his sons had sent Khairion to Eretria in their service, but the indication on the tombstone that Khairion was 'of the Eupatridai' suggests rather that the family wanted to emphasise their claim to be members of the old (pre-Peisistratid) aristocracy. If Khairion is the same person who is commemorated in Athens [**106**], 'it looks very much as if Chairion died as an exile' after Peisistratos succeeded in becoming tyrant (Davies, *APF* 13).

106 *Raubitschek,* DAA *10–12 no. 6* = IG I^3 *618*

Alkimakhos, son of a noble father, Khairion, in performance of a vow
Dedicated me, this statue, to the daughter of Zeus.[1]

Note

1 This inscription of c. 520–510 BC may have accompanied (cf. *CEG* 107 no. 195) the dedication to Athene of a statue of a treasurer, who would in that case have been Alkimakhos's father Khairion. Presumably Khairion was treasurer after Solon's reforms (compare [**104**] above) and hence needed to meet a wealth, but not a birth, qualification (*Athenaion Politeia* 8.1 [**42**]). So his son makes clear that the father here remembered (and by implication he himself) nevertheless belonged to the aristocracy of birth. Friedländer and Hoffleit (p. 51) point out that the address to a 'son of a noble father' in Sophokles, *Philoktetes* 96 suggests that the phrase was almost an aristocratic catchword in Athens. For a reconstruction of the inscription see A. E. Raubitschek, *BSA* 40 (1939–40 [1943]) 17–18, 37 fig. 4, plate 7.1–3; for notes on this family, unknown from the literary sources, see Raubitschek, *DAA* 12, 364–5, 457 and Davies, *APF* 13–15 (noting that the son, Alkimakhos, was apparently recalled to Athens by the tyrant regime; compare Kimon in Herodotos 6.103.1–3 [**99**]).

107 *Raubitschek,* DAA *29 no. 24* = IG I^3 *619*

[M]istress Athene, Timokrates son of Aristaikhmos
Dedicated (this) to you, child of aegis-bearing Zeus.[1]

Note

1 This dedication was set up on the Athenian Akropolis about 510 BC, to judge by the lettering of the inscription (*CEG* 108 no. 197) and the fact that it was cut on an unfluted column (a photograph is provided by A. E. Raubitschek, *JÖAI* 31 [1939] Beiblatt 24 fig. 2). The name of the dedicator's father means roughly 'noble with the spear', carrying overtones of aristocratic birth as well as proficiency in warfare. It is possible that the dedicator is to be identified with the father of a certain Kydrokles who attracted a number of ostracism votes in the 480s: T. L. Shear, *Hesperia* 7 (1938) 361; W. B. Dinsmoor, *Observations on the Hephaisteion* [Hesperia Supplements, 5] (Princeton 1941) 161; Raubitschek, *DAA* 29, 457. As Friedländer and Hoffleit point out (pp. 105–6), 'Mistress Athene' occurs in the same position in the hexameter verse of the Homeric

poems (*Iliad* 6.305) and 'child of aegis-bearing Zeus' is a version suitable for a pentameter verse of the Epic formula 'daughter of aegis-bearing Zeus' (*Odyssey* 3.42, 3.394, etc.; cf. A. B. Cook, *Zeus: A Study in Ancient Religion* 3 [Cambridge 1940] 866 n. 7).

108 *Herodotos 1.59.3, 1.60.1*

When the Athenians of the coast, headed by Megakles son of Alkmeon, and those from the plain, headed by Lykourgos son of Aristolaïdes,[1] were engaged in factional conflict, Peisistratos raised a third faction with the aim of gaining a tyranny . . . . *60* Not long afterwards the factions of Megakles and of Lykourgos united and drove him out. Thus Peisistratos was master of Athens for the first time and lost the tyranny before it had taken firm root. But those who expelled Peisistratos came into conflict with one another again.[2]

Notes

1 This man is the earliest known member of the clan Boutadai. His son Lykourgos (whose namesake in the fourth century belonged to the Eteoboutadai and thus suggests [see Davies, *APF* 349] that the sixth-century factional leader was a member of that clan under its original name, Boutadai) was leader of 'those from the plain', a faction based on the central plain of Attike, in the mid-sixth century.

2 Lykourgos's faction, by combining with the faction led by the Alkmeonid Megakles, was able to remove Peisistratos from the tyranny. But the coalition formed by Lykourgos and Megakles was purely political and the partners soon fell to conflict again. Megakles proposed a marriage alliance with Peisistratos which saw the latter restored as tyrant. More of the context is given in [**51**] (with, especially, note 1) and [**54**].

109 *Aiskhines 2 (*On the Embassy*).147*[1]

Over there is my father Atrometos, now almost the oldest of our citizens; for he has lived ninety-four years . . . . By descent[2] he belongs to the phratry that shares the same altars as the Eteoboutadai,[3] the family from which the priestess of Athene Polias is chosen.

Notes

1 Aiskhines is defending himself against charges brought to trial in 343 BC by Demosthenes, alleging that Aiskhines had been a traitor to Athens when serving on a delegation to Philip II of Makedon in 346 BC.

2 Literally, 'with respect to *genos*'.

3 This phratry (name unknown) evidently had as its core the *genos* Eteoboutadai.

(For the view that it was common for a single *genos* to form the nucleus of a phratry see S. C. Humphreys, *ASNP*[3] 4 [1974] 352–3 = *Anthropology and the Greeks* [London 1978] 196; Rhodes 69, 258; A. Andrewes, in *CAH*[2] 3.3.368; M. A. Flower, *CQ* ns. 35 [1985] 232–5.) As the scholiast (for such commentators see note 1 on [**12**]) on this passage remarks, the 'Eteo-' prefix to the original name of the clan means 'true', 'genuine'. Kleisthenes's tribal reform had as one of its effects the giving of the clan name Boutadai to a deme, which included any other family that registered there in Kleisthenes's time (cf. D. M. Lewis, *Historia* 12 [1963] 26–7). Apparently the clan responded by renaming itself the 'real Boutadai'.

110 *Apollodoros 3.15.1*

When Pandion[1] died, his sons divided their father's inheritance between them. Erekhtheus received the kingdom, while Boutes received the priesthood of Athene and of Poseidon Erekhtheus.[2]

Notes

1 One of the ten national heroes after whom the tribes of Kleisthenes were named (see Herodotos 5.66.2 [**82**] with note 1 and *Athenaion Politeia* 21.6 [**84**] with note 12).

2 Erekhtheus, eponymous hero of another Athenian tribe, was identified with Poseidon at Athens, as is indicated by a fragment of Euripides's play *Erekhtheus* (*Recherches de Papyrologie* 4 [Paris 1967] 39 = *Fragment* 65.90–7 Austin) and by a later lexicographer (Hesykhios, s.v. Erekhtheus).

111 *Pausanias 1.26.5*[1]

There is also [on the Akropolis] a building called the Erekhtheion . . . . As you enter there are altars, one to Poseidon, on which they also sacrifice to Erekhtheus in response to an oracle, a second to the hero Boutes,[2] and a third to Hephaistos. There are paintings of the *genos* Boutadai on the walls.[3]

Notes

1 Pausanias is writing a guide to Athens and Attike in Book I. See also [**76**] and note 1.

2 This is the hero from whom the clan Boutadai took its name.

3 The clan, through its control of the priesthood of Poseidon Erekhtheus (see note 2 on [**110**]), was able to display paintings advertising itself on the walls of the Erekhtheion. For comparable paintings in a building at Delphi, as well as inscribed *hermai* (cf. note 9 on [**96**]) in Athens, commemorating achievements of Kimon of the Philaid family (pp. 195–200 above) in the early fifth century, see R. B. Kebric, *The Paintings in the Cnidian Lesche at Delphi and their Historical Context* [Mnemosyne Supplements, 80] (Leiden 1983) 31–7, 43–4.

BRIEF NOTES ON AUTHORS

Androtion of Athens. Born c. 410 BC, he was the only one of the Atthidographers (local historians of Attike) to be an active politician (mainly in the period c. 386–350). The eight books of his *Atthis* were written while he was in exile in neighbouring Megara (350–340 BC).

Aristotle (384–322 BC). A pupil and a research student in Plato's school, he left Athens after the death of Plato and lived in several areas of Greece, including the court of Philip of Makedon at Pella. In 335 BC he returned to Athens and founded a school in which philosophy and physical science were taught and research conducted on historical, musical and scientific subjects. None of his early popular works (mainly dialogues) survive, nor do any of the large collections of material on historical and scientific subjects made by Aristotle and his colleagues. All the extant works are philosophical or scientific in nature. There has been much debate about the dates of the various parts of the *Politics* and it is not unlikely that the older parts belong to the period of Aristotle's stay in the Troad, Lesbos and Makedonia, while other parts were written after he settled in Athens for the second time.

Athenaion Politeia. This title is simply the Greek for 'Constitution of the Athenians'. The work, attributed to Aristotle, is often referred to as *Ath. Pol.*, by abbreviation of the Greek title.

This document is often mentioned by ancient authors. From these references we know that Aristotle and his students compiled studies of the constitutions (*politeiai*) of 158 states, mainly Greek, as a basis for his *Politics*, a treatise on government. None has survived except the *Constitution of Athens*, which was discovered in 1889 in Egypt, written on a papyrus. Since it is a vital primary source for Greek political development, it was a late and exciting addition to Greek sources.

The extant fragment is incomplete, beginning with the trial of the Alkmeonidai a number of years after Kylon's attempt at tyranny (in the late seventh century). The first part of the document is an historical account of the Athenian constitution; only this part is used here. The second part is an examination of the machinery of government in Aristotle's time.

The work was written about 330 BC, 300 years after the events first described. Most scholars attribute it to Aristotle himself. I personally am not convinced, since such a view entails Aristotle having changed his mind, often for the worse; and he seems to criticise in the *Politics* some of the views put forward here (cf. *Politics* 1273b–1274a [**45**] with the account of Solon in the *Athenaion Politeia*).

Herodotos. A native of Halikarnassos in the south-west corner of Asia Minor, Herodotos travelled widely – to Egypt, Mesopotamia and Skythia, for example. He visited Athens and joined the Athenian colony at Thourioi in southern Italy (founded in 444/3 BC). Scholars differ as to whether his *Histories* were published in Athens shortly before the *Akharnians* of Aristophanes (425 BC) or shortly before the same author's *Birds* (414 BC).

Pausanias. Writing about the middle of the second century after Christ, Pausanias knew Palestine, Egypt, Italy and especially Greece. His *Guide to Greece* survives.

Philokhoros of Athens. Born before 340 BC, he was the most famous of the Atthidographers (local historians of Attike). Almost all the extant fragments of his works come from the *Atthis*, in seventeen books, which reached 261/0 BC. Little remains of his work on religious antiquities and customs.

Plutarch of Chaironeia. Born in the 40s of the first century AD, he lived into the reign of Hadrian (died c. AD 120). He was a priest at Delphi for the last thirty years of his life and was briefly procurator of Greece under Hadrian. Although much of his work has perished, about eighty of his essays, letters, dialogues and lectures are contained in the collection known as the *Moralia*. In addition there are fifty biographies, including twenty-three pairs of 'parallel Lives'.

Solon of Athens. See Chapter II, pp. 40–54 for documents on the man and his outlook.

Strabon (64/3 BC–AD 21 or later). A historian and geographer from Pontus (northern Asia Minor), he resided for periods in Rome and Egypt as well as in his native city. His forty-seven books of *Historical Sketches* are lost, but his *Geography*, in seventeen books, survives.

Thucydides of Athens. His History of the Peloponnesian War (431–404 BC), in eight books, is incomplete. He was born c. 460–455 and was one of the ten generals in 424 BC. As general he failed in the task of relieving Amphipolis from Brasidas and was exiled. He returned to Athens after 404 and died about 400 BC.

INDEX OF SOURCES TRANSLATED

Numbers in square brackets refer to numbered sources in the text; they are followed by page references.

INDEX OF NAMES AND SUBJECTS

References are to pages. When Greek words are used as the main entry, they are normally given in the singular, followed where appropriate by the plural ending in brackets.